MAKING
D
Your Rights and ...
Today

Also by Bowen Hosford

The Grave of the Twin Hills

MAKING YOUR MEDICAL DECISIONS
Your Rights and Harsh Choices Today

BOWEN HOSFORD

FREDERICK UNGAR PUBLISHING CO.
NEW YORK

To my children:
*Bowen Jr. ("Chip"), Kenneth,
Susan, Janet, and Chris*

Second Printing, 1983

Library of Congress Cataloging in Publication Data

Hosford, Bowen.
  Making your medical decisions.

  Bibliography: p.
  Includes index.
  1. Sick—Legal status, laws, etc.—United
States. 2. Medical laws and legislation—United
States. 3. Informed consent (Medical law)—United
States. 4. Physician and patient—United States.
5. Medicine—Decision making. I. Title.
KF3823.H67   344.73′041   81-40464
ISBN 0-8044-5502-3   347.30441   AACR2
ISBN 0-8044-6280-1 (pbk)

Copyright © 1982 by Bowen Hosford
Printed in the United States of America
Designed by Carol Belanger Grafton

CONTENTS

Preface / viii

1. **The Power Struggle between Patients and Their Doctors / 1**
 The Failings of Our Leaders / 3
 The Reach for Autonomy / 5
 The Right-to-Die Movement / 8
 The Fervor for Hospices / 12
 The Reaction of the Law / 17

2. **Refusing Medical Treatment / 21**
 The Right of Bodily Integrity / 23
 The Right of Privacy / 24
 The Free Exercise of Religion / 30
 Fundamental Rights and Their Limitations / 31
 The Abe Perlmutter Case / 33

3. **Discovering Defects before a Baby Is Born / 37**
 Suing the Doctor Who Fails to Communicate / 46
 On Being Paid for Emotional Damage   50
 Babies Who Sue for the Wrong of Having Been Born / 50
 What Must the Obstetrician Ask, and Tell? / 51
 Will We Have a New Eugenics? / 52

On Trying to Stamp Out Sickle Cell Disease / 54
The Power of the New Eugenics Idea / 55
Speaking Up for Diversity / 59
What It Means to You / 61

4. Babies in Trouble / 63
Changes in Doctors' Views / 65
Is Family Suffering a Consideration? / 70
Will the Baby's Life Be Worth Living? / 71
The Legal Framework / 74

5. The Chad Green Story / 81
The First Superior Court Hearing / 87
The Second Court Hearing / 89
In Mexico / 92
A Friday Afternoon in October / 94
The Final Court Appearance / 95
What's a Judge to Do? / 98

6. Teenagers: On Deciding for One's Own Self / 102
The New Age of Majority / 102
The Risk in Treating Minors without Parents' Consent / 103
Adolescent Health Problems / 104
Treatment for VD, Drug Abuse, and Pregnancy / 105
Runaways, Throwaways, and Emancipation / 107
The Mature Minor Concept / 108
Refusing to Be Confined to Mental Institutions / 113

7. Deciding for Patients Who Can't Decide for Themselves / 119
The Doctrine of Substituted Judgment / 122
Patients Who Have No Track Record / 123
What Is Competency? / 124
Relatives Giving Proxy Consent Has Little Legal Foundation / 126
Ethics Committees / 126
Bioethical Counselors / 129

Courts as Decision Makers / 130
The Illogic of Physicians' Taking Exclusive Control / 132
Formal Training in Medical Ethics / 133
Prognosis Is the Doctor's Business / 134
The Complex Motivations of Families / 135
Whether to Continue Treatment Is an Ethical Decision / 136
On Deciding Treatment to Be Withheld: The Use of Code Words; Religious Perspectives / 137
Deciding as the Patient Would / 140

8. Living Wills and Natural Death Laws / 141
Concern for Dying's Living Will and the Christian Affirmation of Life / 143
Naming People to Make Decisions for You / 147
The Medical Care Directive / 147
Natural Death Statutes / 151
Defects of the California Statute / 153
The Arkansas Statute—Vaguest of All / 154
The Kansas Statute—the Best So Far / 155

9. Your Search for Medical Information / 158
A Lack of Time to Talk / 159
Sending Messages from One Subworld to Another / 161
The Legal Doctrine of Informed Consent / 162
Doctors Are Communicating More Than Before / 167
On Not Sharing Medical Records / 168
The Form That Nobody Knows / 170
Getting Information from the Doctor / 174
The Principle of Autonomy / 176
Alert Health Consumers / 177

Notes / 181

Selected Reading / 203
A Selected Bibliography / 203
Cases / 207

Index / 209

PREFACE

I thank my wife, Frances Moore Hosford, R.N., for her loving encouragement.

Storm Whaley, Associate Director for Communications, National Institutes of Health, provided generous and wise advice. Helen Neal, freelance writer, shared her own research and creative ideas and gave welcome support.

Others who provided information or guidance include Judith Bensinger, M.D.; Geraldine W. Blumberg; Donald T. Chalkley, Ph.D.; George Donovan, Esq.; Joseph Fletcher, S.T.D.; Courtenay Hall, Esq.; Josefina B. Magno, M.D.; Charles R. McCarthy, Ph.D.; Richard Roelofs, Ph.D.; Constance Louise Siess; W. Acors Thompson, M.D.; Michael Walker, M.D.; Michael Weisberg, Ed.D.; and Earl M. Weissman, Esq. I thank each of them.

I am also grateful to those who reviewed portions of the book, including Michael J. Bernstein; William Borer, M.D.; Roy Branson, Ph.D.; Fred Finkelman, M.D.; John C. Fletcher, Ph.D.; Philip R. Reilly, J.D., M.D.; Robert M. Veatch, Ph.D.; and Storm Whaley.

I want to express my special thanks to Philip Winsor, Senior Editor, Frederick Ungar Publishing Company, for his perceptive editing and advice.

The case histories related in this book actually happened. But in reporting some state court cases in which identification of the people involved would be embarrassing, I left out their names or changed them. Assiduous students can find the full names by searching out the case reports in law libraries, but I felt a moral hesitance to republish them. I used actual names where I thought participants in court cases wouldn't be embarrassed, in reports of U.S. Supreme Court cases, and in retelling case histories that had already been widely told, either in lawbooks and journals because of their legal lessons or in the public media because of their notoriety.

In some instances, people told me their personal stories on condition that I not identify them. I complied, changing names, family circumstances, and locations. Those instances are noted in the book. In others, people told me their stories and allowed me to use their names. I thank them all.

And I hereby record my appreciation to the research scientists at the National Institutes of Health for the example they have set. For fifteen years, I have observed their work and have reported on their discoveries that have led to better health for all. I hope I have absorbed some of their admirable spirit of inquiry.

In that connection, it is appropriate for me to publish the following disclaimer:

This book was written by Bowen Hosford in his private capacity. No official support or endorsement by the National Institutes of Health is intended or should be inferred.

1
THE POWER STRUGGLE BETWEEN PATIENTS AND THEIR DOCTORS

SOMETHING has happened to the respect that Americans once had for nearly all physicians and many other professionals. One manifestation of the change is malpractice suits. Before World War II, such suits were almost unheard of.[1] After the war, their number increased slowly until the late 1960s and early 1970s, when the number shot upward.

Until then, nearly all doctors could have the warm feeling inside that came from knowing not only that they had superior knowledge but also that people appreciated their motive of helping others. Now, both knowledge and motive sometimes seemed to be questioned.

One doctor, whom a dead patient's family sued, broke down in tears when a jury decided against him. "I've been in practice twenty-five years to help people," he told a reporter.

When those twenty-five years began, people probably forgave doctors readily. They realized that those principled men (and they were indeed nearly always men), who accepted more than their share of burdens, could be expected to nod now and then. And now it had come to this—that jurors, who are traditionally the representatives of and spokesmen for the community, in effect denounced doctors for their presumed mistakes.

Granted, a change in peoples' attitudes isn't the sole cause for the malpractice era. In 1973, a commission appointed by a government department reported that changes in the way medicine is practiced cause some such suits. Technological developments mean that people can be hurt more than before. More potent drugs, for example, mean that people not only can be helped more than before; they can be harmed more too.

The commission nevertheless concluded that social and psychological forces were at work as well.[2] Today, years after the members prepared their report, we can see more clearly some of those forces.

For example, we see a change in respect for all professionals, not doctors alone. We lawyers, the ones who discovered physicians' vulnerability, have joined them as targets of malpractice suits. Officials of one insurance company reported that the malpractice claim rate against lawyers doubled in the mid-1970s.[3]

Accountants and architects have felt the malpractice lash too. Even ministers are vulnerable. In Dallas, a woman filed an $803,000 suit against her pastor, his bishop, and the diocese. She claimed that he had seduced her, and that that was professional misconduct. Although the Texas Supreme Court dismissed the suit, clergymen began buying insurance to protect themselves against lawsuits for giving bad pastoral advice.[4]

The protests from such professionals represent more than a loss of money (much of which is covered by malpractice insurance and thus is passed on to the public generally). It is anguish over the distrust that clients and patients often seem to have for them.

Thus, we are in the midst of a revolt against the professional. I shall examine some reasons for that revolt and look at some additional aspects of its effect on doctor-patient relationships. Then I want to tell you how the law has reacted.

The revolt, illustrated by malpractice suits, reflects a new suspicion of nearly all people who hold themselves out as having special knowledge. "Don't trust the experts!" is a common new slogan, according to writer-chemist Isaac Asimov.[5] The president of the National Academy of Sciences, Dr. Philip Handler, described it as an "antiscientific, antirationalistic trend that should give us pause."[6]

People seem to distrust all authority. ABC News-Harris Poll figures showed the number of Americans expressing "a great deal of confidence" in leadership of selected institutions fell between 1966 and 1979–80. The decline was about 50 percent for higher education, the military, organized religion, and medicine. Confidence in the White House stayed the same but only because it was already low in 1966.[7]

The Failings of Our Leaders

Why do people distrust experts? One reason is that the best and the brightest in all fields seem to have promised to give us untroubled lives and have failed. Granted, some of them, in their failings, have merely reflected the country's disarray. The 1960s especially were years for changes in social institutions.[8] No wonder experts couldn't handle them all and that this led some people to say they'd rather do it their way.

Watergate obviously fostered distrust of national administrations. In addition, Presidents Eisenhower, Kennedy, Johnson, and Nixon, or administrators under them, were perceived to have lied about the sky (the U-2 incident), the water (the Bay of Pigs and the Tonkin Gulf), and the land (the invasion of Cambodia by U.S. troops).

Cancer researchers lost stature because of President Nixon's 1970 declaration of war on cancer. The basic knowledge needed to wage successful war against the cancers wasn't in hand. Scientists gained on them, but failed to rout them. In fact, the cancers increased in incidence, partly because their seeds had been planted in victims years before Nixon started the war.[9]

On the other hand, physicians have also caused some distrust of themselves. Their average high incomes, although presumably showing that people do need them, caused misgivings. Some doctors charge inordinately high fees or else see so many patients that they can't give each enough personal attention.

In the 1970s, some doctors were revealed to have performed unnecessary surgery. A U.S. House of Representatives report concluded that in 1974, physicians performed 2,380,000 unnecessary operations costing $4 billion. Those operations caused 4,900 needless deaths.[10] In 1978, the subcommittee updated the report, finding that unnecessary operations remained " a major national problem, which requires urgent and accelerated attention."[11]

Women, especially, suspected that much unnecessary surgery was reserved for them. They underwent 63 percent of all operations in the mid-1970s. Women in the childbearing years, fifteen to forty-four years of age, had surgery at about two and a half times the rate for men the same age.[12]

The number of hysterectomies per 1,000 population rose by 30 percent from the mid-1960s to the mid-1970s. It fell off somewhat as the 1970s wore on,[13] perhaps because of women's protests. An official of the National Women's Health Network, a nonprofit group in Washington, D.C., said that 1,000 women a year die from hysterectomies and that one-third of the operations are unnecessary.

Among other operations on women, the number of cesarean deliveries jumped from 195,000 to 510,000 between 1970 and 1978. To put the trend in percentages, only 5.5 percent of babies were delivered by cesarean in 1970 as opposed to 15.2 percent in 1978.[14] A Seattle public health specialist, Dr. Helen I. Marieskind, has said that doctors often perform cesareans—at a price of $2,000 to $3,500—despite evidence that a normal delivery would be successful.[15]

In an effort to halt unnecessary surgery, insurance companies and the government now urge patients to get a second opinion before saying yes to a surgeon. Experts argue over whether that has reduced costs of surgery overall.[16] Still, the accusations have branded physicians.

In 1976, Los Angeles County physicians withheld services in a protest against malpractice costs, and the death rate actually fell. Although a reduced amount of elective surgery probably caused the drop,[17] the phenomenon appeared on the surface to confirm the statement of a social critic and priest, Ivan Illich, that the medical establishment itself had become the major threat to health.[18]

Illich's is one of the many articles and books accusing the medical profession, and writers of such material often reach for coloring. "Modern medicine is a nightmare," wrote science writer Belinda Dumont in *Omni*. "Advances often cause disasters worse than the disease. In the United States, deaths from prescription drugs now equal those from breast cancer."[19]

A columnist, Sydney J. Harris, wrote in the *Chicago Sun-Times*: "I am convinced that one of the great American scandals of our time, and perhaps of any time, is the systematic cheating and looting of government funds by the medical profession."

Mr. Harris didn't trim his article with the commentor's usual statement that a few Medicare and Medicaid cheats make all doctors look bad. "What we have here is a monster of mass dishonesty," he wrote.[20]

Doctors themselves have occasionally joined the accusations "There's no more dangerous activity than walking into a doctor's office, clinic, or hospital unprepared," warned Dr. Robert S. Mendelsohn. He explained that modern medicine, in its guise of religion, is the enemy.

"You need appropriate tools, skill, and cunning," he wrote. "The first tool you must have is knowledge of the enemy."[21]

The Reach for Autonomy

There has to be some additional explanation for the revolt against the experts. After all, political leaders presumably have always overpromised or lied, and doctors have always had human frailties.

A major reason is the general move toward individuality, the "I'll-do-it-my-way" phenomenon that annoys some observers. "It's our narcissistic age," a Boston psychiatrist told me. Others equate it with selfishness. But this new individuality is more significant than mere self-indulgence. It grows from mass education, affluence, and improved communications.[22]

Many more persons than in the past have training and an assured competence in specialized occupations. They regard themselves as capable of understanding what other professionals tell them. Thus, paradoxically, professionals themselves revolt against professionals in different fields.

Granted, so far as the doctor-patient relationship is concerned, many doctors are still assertive, and their patients are meek. Americans also rate their doctors high among the professionals in their esteem and report themselves as satisfied with their medical care.[23] A patient might well hate doctors in the plural and admire a doctor in the singular.

Still, the change is real, according to Dr. Seymour Perry, a cancer specialist and director of the federal government's National Center for Health Care Technology. Dr. Perry recalls how it was, twenty or thirty years ago, when a family member was ill. "Everyone clustered around the window, waiting for the doctor to drive up and walk in. And his every word was important."

The doctor was the hope to ward off a threat that, to the family, was obscure in its origins and mysterious in its workings. One did not ask questions, because respect for the doctor almost amounted to awe.

In some aspects, the change in public attitude today is depressing and discouraging, according to Dr. Perry. A classmate—an excellent physician, he says—is retiring early because he's discouraged with the practice of medicine and the way people view him. "It's not as rewarding, and it's not as much fun for him as it was before," Dr. Perry said. "More importantly, medicine is losing a good physician."

European patients are still submissive, said Dr. Perry, who made rounds with another doctor in a Paris hospital. "The patients didn't ask questions," he said. "I was astonished."

The irony is that in an earlier age in America, when patients didn't question doctors, a disease was more likely to be a mystery on both sides. Americans' new questioning of their doctors' authority and competence has come at a time when the doctors' competence has bounded upward.

The reach for autonomy has many aspects. One is the rejection of conventional cancer treatment. Some people charge that surgery, radiation, and chemotherapy amount only to "cutting, burning, and poisoning." Instead, they advocate massive doses of vitamins, enzyme or coffee enemas, and laetrile.

The U.S. Food and Drug Administration has refused to approve laetrile for interstate shipment, and the Supreme Court has upheld the ban.[24] That doesn't apply to shipment inside states, and the demand is so strong that some state lawmakers have legalized its use. About 50,000 to 75,000 people take laetrile regularly.[25]

Some physicians have themselves joined what seems to be a defiance of the medical establishment. A California physician, Dr. James R. Privitera, went to jail because he had recommended laetrile to cancer patients. Dr. Privitera lost his appeal in the California Supreme Court, but earlier, in the progress of his case, a court of appeals judge, Robert O. Staniforth, had defended those who claim the right to use laetrile.

"The issue here is human liberty," Judge Staniforth had written. "The right to control one's own body is not restricted to the wise; it includes the 'foolish' refusal of medical treatment."[26]

Dr. Privitera served fifty-five days of a six-month sentence. Many Californians viewed him as a martyr. On January 1, 1981, California became the twenty-third state with some form of laetrile legalization law.

The U.S. Government has been accused so often of refusing to give laetrile a fair test that the National Cancer Institute has finally supported a clinical trial. Doctors tested laetrile and a metabolic treatment of special diet, enzymes, and vitamins against several types of cancer, such as those of the breast, lung, and colon. They found the treatment to be ineffective. Many patients nevertheless will probably continue to insist on deciding for themselves whether laetrile is foolish.

Another symptom of the new autonomy is the movement towards

holistic health. Although, in its present guise, it started on the West Coast, it had its real beginning with healer and clairvoyant Edgar Cayce, who set up a hospital in Virginia Beach, Virginia, in 1925 and died in 1945.

It is spreading "like an uncontrolled nuclear reaction," according to Dr. John P. Callan in a 1979 editorial in a physicians' magazine. "A remarkable fact is that holism has attracted not only persons of questionable qualifications but legitimate physicians as well."[27]

Holistic practitioners emphasize the inseparability of mind and body. The aim is wellness, rather than a mere absence of symptoms. The main responsibility for health lies with the patient, rather than with a physician.[28] Thus, although physicians have joined the movement, it represents a revolt against conventional medicine.[29]

The women's health movement is another symptom of autonomy. Some women, noting that they've had little to do with running the health-care system, say that as a result they have been victimized. A nonprofit consumer group, the National Women's Health Network, exists in part to wrest more responsibility for women. "Good health care means that an individual participates as a partner with the physician," program director Elaine Clift said. "To a large extent, this still isn't happening with women."[30]

In addition, feminist clinics—owned and run by women—have been springing up. They offer first-trimester abortions, "well-woman" gynecology, Pap smears, contraceptive devices, and health education.

Some physicians tolerate the feminist clinics; others are hostile. Some doctors claim that untrained personnel are being used. Several centers are struggling with money worries. Nevertheless, they continue to come into existence. Some of their leaders plan to go underground if abortions are constitutionally prohibited.[31]

Feeling in some cases almost powerless in traditional medical settings such as medical schools and hospitals, some female health workers have turned to alternative centers. Women with backgrounds in nursing, social work, and health education are forceful in neighborhood clinics and community health centers. They work with the poor, minorities, and the aged. Their participation is significant in promoting autonomy, because the centers emphasize education and self-health practices.

Researchers found that in one area, San Diego, women made up almost half the directors of such centers, all of the assistant directors, more than three-fourths of the clinic coordinators, and 40 percent of the members of boards of directors.³² Women have also led in setting up hospices as a better way to care for the dying, as we shall see.

The Right-to-Die Movement

Among the most striking symptoms of the move toward autonomy was the right-to-die movement of the mid-seventies. For reasons discussed below, people are more likely than ever before to die of chronic diseases. At the same time, doctors have perfected methods to prolong life in some circumstances, meaning they can also prolong death. Doctors have become alarmed by this trend, and laymen have joined in their concern, criticizing the physicians for withholding patients' right to die speedily and naturally at what appears to be their appointed times.

If it is possible to be triumphant in so grim a battle, the laymen clearly have been so. By the end of the 1970s, many doctors were saying they shouldn't prolong life at all costs.

To reinforce the lesson that patients' wishes are to be heeded, many have signed living wills, requesting that doctors forgo heroic treatment at the end of life. And in ten states, legislators have been persuaded to pass natural-death laws, most of them providing that doctors must let patients die without such treatment if they so request.

A slow death is the traditional worst of tortures. Walt Whitman, in a lament for President Lincoln, appealed to the "dark mother" death as follows: "I bring thee a song that when thou must indeed come, come unfalteringly."³³

More people seem to die lingering deaths now than in the past. Why? More people live long enough for chronic diseases to carry them off.

Once, many of them would have died young, of infectious diseases. Little gravestones would have told of their early deaths, like the ones I saw when, each fall, with thirty or so relatives, I would pull grass and weeds from a sandy Georgia graveyard where members of our family lay.

I also picture in my mind the gravestone of Calvin Coolidge, Jr., who was once known as "the first boy of the land." The marker is next to a taller one erected for his father, President Calvin Coolidge, at Plymouth, Vermont.³⁴

In December 1924, President Coolidge sat in his White House office with the editor of the Emporia, Kansas *Gazette*, William Allen White. In four sentences, Silent Cal told of the death, six months before, of his first-born son at the age of sixteen.

"Playing tennis on the soft south grounds of the White House, he got a blister on his toe," the President said. "Blood poisoning resulted." President Coolidge paused. Then, "When he was suffering he begged me to help him. I could not."[35]

Today, antibiotics could save a Calvin Coolidge, Jr., though blood poisoning—which doctors now call bacteremia—is still dangerous.

Still, antibiotics fail to account for the major part of the drop in infectious diseases. Before 1900, improved food was the first and the main reason for the decline. Year by year, other influences came into effect—hygiene, vaccinations, and effective medical care.[36] Today, for the first time in history, parents can expect all their children to grow to adulthood, and so it isn't necessary for them to bear as many as before.

Thus, with the decline in birthrate and the extension of life expectancy, today we have an older population than ever before. The percentage of Americans sixty-five and older doubled between 1900 and 1972 and will double again by 2030. By then, one of every five Americans will be in that age bracket.[37]

Old people have more chronic illnesses than younger ones do.[38] And old people—what with private health insurance and government help—often have the resources to pay for prolonged dyings.[39]

At the same time, physicians have learned to keep their chronically ailing patients alive longer. Weapons against infectious diseases, which have kept many a person from being buried early under a little gravestone now postpone his later burial under a big one.

For example, pneumonia now fails to kill old patients, as it once did. When the twentieth century began, the most popular medical textbook was Sir William Osler's *Principles and Practice of Medicine*. The renowned author stated: "Pneumonia may be called the friend of the aged. Taken off by it in an acute, short, not often painful illness, the old man escapes those 'cold gradations of decay' so distressing to himself and to his friends."

Then, in the 1940s, the ability of penicillin to fight off infectious diseases became apparent. Doctors could prolong a chronically ill patient's life through many attacks of pneumonia.

Along with antibiotics came the science of nutrition. Unconscious patients, some for the first time in their lives, got balanced, nutritious meals through tubes.

Other aids to prolonged existence included a new group of machines.[40] The respirator, which has carried many patients through crises, paradoxically has become a bête noire for those who argue for a right to die. It can keep a patient's heart beating even though the brain has died. Such a machine forces the lungs to function. Red blood cells therefore carry oxygen to the heart, which then marches to its own drummer.

Other techniques and machinery also have been involved in the right-to-die question. A British committee pointed out in 1975 that physicians could resuscitate a body and keep vital organs alive—the heart beating, the kidneys and liver functioning—after a person had been guillotined.[41]

A decade before the Karen Ann Quinlan case hit the headlines, doctors were wondering about the limits to the use of the artificial respirator. In 1966, a Kansas City surgeon, Dr. William P. Williamson, wrote in a doctors' magazine:

> I have seen patients with brain-stem failure, with dilated, fixed pupils . . . and cessations of spontaneous respiration . . . who were assisted by a mechanical respirator. . . . I have never seen such a patient begin to breathe spontaneously and survive, and autopsy always shows . . . the brain . . . "died" several days before the heart did. When did the soul leave the body? Is turning off the respirator murder?[42]

Dr. Nancy L. Caroline, a Cleveland resident in medicine, wrote in 1972 of a seventy-eight-year-old patient, "Eli Kahn," who entered the hospital with abdominal pain and vomiting. His roommate, "Kovanich," who had colon cancer, lay in a tangle of tubes.

"Listen, Doctor, I don't want to die with tubes sticking out all over me," Mr. Kahn told Dr. Caroline.

The next morning, the roommate's heart stopped, and attendants sounded a code. A resuscitation team pounded at his chest and stuck the needles of syringes into him, but Kovanich died.

Kahn was frantic. He made Dr. Caroline promise that nothing such as that would happen to him.

On the fourth day, Kahn suffered congestive heart failure. The house staff kept him alive with morphine, oxygen, intermittent positive-pressure breathing, tourniquets, digitalis, and diuretics. An anesthesiologist fed a tube down his nose and connected the other end to a ventilator.

Sometime during the night, Kahn disconnected the ventilator, and died. Nurses called Dr. Caroline to pronounce death. On the bedside, she found a note. "Death is not the enemy, Doctor," Kahn had written. "Inhumanity is."

The story of Eli Kahn won for Dr. Caroline the *New Physician* award for the best manuscript of the year.[43]

Physicians on a committee of the New York Academy of Medicine in 1973 noted with aversion the prolonged death of a patient who was emaciated with incurable cancer. Doctors rushed him to intensive care when he had a heart attack. He existed there for two weeks before death came. "This futile effort to prolong his life caused severe emotional distress to his family and exhausted their limited financial resources," the physicians noted.[44]

Such incidents have caused doctors to assess their attitudes. In 1973, the House of Delegates of the American Medical Association adopted the following guideline: "The cessation of the employment of extraordinary means to prolong the life of the body when there is irrefutable evidence that biological death is imminent is the decision of the patient and/or his immediate family."[45]

Meanwhile, prolonged dyings were evident to the public, too. Two unrelated persons at separate times told me of the dying of one physician in the early 1960s. I'll call him Dr. Whitledge. He had an automobile accident near the hospital where he practiced. He was thrown from his car, and his head apparently struck a door frame as he flew out. The impact broke an artery underneath the hind part of his brain. Blood poured out of the artery. It put pressure on his brain. Dr. Whitledge lost consciousness.

Not only was the accident close to the hospital. When he arrived in an ambulance, the community's best neurosurgeon was at hand. The surgeon relieved the pressure on his brain, and, unfortunately, that saved his life.

A large part of his brain had been deprived of oxygen. He could breathe, his heart functioned, he could swallow. He could be hand-fed with a spoon. But he was unaware of his surroundings. In the instant, he had been made helpless, and he never improved. He was neither alive, to be paid fees or a salary, nor dead, so that his family could collect his life insurance.

He developed pneumonia several times, but doctors defeated it with antibiotics. Finally, Dr. Whitledge died—five years after the accident. The antibiotics had made his long dying possible.

In 1975 came the Karen Ann Quinlan case. She fell into a coma after a party at a highway tavern, and later, at a hospital, was connected to a respirator. It took her parents a year to force doctors to remove it. And then Karen failed to die after all. Her case has become a famous example of forcing medical treatment on the incompetent. I'll return to it several times in this book.

Resentment by lay people has led to a further change in doctors' attitudes. By 1977, an overwhelming majority of doctors indicated they would support a patient's right to die. About 95 percent of those who responded to an American Medical Association poll said they normally tried to give the care that a dying patient wanted. Seventy percent said they asked the dying patient's wishes.[46]

In 1979, a physician and a statistician showed in a survey of Seattle nursing homes that doctors did not prolong life at any cost there. When patients developed high fevers, nurses often failed to notify doctors, or the doctors failed to order extra treatment. Thus, 40 percent of such patients received no antibiotics or hospital care, and three out of every five of those patients died.

Many of the patients who weren't treated already had notes on their charts reading, "Going downhill," "Failing," or "Losing ground." The ones who received the least treatment included those who were bedridden, in pain, and receiving narcotics. Those who were alone— single, divorced, or separated—also received less treatment than others.[47]

The two professionals who conducted that survey said it refuted accusations that doctors prolonged life at any cost. It seemed to me more significant in revealing that doctors had changed their attitudes in the preceding decade.

I've presented the right-to-die idea as one that occurred to physicians and the general public at much the same time. That's valid, but the movement is also an example of patients' demands for autonomy. Some people accuse doctors of prolonging patients' dying merely because the machinery and other weapons are in place. They also probe into physicians' personal fears of death and their other motives, such as their wills to win over death at whatever cost to patients.

The Fervor for Hospices

Most people die in hospitals instead of at home. But hospital care at the end of life can be cold. Some patients are socially dead before they are physically dead. And so the right-to-die movement has evolved into a fervor for hospices.[48] Although the modern hospice was brought into being in England by a remarkable female physician, the movement in America represents an attempt by lay people to get control over the manner of their dying.

The hospice concept means that, once again as in the past, many patients stay at home during their last days. Their relatives or others care for them there, with visits by a hospice staff. Indeed, some hospices have no building and so are "hospices without walls." Others have inpatient facilities—some of them quite small—so patients may report there when care is beyond their families' ability.

Although other hospices existed earlier, St. Christopher's Hospice in London transformed tender loving care into efficient loving care and was the catalyst for the later hospice movement in the United States and Canada. St. Christopher's opened in 1967, under the medical direction of Dr. Cicely M. Saunders.

She had seen other hospices and from 1948 on regularly worked as a volunteer R.N. in London's St. Luke's Hospital, where patients were dying of cancer and tuberculosis. "The attitude of the staff, the standard of nursing, and, still more, the control of pain achieved by the regular giving of oral narcotics was impressively better than anything seen in teaching and general hospitals," she later wrote.[49]

She had been educated as a nurse and medical social worker, and administrator. After her volunteer work at St. Luke's, she entered medical school and, after completing it, spent seven years developing an improved concept of pain control with the staff of St. Joseph's Hospice, London.

St. Christopher's opened at a watershed time. Developments in pharmacology and studies on the stress of loss influenced Dr. Saunders and others.

Patients at St. Christopher's usually have cancer for which curative treatment has failed. Home care is an essential part of the plan, and thus only about half of the patients being treated under the auspices of the hospice are actually in the hospice itself at any one time.

Personal belongings—photographs, oddments from home—surround patients. The family is regarded as part of the caring team, and visits at any time. For example, a six-year-old boy in shorts and a striped polo shirt reads a comic book alongside his dying father's bed. There is always touching: nurses touching patients, family members touching loved ones. A nurse, on the last day of a patient's life, offers a cup of tea rather than "tubes in every direction," as Dr. Saunders puts it. Loving care in itself reduces pain, and the efficient and regular use of medications adds to its control.

A woman of fifty-five spent her time at St. Christopher's writing and illustrating a children's story. One drawing shows a girl facing a dragon. But the beast is nonthreatening. It flashes no teeth, and flowers are strewn about its feet.

The woman died about five days after completing the drawing.

I met Dr. Saunders in Washington, D.C., at the first meeting of a new U.S. group, the National Hospice Organization. She told me that for most patients in a hospice, the dragon of death loses its teeth. "To the very ill and the very old," she said, "death is not nearly as frightening as it is to us—if the patient has good control of symptoms and knows he's not isolated."

A few people in hospices remain angry at their loss of independence and approaching death. "For them, that is totally in character," Dr. Saunders said. "We can't dictate to people what should happen."

On occasion, death may be pushed back at St. Christopher's and other hospices. "The condition of many of these patients has been so greatly improved by the skilled control of symptoms that they have been enabled to return to further palliative or even curative treatment," Dr. Saunders wrote.

St. Christopher's care has a strong scientific foundation, and knowledge continues to accumulate. For example, the staff performs clinical pharmacology and psychosocial research. Some such studies can only be done in a specialist unit such as a hospice.

Dr. Saunders has been widely honored, having been knighted by the Queen, for example.

Although in England, people such as Dr. Saunders developed the hospice idea slowly, people in America grabbed at the idea. It came to the United States at about the time the right-to-die movement was peaking. Many people were already convinced that their physicians were uselessly prolonging deaths, and here was a new method to avoid death's pain and ostracism.

Lay people—many of them women—took the lead. They called local meetings and enthusiastically announced plans. By the time I met Dr. Saunders at the organizational meeting of the National Hospice Organization in Washington, American hospices were opening fast.[50]

At the meeting, the audience was to break into smaller groups. "All those who plan to attend the workshop on 'Starting a Hospice,' please stand," the chairperson called out. About 500 persons stood.

An author of a book on hospices, Sandol Stoddard, recited from the platform a prayer she said had been handed to her by another woman in a supermarket. Its final words were, "Thou knowest, Lord, that I want a few friends at the end." A pioneer in the American hospice movement, Dr. Josefina B. Magno, said from the platform on the last day, "This has been God's symposium."

The Washington meeting was important in providing guidance, particularly on quality of care, for hospices nationwide. And in the Washington area, where I live, growth has been responsibly directed. In the area, nine out of ten hospice patients die at home, tended by their families and visited at least once weekly by doctors, nurses, or social workers. But home care is impracticable for some patients.

The Washington Home Hospice is a pilot project for treating patients who must have full-time professional care. Group Hospitalization, Inc., and the Vincent T. Lombardi Cancer Research Center of Georgetown University cooperate in it. Six rooms were set aside for the project by the Washington Home, a charitable nursing home that dates back to 1899.

Patients can gather with their families in a sunny and cheerfully furnished lounge, looking out on a garden. Visiting hours are unlimited. Relatives can use a kitchen and stay overnight.

I asked the clinical director, Carol Ann Bingham, whether patients would view with antipathy a place set aside for the dying. Nurse Bingham reminded me that the inpatient facility is an extension of patients' homes, and people don't view their homes with antipathy.

Every patient brings some part of home to the hospice, even if it is only a picture. They can replace all furniture, except for the adjustable beds.

One former State Department employee furnished her room with items from her travels. She placed an Oriental rug on the floor and tapestries on the walls. She had a Scandinavian cane-and-chrome chair, a large, carved wooden trunk, and a rosewood sideboard. She also had someone dig a cluster of three young white birches from her yard and bring them to her room in a tub. Their tops crowded the ceiling.

Hospice care centers on the quality of the patients' lives. The desired quality varies. "For some, it is to sit in the hospice's garden, surrounded by flowers," Carol Ann Bingham said. "For some, the greatest pleasure is a back rub."

She contrasted dying in the hospice with dying in the hospital. She meant no criticism of hospitals, which are set up to rescue patients from death, to cure them, and then to send them home. When a patient dies, depending on the circumstances, the staff may be desperately trying resuscitation. A family might even be in the way at such a time.

In a hospice, death is accepted, and so, when it comes, it isn't fought off. There is quietness, with much holding of hands.

As for the complaint that hospital nurses shun dying patients, Carol Ann Bingham pointed out that a hospital nurse may have ten patients and a hospice nurse three or four, and so the time that can be given to dying patients varies.

Yet, in nursing school, Miss Bingham received no training in care of the dying, except on how to handle a body *after* death. She wrote her Master of Science thesis on how the dying perceive their needs (the patients put physical care first), as contrasted to the way nurses perceive their needs (the nurses think the patients want emotional care first).

She thinks of hospice as a return to earlier patterns, in which people died at home, cared for by relatives. "Hospice is an attempt to rehumanize the dying experience," she said.

It is also an attempt to care for families before, during, and after a patient's death. Washington Home social worker Paul Schniedermeyer pointed out that the loss of a family member or friend causes stress. That might even lead to psychological or physical illness, depending on the family's previous experience with loss, the closeness or intensity of the relationship with the dying person, and the ages of everyone concerned.

"Part of what may be called 'grief work'—that is, working through the experience of a loss—may be accomplished before a death," Schniedermeyer said. "The hospice provides the opportunity to anticipate a death in an open and emotionally supportive environment."

After the death of a patient, Paul Schniedermeyer and hospice staff members counsel the bereaved families for at least a year. Volunteers are important, too, often visiting the families.

Once again, as we have seen, women often lead in setting up and running hospices. Some have channeled their fervor into volunteer work. For example, Mary Frances Brady works two afternoons a week at a nine-patient hospice at Saint Mary's Hospital in Minneapolis.

Some volunteers are unprepared for the emaciation of cancer patients. They have nightmares and drop out. Mrs. Brady, in contrast, knew what to expect. She had trained as a nurse (although she gave up the profession to raise twelve children), and her husband, Dr. Ray Brady, a dentist, died in 1978 of cancer.

"Having dealt with Ray's dying, I thought I could help others," she told me.

Mrs. Brady gives fresh water, serves food to helpless patients, turns them, and puts them in geriatric or wheel chairs.

"I am touching people," she said. "I pray with them or read Scripture to them. I have talks with families in the lounge. And that I can say, 'I lost my husband from cancer, and so I've experienced the same thing you are going through' makes them open up and talk with me."

About 750 to 1,000 hospices exist in the United States today. What do conventional doctors think of the movement? Some have warned that the fast American growth may lead to poor quality control and to shunting patients off to die prematurely. They, and others, have spoken of "Kentucky Fried Hospices." Regardless of whether the criticism is justified, it reveals that some physicians and hospital staff members see hospices as a threat in an area in which they have had exclusive control.

Paradoxically, as we have seen, hospitals are now joining the hospice movement.[51] Their officials use the slogan, "Hospice is not a place; it is a concept." The thought is that the hospice can be set up within the walls of a hospital, thus avoiding empty beds and sharing administrative and medical personnel costs. That would involve, on the other hand, a reversal of attitudes toward the dying by some medical people. But hospitals may integrate and take over hospices in the same way that they integrated natural childbirth techniques in their delivery rooms.[52]

The Reaction of the Law

Lawmakers and lawfinders have responded to people's demands that they have charge of their own bodies. But the former—that is, legislators—are slow to react to social change. If there is no consensus, the lawmakers will reject a proposed statute, or else carve it so as to make it palatable to everyone.

For example, many people who believe in a "right to die" also worry that we might step on a slippery slope of moral values and fall. When California legislators were considering a statute to give people more control over their own dying, opponents said it would lead to killing off useless old people. The lawmakers therefore so limited the new Natural Death law's application that it was almost useless, as we shall learn in Chapter 8.

The legislators and the state officials who administer statutes have been more forceful in the patients' bills of rights now existing as statutes or regulations in seventeen states. These were preceded by the American Hospital Association's Bill of Rights.[53] The AHA's timid document pretended to grant rights, but it was oriented toward the hospitals and merely gave patients what they had already won. "The patient has the right to refuse treatment to the extent permitted by law," the document says, that being an example of its restatement of the obvious.

In 1979, Massachusetts lawmakers adopted a patients' rights statute far superior to that. It gives patients the right to know who is treating them, to reject care by students, to know about physicians' financial interest in hospitals if that would affect health care, to be allowed informed consent, to receive a copy of hospital medical records, and to be told the alternatives for breast surgery.[54]

Patients' rights statutes need to be even stronger. They should require that hospitals appoint patients' advocates who, though paid by the hospitals, would have independence. These persons could obtain medical records and complain to administrators without fear of retaliation.[55]

Beyond legislators' roles in recognizing new customs, the actions of lawfinders—that is, judges—are important, too. They turn social movements into law by interpreting statutes and constitutions and by building a body of case law.

Indeed, judges, sometimes by necessity, respond more surely to social changes than legislators. Their recognition of custom resulted in the English common law, which we in America inherited.[56]

Today, judges continue the tradition. Customs or conditions change, and social theory explains why and persuades doubters. Then judges discover a change in the law.[57]

Many people believe that the process is easily managed—that the law is whatever judges say it is. But, no, it would be unfair and ineffective for courts suddenly to announce revised relationships among people or between them and the state. Thus, judges pay attention to precedent.

In ruling in particular cases, judges don't announce general rules to govern every such case in future. Rather, they move from case to case, finding similarities or differences.[58]

Because a judge's ruling in one case may represent only one step toward accepting a changed social view, it can be acceptable at a time when a generalized statute would fail. Judicial lawfinding, therefore, whether in filling the holes in statutes, interpreting constitutions, or in building a body of case law, points to the way in which much wisdom develops.

That statutes can be interpreted, with judges applying them to disputes that lawmakers never thought of, surprises some people. "That's the law," they say, as if a statute could cover all matters. But their very universality makes them incomplete. Judges therefore must often find the law in statutes' interstices.

As for constitutions, which only vaguely express a society's ideals, judges have much freedom. William O. Douglas learned the extent of his freedom when he went onto the Supreme Court in 1939. Chief Justice Charles Evans Hughes, then seventy-seven, took the new forty-year-old justice into his confidence. "At the constitutional level where we work, 90 percent of any decision is emotional," he said. "The rational part of us supplies the reasons for supporting our predilections."[59]

It was Justice Douglas who in 1965 announced for the Supreme Court that we have a constitutionally protected right of privacy. It's unwritten, but it exists as a "penumbra," according to Justice Douglas. As we shall learn in Chapter 2, the Supreme Court first applied it in declaring a right that seems innocuous today—the right of married couples to use contraceptives in the privacy of their own bedrooms.[60]

Though that ruling is now unoffending, other rulings that grow from the constitutional right of privacy anger people. That is obvious in the abortion controversy.

It exists in other disputes as well. Consider the argument over whether doctors ought to be able to order patients in mental institutions to take medications. Judges may view some patients as entitled to determine their own treatment. Granted, they would not have such a right if they appeared to be irrational ("The CIA sent these drugs") or dangerous if left untreated. On the other hand, their rejection of medications may be rational. Some drugs have such severe side effects that they can cripple inmates. But psychiatrists cry out that they are being handicapped, when they merely want to help patients get well. "They'll die with their rights on," some of the doctors say.[61]

Now to turn to the body of case law that judges build. It contains much of our legal guidance. Private parties who sue each other can make law for others. For example, as we shall learn in Chapter 6, doctors have had to defend themselves against parents who said they had not given permission, but that surgery nevertheless had been performed on their teenage children. Those lawsuits have led judges to declare that some teenagers are old enough to make medical decisions on their own, regardless of the legal age of majority. That "mature minor" rule will probably be applied to even younger children in future.

Lawfinding by American state-court judges has a characteristic not found generally in other countries—that is, the law that they announce governs only as far as the state line. Beyond that line, other judges might rule differently. But the diversity can be beneficial. One judge's soundly reasoned decision can influence others. Thus, a consensus of wisdom can develop.

Supreme court justices in such states as California, New York, and Massachusetts are often influential elsewhere. But, whether on state court benches or in the U.S. Supreme Court, powerful judges can make powerful errors, which then govern for a while.[62]

In this book, I'm going to ask you to examine some court opinions. In the process, you and I must look not only at the issues but also deeply within ourselves.

As we have learned, the revolt against the professional is striking in its effect on medical care. More than ever before, patients insist on being recognized as persons. They have found that they have legal rights that had not been formalized.

Among those rights is the freedom to choose medical treatment—or to refuse it, even if such refusal would mean death. We shall learn in the next chapter about the extent of that freedom.

It only leads, however, to other, equally harsh problems beyond.

2
REFUSING MEDICAL TREATMENT

SHE was a physician herself, this seventy-five-year-old woman who had just been admitted to a hospital in the Midwest. To a resident in internal medicine, Dr. William Borer, still in his early thirties, she represented an earlier era in medicine.

"She was one of the last hard-core general practitioners," he told me six years later. "She was known throughout her area as a loving and compassionate physician. There was a mystique, almost an aura, about her."

She had stayed at home throughout her illness, but now it was difficult for others to care for her there. She had congestive heart failure, which had caused fluid to accumulate in her lungs and elsewhere. Her legs were swollen and ulcerated.

An intern was her primary physician, but as the senior resident, Dr. Borer looked at her medical history and examined her. Listening through his stethoscope, he could hear fluid in her lungs.

Then he noticed a suspicious dimpling of the skin of her breasts. Examining the breasts, he discovered in each a stony-hard lump. Still, she had had no biopsy, and her records disclosed no treatment for cancer.

Dr. Borer said, "Well, you know, Doctor . . ." He began again, "You know, there's a high likelihood that you have breast cancer."

She smiled at the young resident. "Yes, I know."

"Well, what are we going to do about it?" he asked.

When Dr. Borer told me of her answer, he simulated her voice. He dropped to almost a whisper, and half-smiled. "Nothing," was the answer.

Dr. Borer speculates that she had ignored the growing lumps while at home because of the overriding importance of her deterioration from other causes. The cancer would be too slow-growing to kill her.

She died about two weeks after entering the hospital, of her heart trouble. Physicians hadn't objected to her rejection of treatment for those lumps in her breasts.

Cancer patients have often asked that useless treatment be withheld, and physicians have agreed. As we have seen, a basis for the hospice movement is that a time arrives when physicians have exhausted their weapons against a patient's cancer. Then a hospice staff will help that patient live as fully and as pain-free as possible, while omitting further surgery, irradiation, or chemotherapy.

Many other persons in less life-threatening situations decline medical treatment. In fact, studies have shown that patients fail to take the medicines the doctor ordered, or to follow other regimens, about a third of the time.[1] You need look only as far as your own medicine cabinet to confirm that. If all the pills that were not taken were sent back to drugstores for resale, spiders would spin webs around pill-making machines at the drug houses.

Hospital patients also walk out before completing treatment. Alcoholics and drug addicts often seem to have a subtle agreement with the hospital staff that it is all right to leave.[2] Some of them have been carried to the hospital when helpless, and so they depart when they are able. The staff may be glad to see them go, but not before a nurse has run them down, waving a form for them to sign. That document excuses the hospital employees from liability for harm caused by a patient's leaving "AMA"—against medical advice.

Still, doctors sometimes face dilemmas when patients balk at treatment, and therefore they ask judges to issue rulings.[3] On the one hand, if they placed their hands on a balky patient without consent (except in an emergency), they might be accused of a battery. On the other hand, if they agreed to a patient's demands to stop treatment, relatives might sue for damages. Such relatives might claim any release form was ineffective, because the patient (they would say) was incompetent when signing it. Doctors and other medical people might even face criminal charges accusing them of abandoning the patient.

Or, if they agreed to stop treatment, they might be accused of helping the patient commit suicide. A Florida doctor was worried about that possibility when a woman, Mrs. Carmen Martinez, begged for treatment to be stopped. The doctor asked Judge David Popper for guidance.

Mrs. Martinez had been in the hospital for two months because of a blood ailment, hemolytic anemia. The doctor said she needed transfusions and her spleen removed and that she would die in twenty-four hours without treatment.

Judge Popper refused to order it. "Administration of further blood transfusions would only result in the painful extension of her life for a short period of time," he commented. "A conscious adult patient who is mentally competent has the right to refuse medical treatment, even when the best medical opinion deems it essential to save her life."

Mrs. Martinez died within the twenty-four hours. "I hope she died in peace," Judge Popper said. She had, indeed, holding her daughter's hand.[4]

In saying that patients could legally refuse treatment, Judge Popper was observing what today seems to be a revered principle. For about ninety years, judges have been saying that people have a right to control their own bodies.

But in 1891, when the Supreme Court enunciated the principle, the justices meant it to include nothing more than that a woman need not "lay bare her body," as the court put it.

The Right of Bodily Integrity

That case involved Clara L. Botsford, who had been hurt while riding in the lower berth of a Union Pacific sleeping car.

Sleeping cars were essential in the 1890s. "Taking later train," one man wired his family. "Gave berth to old lady." But the lower berth alone was desirable: the train's ceiling pressed down on the upper one like a coffin lid.

Clara Botsford's lower berth turned out to be undesirable. The upper berth fell on her head, "bruising and wounding her, rupturing the membranes of the brain and spinal cord, and causing a concussion of the same," according to Justice Harold Gray of the U.S. Supreme Court.[5]

She sued Union Pacific. The railroad's lawyers wanted their own doctor to see how badly she was hurt, but she refused. A federal court in Indiana awarded her $10,000. That was then such big money that the railroad lawyers took the case to the Supreme Court, still complaining that their doctor should examine her.

She need not bare her body to that doctor, the justices decided. "No right is held more sacred, or is more carefully guarded by the common law, than the right of every individual to the possession and control of his own person . . ." wrote Justice Gray.[6] Union Pacific had to hand over the $10,000.

Aside from that decision, Justice Gray's Supreme Court record is undistinguished.[7] Yet, the case made him famous. In more than 100 other cases, judges have called to mind his words on the right to control one's own person.

The judges have often used their own jargon. They have written about the "right of bodily integrity" or the "right of bodily self-determination." You would think that this right alone would give people much authority over their own persons.[8]

Yet, when it came time for the Supreme Court to rule on whether state governments could regulate married couples' sexual activities, the justices chose to identify a new constitutional right. The words describing it—"the right of privacy"—are catchier than "the right of bodily integrity." The phrase seems to reach out further, to embrace more freedoms.

Also, in adopting it, the justices honored the memory of one of their most intelligent brothers, Louis D. Brandeis.

The Right of Privacy

Brandeis had, as a young lawyer in Boston, helped create privacy as a right that people could enforce through lawsuits. Later, as a Supreme Court justice, he had tried (and failed) in a convicted bootlegger's case to elevate privacy to a constitutionally protected right.

Once again, the story began in the 1890s.[9]

Brandeis and Samuel Warren, a member of a patrician Boston family, had been classmates at Harvard Law School. In the late 1880s, they practiced law together in Boston. Reporters and photographers pried into Warren's marriage to a senator's daughter and their life at a Back Bay home. So the two young lawyers wrote an article, "The Right to Privacy," for the *Harvard Law Review*.[10] It was full of an air of injured gentility, but Warren and Brandeis turned their grudge against yellow journalism into a change in the law.

The gist of the article was a protest against prurient or idle curiosity-seekers who peeked into decent people's back doors. After Warren and Brandeis wrote it, plaintiffs, in varying degrees and in various states, won damages for invasions of their privacy.

Juries now often listened sympathetically when plaintiffs complained that others had intruded by, for example, shadowing them; or that they had violated ordinary decencies, such as publishing a picture of a deformed child; or had put them in false lights, by, for example, signing their names to open letters; or had used their personalities for business purposes, such as printing their pictures in advertisements.[11]

In 1928, Brandeis, by now a Supreme Court justice, tried to give the new right constitutional status. The case that he used as a vehicle had nothing to do with medical treatment but rather was Prohibition's biggest criminal prosecution to that time. It involved a group of Seattle bootleggers, led by Roy Olmstead. Washingtonians called him "the good bootlegger," partly because of his reasonable prices.[12]

Olmstead's men would buy whiskey in Canada, where lawmakers had too much sense to forbid its sale. They would load it onto boats and run it through Puget Sound. In a Seattle office, salesmen took orders over the telephone, thinking they were secure because of a Washington State law that forbade wiretapping.

Federal agents disregarded that law. Without getting a search warrant, they tapped telephone lines for five months. Then they charged Olmstead and his men with conspiracy to violate the National Prohibition Act. Twenty-three were found guilty.

The bootleggers' lawyers went to the Supreme Court with the argument that it had been unconstitutional for prosecutors to use the wiretap evidence. They cited the Fourth Amendment: "The right of the people to be secure in their persons, houses, papers, and effects against unreasonable searches and seizures, shall not be violated . . ."

But those words, when read literally, protect only against officials who enter someone else's quarters. Because the amendment doesn't mention the telephone (which hadn't been invented when it was written), the words cost the bootleggers their freedom.

The words were plain enough to the court's chief justice, the former president, William Howard Taft. "The amendment does not forbid what was done here," he wrote. "There was no searching. There was no seizure. The evidence was secured by the use of the sense of hearing and that only. There was no entry of the houses or offices of the defendants."[13]

That was the winning opinion. Four other justices voted with Taft.

Brandeis could be expected to oppose his old enemy Taft on this issue. He believed the Constitution could be stretched. "Our Constitution is not a straitjacket," he had once written. "It . . . is capable of growth—of expansion and of adaptation to new conditions."[14]

Today, law professors and students skip past Taft's winning opinion and on to the heart of Brandeis's losing dissent, as follows:

> The makers of our Constitution . . . conferred, as against the government, the right to be let alone—the most comprehensive of rights and the right most valued by civilized man.[15]

The right to be let alone—what a plain way to put our right of privacy. Brandeis wasn't the first to use the phrase, but he gave it a throne.[16]

Brandeis was promoting in that case a right of privacy as inhering in a *place*—that is, Roy Olmstead's place of business. In contrast, in that famous law review article, he and his law partner had urged the recognition of a right inherent in the *person*—so people could legally fight off interference with their individuality. As we move along in this chapter, it will be that aspect of privacy that we will be most interested in. And when, a quarter of a century after Brandeis's death, the Supreme Court finally agreed that privacy was indeed protected by the Constitution, the justices used it in a case that involved a *relationship*—that of marriage.[17]

That case came to the court because of what two justices called an "uncommonly silly law" in Connecticut, discouraging contraception. The Connecticut law empowered judges to fine or imprison anyone who used contraceptive devices or anyone who advised another person about contraception.

This relic of the Comstockian era's crusade against vice seemed to prohibit even married couples from deciding whether to have children. But, in fact, police didn't enter bedrooms of middle-class couples to search for condoms. They enforced the law against birth-control clinics, and thus it was poor or uneducated people who failed to get birth-control advice.

The Catholic Church, earlier a strong supporter of that law, was by the 1960s ready to concede that it involved a religious rather than a legal issue.[18] Yet Connecticut lawmakers preferred to let judges handle the risky public execution.

In 1965, by a seven-to-two vote, the Supreme Court killed the law and for the first time established that privacy existed as an independent constitutional right.[19]

The case started when Estelle T. Griswold, director of the Planned

Parenthood League of Connecticut, gave contraceptive instruction and medical adivce (a Yale doctor helped her) to New Haven married couples. A state court fined her and the doctor $100 each.

The Supreme Court overturned the convictions.[20] In the court's view, Estelle Griswold and the physician had merely helped married people in their private affairs.

The spokesman for a constitutional right of privacy was Justice William O. Douglas, onetime sufferer from polio and later a mountain climber, destined to serve on the court longer than anyone else—thirty-six years.[21] To Douglas, the guarantees in parts of the Bill of Rights had "penumbras." Zones of privacy emanate from the guarantees that are written.

Connecticut had violated the privacy of marriage. "Would we allow the police to search the sacred precincts of marital bedrooms for telltale signs of the use of contraceptives?" Douglas asked, pretending that this really was a danger.[22]

No one before then had seen the penumbra that Justice Douglas described. But, to him, it had been there all along. The idea that judges can discover a hidden law, and therefore are not creating a new one, has a long history in courts.

That is not to suggest that the justices ignored precedent. Their path to this conclusion was already worn.[23] Nor did the majority speak with one voice. Their four opinions exploded like popcorn.

Still, five of the justices seemed to support privacy in marriage as one of the Constitution's "fundamental rights." Such rights are those that are implicit in our principles of liberty and justice.[24]

Privacy now had a special niche. As the justices became more familiar with the constitutional right of privacy—their own discovery—they would allow state laws to limit it only for a "compelling state interest." Even then, lawmakers had to select the least restrictive means. Judges would throw out any sweeping laws.

The Supreme Court justices henceforth would give a beady-eyed stare at state laws touching on family matters and sexual activity. In 1972, therefore, they ruled that, when a state allowed distribution of contraceptives to married persons, it must also permit them for single ones. To discriminate against single people would be to deny them the equal protection of the laws, according to Justice William J. Brennan, Jr.

In that decision, Brennan threw in the following remark, which, while it didn't decide the case, showed he thought it was a person's private business to decide whether to have children: "If the right of privacy means anything, it is the right of the *individual*, married or single, to be free from unwarranted governmental intrusion into matters so fundamentally affecting a person as the decision whether to bear or beget a child."[25]

The decision whether to bear a child wasn't at issue in that case, but the Supreme Court had before it abortion cases in which it was. Justice Brennan was letting everyone know his views in advance.

Then, in one of the abortion cases, a Texas woman convinced the Supreme Court that she had had a limited right to an abortion when she had been pregnant three years before.[26] It had taken the case that long to wend its way through the courts. The justices decided to hear her argument anyhow, on the grounds that, if they insisted a woman still be pregnant when such a case reached them, they could never settle the abortion question.

The woman in the case called herself Jane Roe, and that fictitious name is the one still in the lawbooks. Jane lived in Dallas County, was single, had a tenth-grade education, was having difficulty finding a job because of her pregnancy, and feared the stigma of bearing an illegitimate child.[27] Under Texas law, she could have an abortion only if she would die without it.

Her lawyer was twenty-eight-year-old Sarah Weddington, taking on one of her first court cases after graduating from Texas Law School. Lawyer Weddington later served in the Texas House of Representatives, then went on to Washington, where she counseled President Jimmy Carter on women's issues.

Justice Harry A. Blackmun wrote the opinion, drawing constitutional lines at trimesters of pregnancy. His combined medical-and-judicial approach was so unusual that law clerks labeled it "Harry's abortion."[28]

A majority (7–2) of the justices ruled that a state cannot regulate abortions during the first trimester—the first three months of pregnancy. If her doctor agreed, Jane Roe could have had an abortion during that time without any interference from Texas officials.[29]

Thus, the right of privacy had evolved. It now allowed pregnant women to have free choice and self-determination. But that reproductive privacy wasn't unlimited. Texas had an interest in protecting health as well as the potentiality of life. As a woman got closer to term, each of those interests became compelling and therefore overrode her right.[30]

Beyond three months, the justices ruled, abortion was dangerous enough to a mother's health that a state could insist, for example, that a doctor perform it in a hospital. The state could virtually forbid an abortion after the fetus was old enough to live outside its mother's body, though even then the mother could have an abortion to preserve her life or health.

The Supreme Court decision didn't settle the abortion issue in many persons' minds. Those who oppose it often say that God's laws aren't repealable by His creatures. A detailed discussion of the right-to-life vs. freedom-of-choice dispute is beyond the scope of this book.

In 1976, justices on New Jersey's highest court applied the right of privacy to a new issue—a rejection of life-sustaining medical care. By then, the right-to-die controversy was in full swing, with patients claiming that physicians were unnecessarily prolonging deaths. The case of Karen Ann Quinlan, as we'll learn in Chapter 7, seemed to prove the accusation.

It was appropriate for the New Jersey justices to give Karen the benefit of the new constitutional right of privacy. True, she couldn't demand it for herself, since she had no ability to reason or think. Yet, the Supreme Court of New Jersey could pretend that she spoke through her father.

"Presumably this right of privacy is broad enough to encompass a patient's decision to decline medical treatment," commented New Jersey Chief Justice Richard J. Hughes, "in much the same way as it is broad enough to encompass a woman's decision to terminate pregnancy under certain conditions."[31]

And this right is our legacy from Louis Brandeis.

In the Supreme Court building in Washington, I gaze at the bronze head of Brandeis, sculpted by Eleanor Platt. The face is cut in planes; the nose is strong and hawk-shaped, the mass of hair wavy and uncontrolled. His eyes are expectant, his lips pursed. He is poised on the brink of a question, ready for knowledge.

The right of privacy that was eventually protected was more widesweeping than the one he had first advocated. It proved to be what law professor Paul Freund later called a greedy legal concept. It gobbled up within its meaning personal freedoms that judges called by other names.

It now embraces not merely a right of secrecy but also authority to make some—though not all—decisions about your own body without intrusion by the government.

Though he failed to forecast the extent to which the right of privacy would be carried, Brandeis helped us maintain our individuality and personal dignity.[32] He changed our lives.

The Free Exercise of Religion

Patients sometimes invoke the First Amendment guarantee of the free exercise of religion. In contrast to the right of privacy, it has been in the Constitution all along. Jehovah's Witnesses often cite it. Through faith and tenacity, they have enlarged our freedom to control our own bodies.

The Witnesses believe that a divine regulation prohibits partaking of others' blood. In principle, they say, there is no distinction between taking blood by mouth and taking it into the blood vessels.[33] Incidentally, artificial blood—a chemical that Jehovah's Witnesses have accepted in transfusions—may end a long-standing controversy caused by their refusal.[34]

Meanwhile, treating Jehovah's Witnesses must be as frustrating for some doctors as fighting in Korea and Vietnam was for U.S. generals. The generals were told to forgo their best weapons and strategy but to win nevertheless.

Such frustration may have had an effect when a Chicago woman, Mrs. Bernice Brooks, went into the hospital. She had a peptic ulcer and, over a two-year period, had told her doctor she would refuse transfusions. She had given him a copy of *Blood, Medicine, and the Law of God*, a Jehovah's Witness booklet that quoted Leviticus 17:10: "As for any man of the house of Israel or some alien resident . . . who eats any sort of blood, I shall certainly set my face against the soul that is eating the blood, and I shall indeed cut him off from among his people."[35]

When Mrs. Brooks went into the hospital, she and her husband signed a paper excusing her doctor and the hospital from liability when they failed to give her transfusions. But death approached, and, when she was so far gone that doctors felt she was incompetent, they and lawyers for the state went into court. Judge Robert Jerome Dunne allowed a transfusion. She lived.

Mrs. Brooks could not unmix the donated blood and give it back. But she persuaded justices in the Supreme Court of Illinois to consider the case once more, as if she were once again dying.

Illinois state's attorneys opposed her, reminding the justices that people do not have a right to do anything they want in the name of religion. The law would punish a backwoods preacher who handed rattlesnakes to worshippers, for example.

That argument failed to convince the justices. When a preacher hands a snake around, he might hurt persons other than himself. Mrs. Brooks could hurt only herself. She had no young children who would be left motherless if she died. She would not be endangering public health, welfare, or morals. True, as Justice Robert C. Underwood wrote, one might consider her beliefs "unwise, foolish, or ridiculous,"[36] but her right to exercise her religion freely meant she could refuse transfusions, though she might die without them.

That decision must have given Judge Dunne mixed feelings. He had saved Mrs. Brooks's life and in the process violated the First Amendment.[37] If a similar case came before him again, he must obey the upper court and allow the patient to die.

Judges, though, as we shall learn, will search for excuses to avoid what they regard as useless deaths.

Fundamental Rights and Their Limitations

Thus, your refusal of medical treatment can be grounded in one of the following: your right of bodily integrity; your right of privacy; your right of free religious exercise. On the other hand, it's possible to carry the concepts of patient autonomy and death-with-dignity too far. For example, physicians know that a patient in pain or depression may ask to be allowed to die. Wise physicians and patients' families will insist that the pain or the depression be treated. Then the patient can reevaluate the situation.[38]

Another patient may be ambivalent, wanting today to die and tomorrow to live. Still another may have hidden personal problems, such as a feeling of abandonment, or may fear the machinery to be used in treatment. Thus, when a patient says, "I want to die," it doesn't mean doctors and nurses should instantly click off switches or pull out tubes.[39]

Beyond that, no legal right is absolute. Each can be limited because of competing interests. Henning Jacobson, of Cambridge, Massachusetts, found that out in 1905 after he refused a vaccination for smallpox. The local board of health had noted that the disease was on the rise and, using a state statute as authority, ordered everyone in town to be vaccinated.

He had been vaccinated as a child, Jacobson said in objecting, and had suffered for a long time afterward from a disease. The state's statute, he said, was "hostile to the inherent right of every freeman to care for his own body and health in such a way as seems to him to be best."

A local court fined Jacobson five dollars. He fought the conviction to the U.S. Supreme Court, but lost.[40] The reason was that the public's health, not his alone, was being protected against a dangerous disease that might lead to an epidemic.

Similarly, a judge might decide that a patient must accept treatment to protect third parties. For example, a state might have a compelling interest in maintaining productive life for a parent who was the sole support of a child. Otherwise, the child might have to go on public welfare.

Also, physicians have argued in court that the ethical integrity of the medical profession is at stake. It's not the business of doctors or hospitals to let patients die, they have said. On the other hand, many physicians now recognize that life is not the absolute good and death not the absolute evil.

Going beyond those reasons, state's attorneys will argue in court that the state has a compelling general interest in preserving the lives of those within its borders. And so it does, when an illness is curable. But, when a patient's illness cannot be reversed, the state's interest weakens. Judges will refuse to order useless treatment—a mere stretching-out of the death process.

The state also has an interest in preventing suicide. To help another commit it is a crime in most states. Physicians sometimes fear that they will be prosecuted under such laws. On the other hand, many patients who refuse medical treatment are merely willing to surrender to their own illnesses.[41] They have no intention to commit suicide but instead intend to let nature have its way.

But judges may question the mental competence of patients who reject treatment that poses little risk and promises great benefits. "Any person who refused treatment that would save his life is crazy," a judge might conclude, "and a person who is crazy cannot refuse the treatment."[42]

In Washington, D.C., in 1964, Judge J. Skelly Wright visited the bedside of a Jehovah's Witness who had lost two-thirds of her blood because of a ruptured ulcer. The patient's husband had refused to give permission for a blood transfusion on religious grounds. Judge Wright told the woman that doctors had estimated she would have a fifty-fifty chance of living if she'd permit blood to be transfused to her body. She replied. "Against my will."

"It was obvious that the woman was not in a mental condition to make a decision," Judge Wright later wrote.[43] So he examined the problem in her behalf.

She had a seven-month-old baby who needed her, and so the state had an interest in preserving her life. She probably did not want to die, or she would not have come to the hospital. The judge ordered the transfusions, and the woman recovered.

Judge Wright logically could have ruled that her words "against my will" and her commitment as a Jehovah's Witness meant she was refusing blood in a clearly-thought-out way. But, no, he could prevent a tragedy with mere words. He revealed the pressure he must have felt at the time: "A life hung in the balance. There was no time for research and reflection."[44] He need only say she was incompetent.[45] And he did.

In contrast, a judge is likely to agree with a patient's refusal of treatment when it cannot ward off death, when the patient would have a poor quality of life, or when the treatment would be a torture in itself. Medical treatment for a Florida patient, Abe Perlmutter, seventy-three, fell into all three of those categories.

The Abe Perlmutter Case

Mr. Perlmutter was a former New York cab driver and physical fitness enthusiast. He had retired to Fort Lauderdale and then was stricken with a disease—amyotrophic lateral sclerosis—that is nicknamed for a famous baseball player (whom it killed), Lou Gehrig.

"Abe was a tough, wiry man, about five-feet-eight and a hundred-and-forty pounds," said his lawyer, David A. Hoines, of Fort Lauderdale. "He had his own taxicab in New York City and used to get into fisticuffs with truck drivers. A passenger once stuck a knife to his throat, trying to rob him. Abe grabbed the knife, which cut his hand. The assailant went running out of the cab. Abe ran after him and collared him.

"At the condominium where he lived in Fort Lauderdale, he would get up early and go on long runs. He led exercise classes for retired people. He once took on his son Jerry and another young fellow in a three-handed game of handball, two against one. He beat both of them."

With Lou Gehrig's disease, nerves that control muscles degenerate. Then the muscles themselves waste away.

"Here you've got a man who's physical, who's strong, who's outgoing, watching his arms and legs die while his mind is untouched," said lawyer Hoines. "Speech becomes difficult, because muscles in the tongue go. The muscles that cause the lungs to inhale and exhale deteriorate."

It was a crisis in Abe Perlmutter's breathing that put him in a coma in May 1978 and caused his wife, Edna, to have him rushed to a hospital. Doctors saved him from immediate death. They ran a tube into his windpipe to feed air to his lungs, and later performed a tracheotomy (cut an incision in his windpipe) and inserted the tube from a respirator there.

The use of a respirator was standard medical treatment for a patient in his condition. But soon afterward, he began a struggle to rid himself of it. His son, daughter, and grandchildren came from Texas and California to visit him. "I'm miserable; take it out," he would tell his family, mouthing the words, because, except when the respirator was removed briefly, he could not voice them.

Within a few weeks, his wife, seventy years old, died of a heart attack. When he was told, Mr. Perlmutter cried himself to sleep.

He was given an alphabet board, so he could spell out messages by pointing to letters. On one occasion, he spelled the words: "P-U-L-L T-H-E C-O-R-D."

He himself tried to remove the respirator connection. "He could still move his right arm and fingers to some extent," attorney Hoines said later. "He would pull the respirator tube away from the place where it was inserted in the trachea. An alarm would sound, and the hospital staff would plug him back in."

According to one of Mr. Perlmutter's physicians, disconnecting the respirator would result in a reasonable life expectancy of less than one hour. Even with the respirator, the prognosis was death in nine to twelve months.

In June, with Mr. Hoines as his lawyer, Mr. Perlmutter sued the hospital, two doctors, and the state attorney for Broward County. He asked for a "declaratory judgment"—one that would state his rights rather than say anyone had damaged him.

The case was first heard by Judge John G. Ferris, of the Circuit Court in Fort Lauderdale. There, and then in the District Court of Appeal in West Palm Beach, state attorneys argued that Florida had an overriding duty to preserve life. Also, a Florida law makes it a crime to help another person commit "self-murder." Anyone helping Mr. Perlmutter disconnect the respirator would be guilty of manslaughter under that law, according to the state's lawyers, or even murder under a different law.

The doctors and hospital feared they would be sued for damages or would face criminal prosecution if they aided in removal of the respirator. In addition, the doctors pointed to the ethical rule that requires a physician to preserve life. One of them, a pulmonary specialist, later told a presidential commission that Mr. Perlmutter could have signed himself out of the hospital "AMA"—that is, against medical advice—and gone home on a portable respirator. "If [a patient] comes to me, he wants me to help," the doctor said. "If he stays in the hospital, we are going to try to do everything we can."[46]

But the option of Mr. Perlmutter's leaving the hospital wasn't argued in court. Moving him wouldn't have resolved the legal dilemma, according to attorney Hoines. Anyone involved in his removal from the hospital respirator would have been threatened by the Florida criminal statutes.

Judge Ferris visited the hospital and confirmed that Mr. Perlmutter was competent.

"Mr. Perlmutter, do you know what will happen to you if somebody pulls that thing out of your throat?" the judge asked.

"It can't be worse than what I'm going through now," Mr. Perlmutter replied.

In another response, Mr. Perlmutter said he didn't care whether he died, but later he said, "I'd like to live."

"Do you want to have the chance to make the decision yourself?" Judge Ferris asked. "That is, whether or not someone should pull that plug?" Abe Perlmutter nodded affirmatively to each of those two questions and nodded again when the judge repeated: "You want to make that decision yourself?"[47]

In July, Judge Ferris ruled that Mr. Perlmutter's right to privacy meant he could stay in the hospital or leave it, free of the respirator, as he chose. He could ask any other person to help disconnect the respirator, and such a person would not be liable in damages. Nor was the state attorney to bring a criminal charge against anyone.[48]

The appeals judges in West Palm Beach then ruled that Judge Ferris was correct. Disconnecting the respirator wouldn't amount to suicide, they decided. "He really wants to live, but [to] do so, God and Mother

Nature willing, under his own power," Judge Gavin K. Letts wrote. Mr. Perlmutter's children, both of them being adults, had approved his decision, the judge noted.

As for Florida's interest in preserving life, the appeals judge pointed out that Mr. Perlmutter was already in terminal condition. The respirator could keep him alive for only a brief time. Disconnecting it would not harm innocent third parties, because Mr. Perlmutter had no underage children that would be abandoned.

The judge noted that medical ethics have evolved, so that doctors and others can accept a patient's right to refuse treatment under some circumstances.

Judge Letts ended with these words:

> It is all very convenient to insist on continuing Mr. Perlmutter's life so that there can be no question of foul play, no resulting civil liability and no possible trespass on medical ethics. However, it is quite another matter to do so at the patient's sole expense and against his competent will, thus inflicting never-ending physical torture on his body until the inevitable, but artificially suspended, moment of death. Such a course of conduct removes his freedom of choice and invades his right to self determine.[49]

In early October, the Florida Supreme Court refused to delay the ruling's effect. Abe Perlmutter had now been on the respirator five months.

Attorney Hoines continued the story: "After the court issued its ruling, I went out to the hospital and asked Abe again whether he was intent on removing the respirator. He didn't waver. I made him promise not to do anything until his son Jerry could come from Texas and daughter Carol Klaman could come from California. He asked me to thank Judge Ferris for his concern and good wishes."

The next morning, a Wednesday, Carol, Jerry and his wife Lee, and attorney Hoines were gathered in the hospital room. None of the hospital staff was present. At 10:59, Abe Perlmutter himself disconnected the respirator. Alarms went off, until a switch was flipped.

At 3:40 Friday morning, a little over forty hours later, he died.

At the funeral, a rabbi said Mr. Perlmutter had died the way he had lived. That was true. He had been as independent and courageous in facing death as he had been in facing life.

3
DISCOVERING DEFECTS BEFORE A BABY IS BORN

SATURDAY, *September 27*—Paula Sandy is thirty-six years old and has had three miscarriages. She and her husband Richard ("Rich"), "having no luck on our own," have adopted a son, Tommy. Now she is pregnant again.

On October 16, she will undergo an amniocentesis to discover if her fetus is defective. At her age, the expected incidence of Down syndrome (mongolism) is 1 in 300.[1] That is more than three times the incidence for mothers under thirty.

The reason is probably that a woman is born with all the eggs she'll ever have. When Paula reached thirty-six, the eggs in her ovaries were also thirty-six. The egg that gave existence to her fetus had been exposed to X-rays and other outside forces longer than if it had been fertilized when it was younger.

Her miscarriages might have meant her body was tattling, saying the earlier fetuses were defective.[2] Granted, doctors had examined the fetus the last time and found no defects. Still, as a genetic counselor and physician, Dr. John L. Young, informed her last week, the combination of miscarriages and her age mean that there is about a $1\frac{1}{2}$ to 2 percent chance that the fetus she now carries will be defective.

If it is, she will have an abortion. "I know that mongoloids have brought some families happiness," she said. "But I have to look at myself as the kind of person I am. I don't think I'm one of those magic people who can do it. Plus, a mongoloid—or anybody that's retarded—is going to be very dependent on the parents. Twenty years down the road, I'm going to be fifty-six, then sixty-six, and what's going to happen to this child who is dependent on you, and you're not around?"

When she went to Dr. Young for the genetic counseling session last week, she asked, "If I do have to have an abortion, what's it going to be like?" Now she wishes she hadn't asked. He told her a doctor would inject a saline solution into her abdomen and then wait for a process that would be like natural childbirth, except the fetus would be dead. Pain medication may be used, but Paula would choose to be unconscious if she could.

"Even though I believe in the right [to have an abortion], I've hoped someone else would need the right, not me," Paula said. "That's cruelty, to me."

Almost three years ago, she and Rich adopted Tommy. She thinks it is a miracle that they were chosen as adoptive parents, but it is easy to see why they were. They are intelligent and earnest. They are both high school teachers, she having taught biology before resigning to care for Tommy. Rich teaches earth science and does carpentry work on the side.

They live in a Dutch-style house off a country road in the Maryland foothills. At the back is a deck that Rich built. It overlooks a descending forest. Around the house are the azaleas that she loves to tend but has given up for now because Dr. Young has told her she should rest six hours a day and sleep eight.

Only a few years ago, she and Rich would not have faced the harsh choice that they may have to make. But then the U.S. Supreme Court decided that a woman could use her right of privacy, in concert with her doctor, to choose an abortion under certain circumstances. And scientists learned how to discover defects while a fetus is still in the womb.

Now, thousands of women each year undergo the tests that Paula Sandy will have. Doctors perform most such tests in university-affiliated hospitals. Paula will have hers performed by Genetic Consultants, one of the first clinics of its kind. It was formed by Dr. Young and Dr. Mark R. Geier. Dr. Young, having recently completed his training at Johns Hopkins Hospital, brought to the new clinic a background as an obstetrician. Dr. Geier earned his Ph.D. in genetics, then earned an M.D., and is an assistant professor of obstetrics and gynecology at Johns Hopkins Medical School in Baltimore.

DISCOVERING DEFECTS BEFORE A BABY IS BORN 39

The problem of congenital defects and hereditary diseases is enormous.[3] About 100,000 to 150,000 babies are born each year with such troubles. About a fourth of young patients—under eighteen—who enter acute-care hospitals have such disorders.

They also cause much of the nation's mental retardation. Two out of every five people with IQs less than 50 ("normal" is about 100) have a chromosomal disorder, such as Down syndrome; a single-gene disease, such as Tay-Sachs; or a severe malformation, such as open-spine or related defects.

Many persons, such as Paula Sandy, would choose abortion if a fetus were defective. In 1975, 86 percent of white Protestants and 77 percent of white Catholics thought a pregnant woman should be able to obtain a legal abortion if there were a strong chance of a serious defect in the baby. The number of Catholics who favored this had about doubled in thirteen years.[4]

Specialists advise pregnant women over thirty-five to have amniocentesis. And the number of women who have children at such late ages is increasing. From 1975 to 1978, those having their first babies between the ages of thirty-five and thirty-nine increased by 22 percent.

Women gave various reasons for those late starts. The right man hadn't been available, or else they were making late-in-life gifts to themselves. And they said they were influenced by the availability of tests to determine if a fetus was defective.[5]

Doctors first used amniocentesis in 1968, and already it is a household word. It means "puncture of the amniotic cavity," that is, the sac containing the fluid within which a fetus floats. Dr. Young will push a hollow needle through Paula's abdominal wall, into the sac, and withdraw a sample of yellow fluid.

He and Dr. Geier will use the fluid for two purposes: to determine if the chromosomes in the fetus's cells are abnormal and to discover whether the fluid contains too much of a certain protein, alpha-fetoprotein, or AFP.

On the average, mothers who have undergone amniocentesis have had no more miscarriages than others. Nor have their babies had significantly different birth weights or more complications than others.[6]

Still, the process is not error-free. Ironically, lab mixups cause mistakes. Technicians occasionally switch microscopic slides, or secretaries mistype letters telling obstetricians or parents the results.[7]

And mishaps occur. The needle could cause infection or stab the fetus. It could puncture the mother's small bowel, her bladder, or a blood vessel in her uterus.[8]

The accidents are rare enough that a pregnant woman at risk for bearing a defective child will usually decide to go ahead. The dangers are a good reason, on the other hand, why amniocentesis isn't for every pregnant woman. Young women with no background that would suggest they will give birth to defective children would do well to avoid it.

Another detection technique—which is still experimental and won't be used on Paula Sandy—is fetoscopy. A doctor pushes a small telescope (called a "fetoscope") through a pregnant woman's abdominal wall and down into the amniotic sac and peers at the fetus. The fetoscope has a narrow field of view and therefore cannot show the doctor the entire fetus, floating inside its private world. Rather, the doctor may see three toes, blobs, filling the view.

The doctor searches for a tiny blood vessel on the surface of the membrane surrounding the sac. He finds it and feeds a flexible, hollow needle through the fetoscope. The needle is as fine as a mosquito's proboscis. The tip touches the vessel, penetrates, and sucks in a small amount of blood. Technologists will later test it, looking for disorders.

Fetoscopy is so risky for fetuses that scientists have tested it only when mothers already planned to have abortions, or when the risk of having a seriously abnormal fetus was high.

Another method for looking at the fetus doesn't require any invasion of the mother's body. That is sonography, and in a few years its use has boomed.[9]

Paula Sandy has already undergone two sonograms. At nine weeks, physicians checked her fetus's age by measuring its head. At thirteen weeks, they looked it over again.

Bats have always used the sound-echoing technique that humans discovered how to use only in the twentieth century. In the darkness, a bat emits squeaks and listens to their echoes so as to dodge obstacles.

The medical use of sonography developed from World War II experience. Aboard a destroyer escort, a technician would send sound waves streaming into the depths and listen to their echoes. If the waves returned more quickly than they ordinarily did from the ocean floor, the technician might decide an enemy submarine was lurking below.

At the Clinical Center, the research hospital of the National Institutes of Health, I watch as a modern hunter searches for defects in a human

DISCOVERING DEFECTS BEFORE A BABY IS BORN   41

heart. The hunter, a physician, poises a "transducer," which is like an oversized pencil, over the patient's chest. The sounds it emits are too high in pitch for human ears to hear. They go through the skin, strike internal and external surfaces of the heart, and send echoes back. Now I raise my eyes to what looks like a television screen. Machinery has converted the echoes into images, and I see into the inner chambers of the living heart.

Similarly, sonography permits doctors to peer through a mother's abdominal wall and see her unborn child. They have seen defects such as water-on-the-brain, kidney trouble, blocked intestines, and neural-tube defects.

And, with a high-speed unit, the doctor can watch the fetus as it moves about inside its mother's body.[10] That unit feeds flicker-free images to the screen.

Thursday, October 16—Paula Sandy had her amniocentesis today, lying on an examination table in the doctor's office. The dramatic part was not the insertion of a needle to withdraw amniotic fluid but rather the image on a screen of her developing child. It was revealed as Dr. John Young passed a six-inch-long, domino-shaped transducer over Paula's abdomen.

Rich Sandy watched as Dr. Mark Geier pointed to the hemispheres of the brain, the parts of the heart, the spinal cord.

"That was thrilling to my husband," Paula said later. "I wanted him to see inside, to see what it was all about. It was like a TV picture of the baby. And the baby was moving around like crazy."

Dr. Geier once again calibrated the size of the fetus's head, thus confirming its age. At birth, one baby's head size is different from another's, but earlier, during pregnancy, they are similar at similar ages. The measurement is important, because the doctor must know the fetus's age to determine whether the amount of AFP is excessive. AFP decreases in amount as a fetus grows. An amount that would be tragic for a sixteen-week-old fetus—indicating a severe malformation—would be normal for a younger one.

Dr. Young used the sonogram to reveal to what depth and where he should insert a needle. He pressed the flat of a penny into Paula's skin there.

The doctor washed Paula's swollen abdomen and swabbed it with an iodine-colored antiseptic. He draped her with a sterile sheet with a hole that left bare the spot where he would insert the needle. Paula looked away when he picked up a hypodermic needle.

Rich watched as Dr. Young injected an anesthetic under Paula's skin, then inserted a larger needle through the place where the penny had left a dent, pushing down for more than two inches. Rich didn't cringe. He had no fear that the needle would stab his child because he understood the method used to find the proper place and measure the depth.

Dr. Young said, "This will cause a slight cramping," but, if he hadn't said it, Paula might not have noticed. It was like a slight menstrual cramp.

Dr. Young connected one vial to the needle, drew off a small amount of liquid, and then discarded it, because it would be contaminated with Paula's own cells and perhaps blood. Then he drew two more vials of a yellow fluid, applied a Band-Aid, and examined the fetus again with ultrasound.

The doctors said this final sonogram was to enable Paula and Rich to see their child once again, but Paula thought instead that they were checking to make sure the fetus was all right. Then Paula dressed. Before she left, the doctors told her to report any leakage or cramps.

She and her husband had expected the process to take longer. Now, with three-year-old Tommy in good hands back home, they went out to dinner. In about four hours, her body replaced the fluid that had been taken.

Some of the yellow fluid taken from Paula Sandy's amniotic cavity went to a laboratory in California for an AFP measurement. An occasional fetus has a neural-tube defect, in which the backbone that should have folded over the spinal cord like a tube has failed to do so. The spinal cord or brain then may be unprotected by skin or bone, and will leak AFP into the amniotic fluid. If carried to term, a baby with such a defect might be paralyzed below the waist or have such an incomplete head, brain, or spinal column as to be unable to live. Neural-tube defects are among the most common birth defects, yet are scarcely known except—tragically—to parents to whom the babies are born.[11]

A blocked intestinal tract might also cause an elevated AFP reading. In such a case the fetus would be unable to digest AFP, and so it would go into the surrounding fluid. Such a fetus can survive in the womb because it receives its food through the umbilical cord, but at birth it would need an operation or else would starve.

If Paula's AFP reading were more than three times normal, doctors would repeat the test.[12] They would also look even more carefully than before with ultrasound, to make certain she wasn't carrying twins (two fetuses put out more AFP than one), or to discover abnormal body protrusions or missing parts. They could also put a dye into her amniotic fluid and take X-ray pictures to find whether it entered the fetus's spinal column at the wrong place, indicating an abnormal opening there.

Careful checking is important. An occasional fetus is aborted because the AFP level is high, and then doctors find it has no abnormalities.[13]

Friday, October 31—Paula Sandy received the report on the AFP level today. She had thought she'd receive it earlier. Today, she was "climbing the wall," so she called the clinic and found that she had failed to understand that it operated on a no-news-is-good-news procedure. "We have the results, and they are normal," she was told. "We don't usually call you if they are normal."

Thus, her fetus apparently has no neural-tube defect. That is nevertheless only half the news that she must wait for. She has yet to learn whether her fetus has abnormal chromosomes. The laboratory process is slower for that determination.

October 16 to early November—Part of Paula Sandy's amniotic fluid was sent to a Baltimore laboratory. Technicians transferred it from its syringe to a plastic flask, mixing it with a pink nutrient. The procedure is based on the knowledge that Paula's fetus has shed living cells, and that some were floating in the amniotic fluid when Dr. Young pulled a sample of the fluid into the syringe.

The flask is now in an incubator, set at 98.6 degrees, with high humidity and carbon dioxide. Thus the conditions are like those in Paula Sandy's body—just right for her fetus's cells to grow.[14]

A technician adds fresh medium as food every three to four days. After a couple of weeks or so, there'll be enough cells so they can be tested. The technician will then add an inhibitor to stop their development.

When enough are in suspended animation at the point of division where their chromosomes are visible, the technician will break open some of them and mix them with a fluorescent stain on a glass slide. Each chromosome will then glow with alternate dark-and-light stripes, like a sergeant's hashmarks, in a different pattern from other chromosomes.

The technician will photograph them and then cut out their images and arrange them in pairs, in rows, on a sheet of paper. The images of the biggest chromosomes will be at the top left, with each pair becoming smaller until, at the bottom right, the specialist will mount the images of the sex chromosomes. That arrangement is called a karyotype. There should be twenty-three pairs of chromosomes, in X or Y shapes. Rich will have contributed half—one of each pair—and Paula half.

A specialist will examine the small chromosomes at the bottom of the page first.[15] Are there three No. 21 chromosomes instead of the expected pair? If so, that fetus has Down syndrome, which many persons still call mongolism. A child who has it will be mentally retarded and may have eye cataracts, heart troubles, a blocked intestine, or a predisposition to leukemia.

Now the specialist will move a finger to the next row up, where the chromosomes are larger. Are there three No. 18s instead of the expected pair? Even if such a fetus survives to birth—and that might not happen, because the mother's body would probably reject it—it might have no fusion of the face. It might have a cleft lip and no nose. If born alive, such a baby would probably die inside a year.

The specialist will point to the sex chromosomes at the bottom right of the sheet. If the fetus is a female, there will be two large X chromosomes. If there is only one, then the fetus will have only a single dose of femaleness. That deficiency—Turner's syndrome—will mean she has no ovaries or almost none and will be short in stature. She will suffer almost no handicap in intelligence, however.

If the fetus is male, there should be one large X female sex chromosome and one small Y male one. If, instead, there are three sex chromosomes—XXY—he will have an extra dose of femaleness. The extra dose, called Klinefelter's syndrome, will mean that even when grown he will have skinny legs, small testes, and larger breasts than most men. He will have a high voice and never spend much for razor blades.

If, in contrast, the three sex chromosomes include an extra dose of maleness—XYY—it may lead to criminality in later years, according to some observers, although that is open to doubt. Some people point to the rumor that Richard Speck has that disorder. Speck killed eight nurses, one by one, during a 1966 night in a Chicago apartment that he left drenched in blood.

In fact, Speck has no extra Y chromosome. It is true that more XYY men are in mental and penal institutions than you would expect from their numbers in the general population, but the reason isn't known.[16] There's no proof that they're less intelligent and therefore more likely to be caught than others. Some observers have suggested that, because they're usually taller than other men, judges see them as more of a threat than shorter ones and therefore send them to jail more often.

Thus the images of the threadlike chromosomes, in their X and Y shapes, will form a picture of Paula Sandy's fetus.

Thursday, November 13—Paula had the amniocentesis four weeks ago today. Today she was jumpy. "Every time the phone rang, I said, 'Oh, that's it,'" she said. "My husband comes home every night and says, 'Well, did you hear?'"

She has been pregnant for twenty weeks now. That's halfway. The doctor has told her she can resume some of her normal activities, but that it's too risky to travel to Pennsylvania to visit relatives at Thanksgiving and Christmas.

"There has been so much stress in this pregnancy," Paula said. "It just seems like I've been pregnant forever."

Sunday, November 16—Dr. Mark Geier called today, with news about the chromosomal makeup of Paula Sandy's fetus. She hadn't expected the call on a Sunday. The picture of her fetus's chromosomes came in Friday, and Dr. Geier was finishing up the week's work today.

He had the photograph (the karyotype) of the chromosomes in hand and had confirmed the information given him by the Baltimore laboratory. He had glanced at the chromosomes in the No. 21 location. There were only two. Good. The fetus didn't have Down syndrome. The other chromosomes were also arranged, two by two, in rows—no triple chromosomes, no missing ones, and no fragments lying about or attached to other ones. He looked at the sex chromosomes at the lower right corner of the karyotype and saw a large X and a smaller Y one.

"Your baby has no chromosomal defect," Mark Geier told Paula. "It's a boy."

Paula recognized that her baby might still be defective. "I know they can't check for everything," she told me later. "It is misleading for families to think that this identifies all possible defects." Still, her voice had less nervousness than before, as if the test had merely confirmed what she had known all along.

She refuses to give her fetus a name, even though she knows the sex. "This baby will have a name long enough," she said.

I got the impression she didn't want to personify the fetus and thereby show too much confidence. Her attitude was like that of spectators at a baseball game who see a no-hitter in the making but won't jinx it by saying so.

Saturday, March 28—Paula Sandy gave birth to her baby, a boy, today. Weight: 8 pounds, 10¼ ounces. She and Rich named him Matthew Paul Sandy. He is normal. "You couldn't ask for a better baby," Paula told me.

Suing the Doctor Who Fails to Communicate

A Washington, D.C., area woman, almost thirty-five, told her obstetrician on her first visit that she thought she'd have an amniocentesis. He replied that it was only after she reached thirty-eight or so that she'd have to worry.

"I'm not going to tell you not to," he said, "but, if you were my wife, I'd say don't bother."

"I'm not your wife," she replied. She had the amniocentesis. It revealed a fetus with Down syndrome, and she had an abortion.[17]

Women who, in contrast to that mother, didn't know of the availability of tests and who bore defective babies, have sued. That news has flashed among doctors. True, they have garbled their accounts of the cases. Obstetricians have told each other that they must persuade older women to have amnioceteses.[18]

Actually, the court rulings that have excited doctors so mean only that obstetricians and genetic counselors should *inform* parents. Doctors should tell at—risk parents about a prenatal test, the conditions under which it is indicated, and the possible consequences of the decision on whether to undergo the test. Physicians who have failed to inform women about prenatal tests may be forced to pay for the costs of medical and institutional care of defective children that they bear, if the children are born with conditions that could have been detected during pregnancy.[19]

At a meeting in Washington, D.C., Dr. Philip Reilly, of New Haven, Connecticut, told an audience of obstetricians, geneticists, and others about their new legal duties. Anguished physicians said, in effect, "We're bringing new scientific knowledge to mankind, and as a reward we're being sued."

That was no news to Dr. Reilly, who is both an attorney and a physician, who has written and lectured on legal aspects of genetics, and who edits a monthly newsletter on malpractice. He later told me that suits by parents of defective children would continue to amount to only a small percentage of the total number of malpractice suits, but that awards against physicians could be huge. "The largest damage awards in medical malpractice now include suits involving birth defects," he said. "There are damage claims as high as two to four million dollars."

Such a suit has had a chance of succeeding only since abortion was no longer illegal. That was illustrated when, in 1968, a Texas woman, Carla Bechtel,* became ill on a vacation trip. When she returned, she consulted a doctor and found she was pregnant. She later said that she asked the doctor whether her illness could have been German measles (rubella), and that he said no. But, when she gave birth, it was apparent that it had been German measles, because her daughter's major organs were defective.

When the new baby girl was three months old, surgeons operated on her heart. Other operations and treatments followed in Houston, Dallas, Baltimore, and Washington. Medical costs climbed to more than $21,000.

Mr. and Mrs. Bechtel filed suit. If she had been better informed, Mrs. Bechtel said, she "would have done the kindest thing that I could have known to have done for her, and that would have been to terminate the pregnancy."

When the Bechtels presented their case before a district court judge in Wichita County, Texas, abortion was illegal in the state. The judge threw their case out of court for that reason. The Bechtels appealed.

While their case was moving through the Texas courts, the U.S. Supreme Court declared the Texas abortion law unconstitutional. Two years later, in 1975, the Bechtels' appeal arrived in the Texas Supreme Court.

In that changed climate, the Texas justices ruled that, if the Bechtels could prove their contentions, they could recover from the doctor the

* Not her real name.

expenses for care and treatment of their daughter's impairment. Justice Thomas M. Reavley wrote that the court had to assume that Mrs. Bechtel could have obtained a legal abortion.[20]

It was the first case in which a state's high-court judges ruled that a doctor could be ordered to pay damages for negligent failure to tell parents about risks of their bearing a defective child.

A physician needn't tell mothers about prenatal tests while they are merely experimental. Still, a turning point occurs, after which a test is accepted as routine. Usually, that means some authoritative group of physicians has decided it is safe to call the test standard. An example is amniocentesis, which doctors first used in 1968. By 1974, it had become routine.[21]

In 1975, a retarded and brain-damaged Down syndrome daughter was born to a Long Island couple, Niles and Eileen Groves.* Mrs. Groves was thirty-seven when she conceived the baby. She said doctors had never told her that women her age had an increased risk of bearing such a child, or about the use of amniocentesis to reveal Down syndrome. She and her husband sued for damages.

The test had become so routine by then that a majority of judges on New York State's highest court ruled that doctors who didn't tell older mothers about such matters were negligent. If the Groves could prove their allegations in a lower court, they could collect for the long-term institutional care of their daughter.[22]

It isn't just physicians who must warn of risks and tell about tests. Prenatal counseling doesn't necessarily require clinical training. In future, obstetricians will guide pregnant women to white-coated counselors who will have Master of Science or Ph.D. diplomas (not M.D.'s) mounted on the wall, and all such experts must keep pace with new knowledge.

And knowledge is accumulating fast. For example, you'll recall that specialists can test amniotic fluid to see whether a fetus is leaking AFP into it. Today, scientists have learned that, when a fetus has open spine and other such neural-tube defects, the extra AFP moves into the mother's bloodstream.

In the near future, obstetricians will routinely take blood samples from pregnant women for that test. Millions of pregnant women will

---

* Not their real names.

then go through anxious times during their sixteenth to eighteenth week of pregnancy. Of 1,000 such women, 50 will have high AFP readings. However, only 2 of the 50 will be carrying defective fetuses, and it may take another blood test, a sonogram, and perhaps an amniocentesis to find the afflicted ones.

Experts will fully inform such women, because good professional practice will demand it. "At each stage, counseling is essential," Dr. Barbara Gastel advised the audience at a conference in Washington, D.C. "Whenever a test is offered, it must be explained to the woman in a clear, balanced manner that allows her to make an informed decision; and all test results and their implications must be carefully discussed."[23]

I've been writing here as if a counselor had a duty to fully inform a woman only after she became pregnant. But a New York couple, Cecil and Jane Kurtz,* claimed in court that doctors hadn't given them accurate advice about their chances of conceiving a child with polycystic kidney disease. In that disease, the child's kidneys are filled with sacs, as if hollow marbles were embedded in them.

They had had one child with the disease. It had died five hours after birth. The Kurtzes said they had asked their obstetricians about the chance of having a second child with the same trouble and were incorrectly told polycystic kidney disease wasn't hereditary, and thus the chances were "practically nil." So they conceived the second child. But it had the same kidney disease and died after two and a half years.

New York judges ruled that, if the Kurtzes could prove all their allegations, they could recover the money they had spent for the care and treatment of their second child until its death.[24]

None of this means that parents automatically recover damages when they go to court. In fact, the Kurtzes weren't awarded the $67,358 they were trying to collect. When the case went to trial, the jurors chose to believe that the doctors had warned the parents about the danger of kidney disease in their second child. So they awarded them nothing.[25]

Doctors win most informed consent cases. They are helped by laws in twenty-three states that favor them if they obtain signed consent forms.[26] That, of course, means prospective mothers shouldn't sign such forms until they've received full information.

---

* Not their real names.

On Being Paid for Emotional Damage

Judges in various states disagree with each other on how to measure the damages that a physician must pay. For example, in addition to medical and other expenses, should a couple collect from the doctor for their shock when the mother delivers a defective child?

Only the New Jersey Supreme Court has allowed parents to claim payment for such emotional damage.[27] Judges in other states have said they couldn't balance the parents' anguish against the benefits of parenthood and determine how much any difference was worth.

Still, judges have never hesitated in other situations to calculate the value of intangibles. Aside from saying, "I'm sorry," you can't repay someone for emotional injury other than with money.[28] It would therefore be appropriate to judges to calculate the worth of the emotional damage to parents and to order them to be recompensed.

Babies Who Sue for the Wrong of Having Been Born

Sometimes a baby sues a doctor, asking for damages on the grounds that it should never have been born.[29] Such babies don't themselves retain lawyers. Rather, their parents sue and throw in a claim that the baby ought to recover damages, too. Thus, they use this method to ask for extra money.

Such a suit could cause the judge's head to whirl. The baby in effect is saying, "I shouldn't be here, and therefore I'm suing for damages." The judge's reply could be, "If you're not supposed to be here, you can't sue, because we can't accept suits from wraiths."

But judges don't waste time on such mental exercises. They generally oppose such lawsuits. Such judges may feel that it's better to be born, even in unhappy circumstances, than not to be born at all.

A judge may state that it is impossible to measure the difference between a defective baby's life and nonexistence. A New Jersey baby sued a doctor because it had sight, hearing, and speech defects due to the mother's having had German measles. The mother said the doctor had told her the illness would not affect her fetus. But the chief justice of New Jersey's Supreme Court, explaining why the baby itself could not collect, wrote:

> Ultimately, the infant's complaint is that he would be better off not to have been born. Man, who knows nothing of death or nothingness, cannot

possibly know whether that is so. To recognize a right not to be born is to enter an area in which no one could find his way.[30]

What Must the Obstetrician Ask, and Tell?

Obstetricians and other professionals needn't tell parents about every minor risk. A geneticist showed me a thick book listing more than 2,000 genetic defects—those that have been identified so far—and the list is growing.[31] A doctor needn't read that entire book to a pregnant woman.

In most states, judges would probably say that the doctor must tell as much as other doctors do. In other words, they can set their own standards. They will tell as much as a "reasonable medical practitioner" would tell under similar circumstances.

An obstetrician, on reading that, might say, "The field is so new that we don't have any firm standards." True, and therefore wise doctors will follow a newer legal rule. They will tell reasonable parents everything that is material to the decisions they have to make.[32]

First, to be able to give advice, the doctor must ask the proper questions. "It's amazing what isn't asked by obstetricians," said Dr. Mark Geier. "When they ask about a family history, they don't even say, 'Have you or any close relatives ever had a defective child?'"

Let's assume a professional has asked the right questions, given appropriate advice, and a pregnant woman has had an amniocentesis. The question now arises whether the professional can choose among facts, revealed by the test, that will be told to the couple.

The answer is no. The parents, not the physician or other counselor, must live with any decision. Therefore, a wise counselor will tell the parents whatever they or a reasonable person in their place might feel is germane to their decision.[33]

Some physicians oppose abortions. They may believe therefore that they have a moral duty to do more than merely lay facts on the table like fish for customers to choose. Other counselors may believe, in contrast, that they should refrain from telling people what to do.[34] The law doesn't take a position either way. It doesn't demand that physicians be neutral.

Incidentally, even if both the parents and the doctor oppose abortion, there is good reason to choose to have prenatal tests when the risk is high that a mother will bear a defective baby. If the tests show that a

52 MAKING YOUR MEDICAL DECISIONS

fetus was indeed defective, the parents could prepare for its birth mentally and financially. They could also arrange for the baby to be born at a center specializing in treatment of the disorder.

Will We Have a New Eugenics?

The new ability of medicine to detect defects while a fetus is still in the womb, coupled with approval by most people of abortion for such defects, points to a disturbing possibility—that state lawmakers may try to improve the race through legislation.[35]

Don't dismiss the possibility. In the past, when scientists pointed to ways that they thought would improve the race, lawmakers embraced the techniques. Granted, their statutes have now been abandoned, but only because the scientific theories that supported them were shown to be erroneous.

Consider eugenics,* which taught that retardation and criminal tendencies could be reduced by sterilizing mental institution inmates. In 1927, the U.S. Supreme Court, in an eight-to-one decision, approved the practice. The Court announced that it was acceptable for doctors in Virginia to sterilize a teenage mental patient, Carrie Buck.

Carrie was an inmate of the State Colony for Epileptics and Feeble Minded. Her mother was an inmate in the same institution, and Carrie herself was the mother of "an illegitimate, feeble-minded child," according to the Supreme Court record. Justice Oliver Wendell Holmes, who wrote the Court's decision, pointed to an even earlier decision—the one I told you about on page 31, in which Henning Jacobson was forced to pay his hometown a fine of five dollars for refusing to have a smallpox vaccination. The reason, you'll remember, was that Jacobson might infect others.[36]

It would similarly be acceptable for a surgeon, acting under authority of a Virginia law, to cut Carrie Buck's Fallopian tubes. Otherwise, she, too, would transmit her trouble to others. "Three generations of imbeciles are enough," wrote Justice Holmes, and therefore he and other justices ruled that the Virginia law was constitutional.[37]

The old justice (he was then eighty-six) was one of the giants of the Supreme Court. Law professors and students love his trenchant opin-

---

* In this section, eugenics refers to negative eugenics, that is, the science that is aimed at eliminating or treating inherited genetic diseases. Positive eugenics, not covered in this book, tries to perpetuate desirable features by the mating (perhaps through artificial insemination) of men and women who are believed to be superior.

ions, and that's one reason why his face, with its walrus mustache, looks at me from a postage stamp on my desk as I write this. But, in this case, Holmes decided a constitutional issue with a flip epigram.

Moreover, the case before the Supreme Court didn't involve three generations of imbeciles. In 1953, Dr. J. E. Coogan, a Detroit sociologist, discovered that Carrie's mother, the supposed first-generation imbecile, had been only mildly retarded. He also noted that Carrie Buck's baby daughter had been only one month old when a Red Cross nurse appraised her as mentally defective. Dr. Coogan learned that, actually, she had been very bright. She finished the second grade, which would have been unlikely if she had been an imbecile and then, in 1932, died of measles.[38]

Was Carrie herself truly an imbecile? In 1980, she was discovered, at the age of seventy-three, living near Charlottesville, Virginia. By today's standards, according to the superintendent of a state mental health facility who became interested in the old case, she would not be considered retarded.[39]

By the time the superintendent found her, however, the Supreme Court's decision concerning her had bolstered state laws under which officials nationwide had ordered the sterilization of 70,000 inmates of mental institutions. Oftentimes, staff members at the institutions had explained that an inmate was merely having an appendix removed. Thus, they called the sterilizations "Mississippi appendectomies."

"Three generations of imbeciles are enough" seems to say that transmission of retardation is inevitable. But the average child of retardates tends to be brighter than the parents. Scientists know this as a regression to the mean.

Granted, the evidence isn't conclusive. People can use the data to show either that retardates give birth to retardates or, in contrast, that seven-eighths of their children are normal. In any event, normal parents produce most retarded children.[40]

State programs to sterilize mental institution inmates trailed off by the 1970s.[41] And today, even when families demand that their own retarded daughters be sterilized, doctors are hesitant. Judges demand such procedural safeguards that the families often give up.[42]

You shouldn't assume, however, that eugenics is dead. Granted, we laugh when we read old statements that our genes cause not only insanity and imbecility but also criminality, prostitution, and alcoholism.[43] But, as our fathers were swayed by the "scientific" knowledge that people inherited such characteristics, we are swayed by what seems to be surer knowledge. For example, lawmakers in several states in the early 1970s passed legislation with the intention of attacking sickle cell disease.

On Trying to Stamp Out Sickle Cell Disease

Once again, however, the lawmakers acted on erroneous information. In their discussions and in the laws that they enacted, they gave a false impression that most blacks had a crippling disease.

Many blacks carry a sickle cell *trait*, in common with Arabs, Egyptians, Turks, Greeks, Italians (chiefly Sicilians), Iranians, and Asiatic Indians.[44] It causes no trouble. The trait probably helps protect children in Africa and southern Eurasia against malaria.[45]

It is only when two persons with sickle cell trait mate and give some of their children a double dose that such children have sickle cell disease. When such a child's red blood cells mature and then are occasionally deprived of oxygen, some of them take on the shape of a sickle. Ordinarily, red blood cells are so small that they flow through the tiniest blood vessels, but when they take on a sickle shape, they cause log jams. That can damage the body's organs. Even as a baby, a sickle cell victim can have pain, tiredness, pallor, jaundice, fever, or pneumonia.

Some patients may be free of serious illness and lead productive lives until an advanced age. Others die young.

One out of every 12 blacks has the sickle cell trait, but on average only 1 out of every 576 babies is born with the disease.[46] It is a serious problem nevertheless, affecting about 50,000 Americans. It was therefore understandable that, in 1970, a black civil servant in Washington urged programs to deal with the disease. In 1971, President Nixon put a sickle cell plank in his annual health message. Blacks had emerged as a political force, and he was facing reelection.[47]

With the disease suddenly politicized, twelve states and the District of Columbia rushed to pass laws.[48] The idea was to find those who had the trait and warn them. It was quickly apparent that some of the laws were based on false assumptions.

Even in the District of Columbia, with its large black population, lawmakers incorrectly labeled the disease as communicative. In three states, they equated it with syphilis. And, everywhere, lawmakers and physicians confused the trait with the disease.

Black leaders criticized the new laws, and states repealed some of them. Other screening laws, even mandatory ones, stayed on the books, but officials didn't enforce them.[49]

Today, it is possible to detect a fetus afflicted with sickle cell disease while it is still in the womb.[50] But oftentimes black parents don't volunteer to be tested for the trait, to determine whether they might have given their offspring a double dose. "The reasons are complex," a scientist told me. Much of it probably stems from the bad name that legislation of the early 1970s erroneously gave to sickle cell trait and disease.

The Power of the New Eugenics Idea

Those who imagine that such programs have doomed any New Eugenics have failed to consider the power of the idea. Reproduction is society's business, not just the parents', according to Nobel laureate Francis Crick.[51]

Crick is British and would seem to be far removed from mainstream America. But University of Dayton (Ohio) philosophy professor Lawrence P. Ulrich published the following statement in 1976: "Those who are at high risk for passing on clearly identifiable and severely deleterious genes and debilitating genetic diseases should not be allowed to exercise their reproductive prerogative."[52]

Three years later, at a meeting in Boston on genetics and the law, a widely known thinker on ethical problems, Joseph Fletcher, asked, "Why should this particular wrong—the wrong of knowingly transmitting grievous genetic disease—be an exception to the general principle that a sane society prohibits by law substantial injuries by any one member of the society to innocent others?"[53]

Thus a New Eugenics could arise. Let's focus on the constitutionality of possible new state statutes that would apply at the following times in people's lives.[54] Premaritally, the state could refuse to issue a marriage license until a couple underwent a test for harmful genetic traits. Prenatally, the state could insist on testing pregnant women and could compel the abortion of defective fetuses.

Statutes aimed at characteristics that are governed by genetics can offend our sense of decency, according to Alexander Morgan Capron, executive director of the President's Commission for the Study of Ethical Problems in Medicine and Biomedical and Behavioral Research. "Here is a fact about people that is inherent in them," Professor Capron told me. "It is immutable—it is not anything they can change."

Judges might liken such laws to those that have discriminated among races. In a famous decision, the Supreme Court declared unconstitutional a Virginia law that forbade racially mixed marriages.[55] The law violated the equal protection clause of the Fourteenth Amendment.

Professor Capron pointed out that the justification for such laws aimed at blacks was palpably thin, it being clear that those in power wanted to exclude blacks or keep them down. However, laws aimed at transmission of genetic diseases *could* in contrast be based on rational considerations. For instance, since society bears some of the burden of genetic diseases, through medical assistance, hospital support, and school programs, detection of carrier parents or defective fetuses could reduce the burden.

Judges therefore might well reject a comparison of genetics laws with those aimed at racial minorities. In that case, they would forgo the suspicious scrutiny that they now apply to the latter type of legislation. Instead, they might apply a "rational relationship" test to the genetics laws. If lawmakers had stated a legitimate purpose in passing a statute aimed at transmission of genetic defects, the judges would be inclined to approve it.[56]

But such statutes would have to pass further tests. In considering their constitutionality, judges would point to two fundamental rights.[57] One is the right of privacy. It includes a woman's control over her body and a couple's freedom to marry and have children. The other is the right of free exercise of religion. For example, a religious belief forbidding medical treatment could extend to the taking of blood for testing.

Judges look with eagle eyes at laws affecting those fundamental rights. To be constitutional, the laws must be justified by a compelling state interest, and they must be narrowly drawn to express only the legitimate state interests at issue. If alternative means would invade the rights to a lesser degree, they would have to be used instead.

"We would have to examine in detail any actual program," Professor Capron said. "What is its justification? What is the burden that it imposes? Is the burden excessive in light of other ways of reaching the same goal?"

Let's therefore consider some possible statutes.

A state law that required all persons applying for marriage licenses to undergo genetic testing would probably be constitutional. The invasion of their bodies—a mere needle prick—would be minor. A compelling state interest would be served by a reduction in genetic diseases.

Many couples, using the information the test gave them, would act to reduce the chance of bearing defective children.

Some misguided state lawmakers might go further and pass laws prohibiting marriage between carriers of defective genes. They would try to justify them by comparing them to laws that now prohibit marriage between close relatives or to other laws also on the books that require would-be husbands and wives to be tested for syphilis.

But neither of those two types of statutes is truly pertinent. For example, in Virginia, a person who has syphilis isn't forbidden to marry but rather must merely promise to be treated afterward.[58] In contrast, a person who has a harmful genetic trait would be able to make no such promise, because no treatment is available.

Laws forbidding close kin to marry each other are more pertinent. They probably had their beginnings in our ancestors' discovery that marriage between a brother and a sister or a parent and child often led to defective children. The prohibitions were included in the Bible.[59]

A more crass motivation came into play when rulers imported the Biblical ban into Western Europe. They wanted to prevent tribes from concentrating their wealth. Later, in the seventeenth century, writers declared that marriage among close relatives was against the law of nature.[60]

A judge can find in our history or basic morality a good reason to approve as constitutional a law that forbids a father and daughter from marrying each other. That judge would be hard put to find an equal justification for a law that forbade marriage between carriers of a genetic trait.

The judge would be influenced by the less-than-even chance that a child born to two carriers would be defective. The odds are only one in four that a baby will have a disease when both of its parents carry what is known as an autosomal recessive trait. And the couple might reduce the odds further. They might forgo childbearing. The vagaries of chance might mean all their children would escape the disease. Nature might cause miscarriages, so that diseased children would fail to be born. Or the woman, having been warned that both she and her mate were carriers, might voluntarily go for prenatal testing when she became pregnant.

Now to move on to the constitutionality of possible laws that might force obstetricians to test pregnant women. Lawmakers would be influenced by the ease with which technicians could take a sample of a mother's blood and test it for AFP, to reveal open-spine or related defects. A compelling state interest would be served by the information on defective fetuses the test would yield.

Still, such a law would have to pass a second constitutional requirement—that other, less restrictive means wouldn't lead to the same end. Even without compulsion, private doctors, supplemented by, say, free public clinics, might give blood tests to so many pregnant women that compulsory blood tests would be redundant.

Any statute that went still further and required amniocentesis would probably be unconstitutional. Pushing a needle into the sac where the fetus floats is a greater invasion of a woman's body and poses more risks than a mere blood test.

Judges would also throw out any law that compelled pregnant women to undergo abortion. For one thing, it would be impossible to draw guidelines on which disorders were serious enough for compulsory abortion. Thus, such a law would be too wide-sweeping to pass the constitutional test.[61]

To sum up, judges might accept as constitutional laws that forced couples to be tested before marriage and, perhaps, those that required blood tests of pregnant women. They would throw out stronger laws.

Would they accept the stronger laws in the future? Constitutional interpretations, as we have learned, change with changing social views. Who could have confidently predicted fifty years ago, for example, that Supreme Court justices would strike down laws forbidding abortion? Similarly, the justices might someday accept a New Eugenics. If so, they would be influenced by a social disapproval of those who refused to use prenatal tests and therefore bore defective children.

Now to turn to the possibility of other action, falling short of statutes, that might lead to the same result. In the mid-1970s, a Harvard pediatrician and geneticist, Dr. Aubrey Milunsky, thought it was likely that insurance carriers would enter the picture. Your health-and-accident insurance policy would have a clause such as this: If you, a pregnant woman, were over thirty-five, the policy would pay for amniocentesis and an abortion. But if you chose to skip the test or to bear a baby that the test had shown was defective, the insurance company would refuse to pay for its care.[62]

Alexander Capron agrees that screening and abortion requirements seem far more likely to occur first in health plans than in statutes.

Rita Theisen, a Chicago-based lawyer for the Health Insurance Association of America, was surprised when I told her of the suggestion. "I can't imagine that the insurance industry would try to manipulate social policy by varying insurance provisions," she said. "Usually, it's the other way around: social policy dictates to the insurance industry, saying, 'This is what we want.'"

Whether social policy will dictate insurance policy to that effect remains to be seen. It is certain, on the other hand, that people will continue to put the pressure of disapproval on those who bear defective children. We can hope those who disapprove will instead come to realize that it is diversity that marks us as free.

Speaking Up for Diversity

With their facial expressions, people often in effect say to defectives: "Why did God allow you to be born?" Sondra Diamond, born into a Canadian family, had cerebral palsy, extensive brain damage, and was unable to walk or dress herself. Later, at the age of thirty-six and working toward her Ph.D. degree, she told Canadian television viewers of an incident that had happened when she was nine.

She had gotten off a special school bus, with her mother waiting for her, and noticed a woman staring. "And the woman was standing there, saying 'Oh, my God, oh, my God,' and shaking more than I shake. . . . And my mother said to her, 'I charge a quarter for this [to look at Sondra].'"

Once in the house, Sondra's mother explained to her that the woman had been looking on her as a freak. Sondra knew what that meant. She had been to the circus.[63]

As the capability to diagnose defective fetuses increases, the unspoken question may be, "Why did your *parents* [rather than God] allow you to be born?" Parents who are told they have bad genes that can lead to such defective children already bear a load of guilt.[64] If a defective baby is born, they may feel that the evidence is there—in that Rosemary's Baby—for everyone to see, not only of the horned, evil influence in their bodies but also that they are unheedful of whether they taint the race.

But a defective child is no evidence of a shameful condition in its parents. If genetic health means having no harmful genes, virtually no one is healthy. On average, every person carries 2.2 deleterious genes, of a total of 100,000, although some carry none.[65] We are complex people, with diverse characteristics.[66]

Genetic defects have existed through man's existence, and they have failed to spoil the race. To reduce them significantly, all carriers of deleterious traits would have to refrain from having children or else abort those who promised to be carriers like themselves.[67]

In any event, we need to realize the value of pluralism, according to Dr. Michael M. Kaback, professor in the Departments of Pediatrics and Medicine, University of California, Los Angeles, School of Medicine. People can't be dealt with as being identical, he said, like E. coli bacteria or Wistar strain laboratory rats. "They are individual persons and must be able to make a decision that is for them best and legal within the society in which they live," he said.

In the early 1970s, Dr. Kaback led a successful voluntary effort to screen for Tay-Sachs trait among Ashkenazi Jews in the Washington-Baltimore area.[68] Tay-Sachs disease (not the trait) causes brain degeneration, always killing the children who have it at an early age, but not before breaking the hearts and the pocketbooks of their parents. It is 100 times more frequent among infants of Eastern European (Ashkenazic) Jewish descent than among other persons. If both a woman and her mate have the trait, the risk is 25 percent in each pregnancy that the fetus will have the disease.

Through counseling ahead of marriage or pregnancy, the couple may consider any of several options. They may refrain from having children, adopt them, or have artificial insemination of the woman with sperm from a noncarrier man. Or they may conceive children, because they know each fetus has a 75 percent chance of escaping the disease and they can have amniocenteses to check for it.

Dr. Kaback now directs the California Tay-Sachs Disease Prevention Program and the Prenatal Diagnosis-Genetic Counseling Center at Harbor-UCLA Medical Center.

"I don't want to see legislation requiring noncompletion of pregnancy for Defect A, B, C, or D," he told me. "What I would much prefer to see is legislation to make information, excellent technology, and counseling and related services available to people, and let them make informed decisions for themselves."

This pioneering scientist sees great value in scientific education beginning in lower school grades than today. He points out that in ten or twenty years, obstetricians will be able to offer every pregnant woman a battery of tests to find defects in her fetus. Those will involve a minimum invasion of her body. If she has been well educated in biology,

DISCOVERING DEFECTS BEFORE A BABY IS BORN 61

she and her mate will understand the implications and make informed decisions without requiring a new education from the doctor.

An important right will be that of refusing information or failing to take the tests. "People have the right not to have information if they so choose," Dr. Kaback told me. "As long as it's an informed decision that leads to that conclusion, then fine—they have that right. That's their option."

Many persons have religious or ethical objections to abortion. Thus, leaving aside the fact that most defects in fetuses cannot as yet be detected, the existence of a defective child does not necessarily indicate an uncaring attitude on the part of parents. It may indicate just the opposite. And, as a wise ethicist, Daniel Callahan, has said, we need to take the idea of freedom of choice seriously, bearing the costs and accepting diversity.[69]

What It Means to You

As scientists leap forward in their ability to diagnose defects before a baby is born, your legal rights are moving in step. An important recent change is an enlargement of your right to knowledge.

If you are a husband, you have the same legal right to knowledge as your wife, but, if you disagreed with her on whether to have a prenatal test or an abortion, her decision would control the outcome.[70] If you are the unmarried lover of a pregnant woman, you probably have no legal right to information from the doctor.[71]

You cannot be sure judges in every state will rule precisely as those who have heard other such cases, but you, the parents, probably have the following rights:

1. Even though you fail to ask for the information, to be informed by the physician attending a pregnancy whether you have more of a risk than other people of bearing a defective child.

2. To be told of tests that can reveal a defect and of material risks that the test itself can hurt the fetus or mother.

3. To decide whether to have the test performed.

4. To have the test performed skillfully, at least up to par with good medical practice in your area. (A doctor who does not have the proper skill should refer you to a specialist.)

5. To know the results.

6. To keep others from knowing. (If your relatives ran a risk of having

children with the same defect, the doctor could probably tell them without legal risk, even though you objected.)[72]

7. In concert with a doctor, to choose abortion, through at least the first six months of pregnancy, within guidelines that the state may, to a limited extent, prescribe.

8. To refuse to take any action, even though the test has revealed a defective fetus.

None of this means that the birth of a defective baby is in itself proof of medical malpractice. The usual outcome of a pregnancy is a normal baby, and it would be a misuse of medical resources to require an obstetrician to discuss every conceivable risk with a pregnant woman. Tests now available cannot detect all defects, and every medical test has inherent errors. Thus, even skillfully tested women may bear babies whose defects were unknown before birth.

4
BABIES IN TROUBLE

WHEN Miles was three-and-a-half months old, his life or death depended on whether his mother and father wrote their names on a consent form. Like a third of all Down syndrome (mongoloid) children, Miles had a heart defect. He needed an operation. His parents needed only to refuse to sign the form and, unless the hospital took them to court, they would be free of Miles forever. To relatives, they could say, as a relative once said to me after the death of a deformed baby, "God took him home to finish making him."

There was a time when such deaths were always God's fault; doctors were helpless. But now surgery and anesthesia have advanced to the point that operations on infants are routine.[1] Surgeons, using stereoscopic magnifying lenses that poke out from their glasses, manipulate tiny tissues as human forms, some scarcely larger than footballs, lie on operating tables before them.

Should the parents give permission? "We did sit down and talk about it some," says Miles' mother Elisabeth* today. But ten years ago parents rarely challenged doctors. "We really weren't given any choice."

They signed—and the operation was successful. Granted, Miles still has a heart murmur, but so does his mother Elisabeth ("worse than he does," she says), and he'll probably outlive her. He still has the Down syndrome, of course.

This chapter describes some babies, who like Miles, have double

---

* Names and other identifying details have been changed.

trouble. They are deformed or brain-damaged and in addition have a life-threatening defect. The question is whether parents should authorize doctors to operate on them and give them other active treatment. The question extends to other babies as well who have major medical problems.

Now that Miles is ten, you'd probably like to look in on him, to try to guess whether Elisabeth and her husband would consent to his surgery if they had it to do over again. Elisabeth doesn't want the intrusion. The subject is painful, she says over the telephone from their North Carolina home. They have no plans to have other children. "We screwed up once," she says, indicating that one sin is enough.

Is Miles intelligent? "He reads," says Elisabeth, "and his writing is getting better. His spelling isn't so great. He hasn't got the hang of vowels, so it's all consonants."

I say I have heard that Down syndrome children can be lovable. "He has his moments of being adorable," she says. "Like all kids, you want to strangle him now and then."

When such children are denied continued life, she says, they can never show whether it would have been meaningful. "You can't judge that with a teeny-weeny little kid."

Still, she could understand it if parents decided to "let a kid go," as she puts it, especially if they already had one that was retarded. "You have to make a case-by-case judgment. You can't enunciate general principles. There are too many factors."

An instant judgment about a child who was only a "teeny-weeny little kid" was made by its mother, a nurse, thirty-four years old, when it was born in a Baltimore hospital in 1963.

"I believe that child is a mongol," said the doctor, just after delivering the baby.* "I don't want it," said the mother at once.

Soon after birth, it was apparent that the baby had a blocked opening to the small intestine. Such a baby has telltale signs—it vomits and spits up bile. Whether given food or not, the child will starve. Nurses must put a sign on such a baby's crib: "NPO"—*nil per os*—meaning nothing by mouth.**

An operation would have opened the intestine so the child could

---

* These and other quoted words are approximations. I know what was said but not the exact words.
** I don't know whether such a sign was hung on this particular baby's crib.

receive nourishment. The chance for success was nearly 100 percent, but the chance that the baby would remain afflicted with Down syndrome was precisely 100 percent.

The mother refused to give permission. "It would be unfair to the other two children to raise them with a mongoloid," she said.

Her husband, a lawyer, thirty-five, supported her. "She knows more about these things than I do," he said.

Their doctor tried without success to talk them into signing the consent form. "They're almost always trainable," he told them. "They can hold simple jobs. And they're famous for being happy children."

But he also told them a fact that could have hardened their refusal—that is that Down syndrome children can live a long life. This one didn't. The hospital staff put it in a side room, where, over a period of eleven days, it starved, then died.[2]

The case wasn't unusual. Dr. Anthony Shaw, professor of surgery and pediatrics at the University of Virginia Medical School, told *New York Times* readers in 1972 about others. He revealed that a mother's decision is often tipped in favor of an operation when her Down syndrome baby is placed in her arms.

A mindless condemnation of parents who choose the other way isn't warranted, according to Dr. Shaw, who today is director of the Department of Pediatric Surgery, City of Hope National Medical Center, Duarte, California. He wrote, "In many cases, if it were my own child, I would refuse to allow any measures other than simple procedures to relieve terminal suffering." Still, he found it impossible to adopt a rigid view one way or the other.[3]

The term that will be used in this chapter is "no active treatment." That would apply if those on the medical team performed no operations, gave a baby no antibiotics or oxygen, employed no tube feeding, or withheld resuscitation when it was dying.

Changes in Doctors' Views

In the early 1970s, pediatricians on both sides of the Atlantic opened doors of hospitals to reveal a change in their attitudes. They no longer believed it was prudent to try to save every baby, regardless of its afflictions. They told the story in medical journals. It soon moved to the more popular media.

In 1973, two pediatricians, Drs. Raymond S. Duff and A.G.M. Campbell, revealed that some babies were allowed to die in the special-care nursery of the Yale-New Haven Hospital, in New Haven, Connecticut. This is a renowned institution. Pediatricians all over the state refer children with major problems to it.

In the past, the staff hadn't disclosed that they did not always take advantage of medicine's ability to maintain existence for even the worst cases. But by the early 1970s, parents and staff began to question openly the wisdom of this policy. A nurse asked a significant question about a baby whose life was flickering. "We lost him several weeks ago," she said. "Isn't it time to quit?"

The staff always had had full discussions with families about treatment decisions, and now they explored whether active treatment should be continued for certain children. Some parents wanted the suffering stopped, and, over a two-and-a-half-year period, forty-three babies died as a result.

One baby, for example, had what doctors called respiratory distress syndrome. Twelve thousand babies a year die of this trouble, which usually is associated with premature birth.

When this baby was a newborn, doctors hooked up a respirator and later, when he could breathe on his own, they dialed as much as 40-percent oxygen into his air. Even so, he would pant to take in more air. His skin stayed a blue or purplish color. His heart worked overtime, sending blood to the lungs for more oxygen, and one of its chambers grew larger.

Doctors and nurses bent over him every day for five months, and grew to love him. They sometimes said to each other that it was cruel to continue. Still, it was difficult to stop.

The parents were quarreling with each other by now. The hospital bill was $15,000 and growing. Their other children were showing signs of disturbances.

After talking to the parents, the staff stopped mixing extra oxygen in the baby's air. He died in three hours.

Dr. Duff and Dr. Campbell told the story in the *New England Journal of Medicine*.[4] It soon received wide publicity. Some people were hostile to the doctors. In 1979, six years after they published the article, I asked Dr. Duff about the reaction.

"It is correct that I have been called 'Nazi doctor,' 'murderer,' or other things in letters sent to me and in a few public forums," he answered. "My reaction has been disappointment that people can be so misled or blind as to permit an ideology (usually 'pro-life' combined with enthusiasm about technologic possibilities) to dominate their reasoning. Then, the larger picture of tragedy in human existence is ignored, and the virtues of intelligence and compassion cannot be used in deciding care."

One of the babies who died at the special-care nursery had defects of every organ in the lower part of the abdomen, plus a ruptured spinal cord and a swollen head, from the pressure of fluid. This ailment has a name that is as forbidding as it is—"meningomyelocele" (min-NIN-joe-MY-eh-lo-SEEL), which, translated from the Greek, means "membrane and spinal cord rupture." This is the neural-tube defect that I told you about in the last chapter. It is a form of spina bifida, which can exist as a mild and untroubling defect or can be a crippler.

Ordinarily, when a fetus is growing in the mother's womb, its backbone folds around the spinal cord, making a tube. But at about the fourth to sixth week of pregnancy, one or more of the backbones may fail to close.[5] In the worst form, the sheath—the membrane—that encloses the spinal cord balloons out from the baby's lower back, perhaps bringing with it the spinal cord. Inside the balloon, the spinal cord is like tortured rope, with its fibers separated.

The baby's feet may not wiggle. If the mother were to pinch its buttocks, it might not cry. At one time, 40 percent of such children in London were "born dead."[6] That probably meant adults killed them.

Doctors in Britain and America gave surviving babies mere routine treatment, and many died.[7] Fluid could leak from the balloon in such a baby's back, and bacteria might infect it, leading to meningitis. Or urinary tract infection might kill it.

Doctors could not control the swollen heads that many such youngsters had. When I was ten, I and other Atlanta boys sat on a porch and looked out the corners of our eyes at a baby with an enormous head. His nine-year-old sister, sitting in a wicker swing, cuddled him. Veins showed in the pink skin that was stretched over his skull. The head moved ponderously. Pressure had damaged his brain. He would die soon.

My Atlanta relatives called that trouble "water on the brain." Doctors call it "hydrocephalus," which means almost the same thing.

There came, in 1957, a medical breakthrough in the form of a tube, several inches long, incorporating either two valves near the center or, in another variety, a valve in one end. Surgeons implanted these in some children with hydrocephalus associated with spina bifida—one end in the head, with the rest of the tube running through the neck to the heart. Presto: an end to water on the brain. The fluid would drip into the heart and eventually be excreted by the body.

For the first time, surgeons could save many such babies, and that led to a revolution in treating them. At Sheffield, England, Professor John Lorber and his colleagues would receive babies still in their first hours of life. Pediatricians would send them from all around England. The babies had large, open lesions on their backs. They were rushed to surgery, where doctors put the spinal cord back in its place and closed the lesions. When signs of hydrocephalus developed, they inserted the tubes.[8]

More babies than before lived, but some were paralyzed in the lower part of their bodies, had deformed legs, hunched backs or crooked spines, and even when they were older would be unable to control their bladders or bowels. The tubes became blocked or infected, and the surgeons operated again and again. In the worst cases, the children were blind, subject to fits, or retarded.[9]

Professor Lorber decided it was possible to identify, even on the first day of their lives, the children whose outlook was particularly unfavorable—those who had extensive paralysis, big heads, and gross hunchbacks or other major deformities.

He and his colleagues started what they called a second revolution. In the first twenty-one months of this new policy, they recommended to parents that twenty-five babies not be treated. All died before reaching nine months. In contrast, the doctors recommended that twelve babies be treated. Eleven lived. They turned out to be normal or only partly handicapped.[10]

Professor Lorber's views were revealed and debated in journals that American pediatricians read and meetings they attended.

It is undoubtedly true that today babies with severe trouble are allowed to die in various U.S. hospitals. The extent cannot be documented. The hostile reaction by some people to the 1973 article by Drs. Duff and Campbell and the warnings of prosecution probably caused a few pediatricians and parents to continue treatment, regardless of babies' defects and interests. Perhaps more of them withdrew active treatment from severely defective infants. "My guess," Dr. Duff wrote me in 1979, "is that the latter prevailed more than the former because the majority of physicians and informed laymen realized the prudence in the policy we proposed and dared to adhere to it in part because we were never prosecuted."

Dr. Duff remained convinced of the policy's correctness. Twentieth-century trends, he believed, had involved the medicalization of society. That included crusading efforts to defeat disease, death, and even discomfort. Every baby had to be saved.

A better view "acknowledges tragedy and proposes a reasoned approach to it," he wrote me.[11]

Still, revolutions at individual treatment centers didn't alter the views of some doctors. A Chicago neurosurgeon said that in only one of more than a hundred cases of open-spine babies had parents told him not to operate. In that one instance, he prepared to seek a court order to force them to give permission. Then they submitted.[12]

Doctors may seize control from parents who are upset and confused by a ruined natal event. Robert and Peggy Stinson's son Andrew, for example, was born four months early and weighed only twenty-eight ounces. Doctors at a pediatric hospital then tried to complete the development that Andrew should have had in his mother's body. Less than a third of such tiny babies live, even in the best hospitals.[13]

The parents later described Andrew's hospitalization as "disastrous" and said most of his afflictions were iatrogenic—that is, caused by physicians. "Andrew had a months-long unresolved case of bronchopulmonary dysplasia, sometimes referred to as 'respirator lung syndrome,'" they wrote. "He was 'saved' by the respirator to endure countless episodes of bradycardia and cyanosis, countless suctionings and tube insertions and blood samplings and blood transfusions, 'saved' to develop retrolental fibroplasia, numerous infections, demineralized and fractured bones, an iatrogenic cleft palate, and, finally, as his lungs became irreparably diseased, pulmonary artery hypertension and seizures of the brain. He was, in effect, 'saved' by the respirator to die five, long, painful, and expensive months later of the respirator's side effects."

The hospital collected $102,303.20 from the Stinsons' insurance company.

The medical staff had assumed they controlled Andrew's treatment, because Robert and Peggy had signed a general consent form. (Read

Chapter 9 to learn the legal effect of such forms.) When the Stinsons protested, a doctor accused them of wanting to play God and of going back to the jungle.

The Stinsons now have a new baby boy. "I had no fear of having a pregnancy again," Peggy told me. "In Andrew's case, man took over and tried to rectify nature's error."

After this couple told their story in *Atlantic Monthly*,[14] physicians wrote them, criticizing the "nonhumanistic" response of young doctors to such problems. "But I am worried," Robert told me, "that some doctors seemed to think it was not an ethical problem but merely a communications problem. They seemed to think that, if they were going to do this sort of thing [force treatment on a foredoomed baby against the parents' wishes], they should do it more nicely."

In any event, physicians strongly influence parents of babies in trouble, either for or against active treatment. Parents may surrender control. Despite stress, the family is probably wise to accept the burden of making the decision. Aside from being their moral responsibility, it is a preventive health measure for them to take part. When they are isolated from participation in the life or death of one of their own, their feelings of guilt may be multiplied. Heart troubles may worsen, and even resistance to cancer may be lowered. Besides, it is the family's touching of the problem with emotional feelers that removes it from dispassion. Family members will, of course, consult the physician, and will also want to know what others have thought about similar problems.

Is Family Suffering a Consideration?

Physicians have seen families emotionally drained, financially ruined, and torn apart by the presence of defective children.[15] But the degree of suffering varies.

Dr. Milton D. Heifetz, Clinical Professor of Neurosurgery, University of Southern California, felt that babies doomed to live a subhuman existence would draw some families together and destroy others. "Parents—usually the mother—frequently adopt a martyr role, ignoring the rest of the family and household to devote full time to the handicapped child," he wrote. "Parents have mental breakdowns. . . . Some kill the child and themselves. . . . Separation and divorce are common. Many brothers and sisters leave their homes as early as possible."[16]

Those who view state institutions as alternatives to home care have not seen those that are "mere stalls, furnishing hay, oats, and water," as a juvenile judge described them.[17]

A different alternative is adoption. Stephen B. Parrish, spina bifida coordinator for Loyola University, is a member of a voluntary group that helps families.[18] He acknowledges that a very small percentage of open-spine babies are untreatable but told me that his group has a waiting list of parents who are willing to adopt others. Incidentally, he has a child with spina bifida.

As for another affliction, Down syndrome, a variation in intelligence may be one reason you hear conflicting reports about its impact on families. Down syndrome children may have IQs as low as in the 30's, meaning they are scarcely able to dress themselves. Or they may have scores as high as the seventies, and can then be classed as mere slow learners.[19] They repay love with devotion of their own and, provided they are trainable, with skills.

The availability of counseling, therefore, or the presence of a parents' group to give mutual support can help.[20] Beyond that, the impact on a family depends on the baby's handicap, its parents' outlook on life, and the stability of their marriage. Assured, well-educated persons may be more confident than others that they can handle such trouble. Paradoxically, though, some professionals may reject mentally deficient children. "This baby is not *me*," a professional might say in effect, thus labeling it as nonhuman.

If the family itself would be destroyed by the presence of a defective child, that fact might well influence parents. But they should also remember that they may create a conflict of interest—measuring their own interest against that of the baby—when they enter their own suffering into the decision.

Will the Baby's Life Be Worth Living?

If a baby's life will be one long experience of pain, perhaps caused by medical treatment, then its parents may bear its death with equanimity. They may open their Bible, to the place where an inspired sage says there is a time to be born and a time to die. That sage—thought to be Solomon—implies that we should not abuse the seasons for such matters.[21]

Dr. Judson C. Randolph, surgeon-in-chief of the Children's Hospital National Medical Center, Washington, D.C., gave the example of a child who was on kidney dialysis for three years. The child simply could not tolerate anyone else's kidney: three kidney transplants had been rejected. There were other medical problems and only minimal conscious existence. The child's parents were in despair. The doctors could offer to keep the child alive for only a limited time.

Even the most conservative physicians, judges, or laymen wouldn't contest a decision to forgo further treatment for that child, Dr. Randolph told an interviewer. As for withholding treatment for severely retarded babies with life-threatening defects that could be corrected by surgery, he thought the decision should depend on the potential quality of life. If the children had *any* chance for a meaningful relationship to their families and their fellow men, all efforts should be made to save them.

Thus the child's potential quality of life might influence the decision. "If a severely handicapped child were suddenly given one moment of total omniscience and total awareness of his or her outlook for the future, would that child necessarily opt for life?" Dr. Randolph asked. "No one has yet been able to demonstrate that the answer would always be 'yes.'"[22]

Some observers have said that the quality of life of a baby should not be taken into consideration. They mean that parents should not make decisions based on babies' social worth, because that would be to judge their quality of life in an interpersonal sense.

The other question in determining quality of life is whether a life is worth living to the person concérned. It is an internal or intrapersonal viewpoint and is a justified ingredient in making a decision.[23] Thus to that exhausted baby with end-stage kidney disease, life might not be worth living.

Granted, this seems to demand that the parents must determine the wishes of a baby who hasn't lived long enough to have an attitude toward life. So, in acting in the baby's behalf, they may decide to use the "resonable person" test.

A reasonable human would wish, for example, to be able to relate to other humans. A legal philosopher, Lon L. Fuller, said that none of us would regard as desirable an existence in which we had no meaningful contact with other human beings. "Communication is more than a means of staying alive," he wrote. "It is a way of being alive."[24]

In making decisions, parents obviously need full information. In two cases, parents who had raised handicapped children told me they thought the advice given them by doctors had been insufficient.

Carol Buchholz is the chairman of the board of the Spina Bifida Association of America. Sixteen years ago, her daughter Karen was born with spina bifida. Doctors told Mrs. Buchholz and her husband that Karen would be a rag doll. A priest told them that the extent of Karen's defects meant there was no moral obligation to have her treated. Still, the parents found a surgeon to close the lesion in Karen's back. He did it, he said, only because he looked on it as a research project, not because it would do any good or save Karen's life.

When Karen was six months old, surgeons inserted a shunt between her head and chest to control her hydrocephalus. She was six years old before she got out of a wheel chair. She now walks with short leg braces and crutches. She has had twenty-two operations.

Karen has learning disabilities, but she is in the tenth grade, only one grade behind her age level. She insists on going to public school, though it has no elevators, so as to make friends in the Buchholz's community.

She can program and run a computer, and a high-school counselor has suggested she go into data processing or airline reservations.

"Families shouldn't have to search out the information as we had to do," Carol Buchholz said. She added that the information must be given in an unbiased way, though she said that may be difficult for the physician, who sees the child only when it is ill or in trauma rather than in an active, daily-living situation.

Carol Brown, of Lithonia, Georgia, the mother of a Down syndrome son, said doctors "just give you the bleakest, darkest news and no optimism whatsoever."

She knows parents in another Georgia city who allowed their Down syndrome baby to starve. It had an intestinal obstruction and a heart defect, both of which would require surgery. A doctor told the parents that the odds of its living to three years were 10 to 20 percent.

Carol feels that the decision was up to the parents but that they weren't told enough. "Such a decision should be based on sound information—all the good and the bad—everything available."

She and her husband Gene faced no such decision for their son Chad, because he had no secondary defect. Still, soon after Chad was born, a doctor told Gene the baby had Down syndrome, painted a dark future, and said he should be put in an institution.

When Carol could leave the hospital (she had had a cesarean), she and Gene visited a private institution. Two adults were caring for sixty defective children. Teenage Down syndrome boys were tied to beds that had plywood mattresses. Carol and Gene rejected the place (which has since closed) and brought Chad home.

They worked with him themselves through the guidance of a parent-infant program funded by the educational system. He's in speech therapy, a full-day, early-childhood class, and his parents plan to put him in vocational training. "We expect him to be a productive citizen," Carol said. "He's a lot more normal than he's not. He's brought a lot into our lives."

Carol and Gene took the initiative to learn realistic information about their son and to seek out supportive resources that were available in their community before making a life-altering decision. They expressed concern, however, about those parents who, for many reasons, would not or could not explore such alternatives. Pediatricians, obstetricians, nurses, or other professional persons should be well informed about supportive services, they said.

The Legal Framework

Judges usually assume that parents have authority over their children. A child's biological and psychological needs are served in a family environment in which adults furnish protection and guidance.[25]

The state has never left parents entirely on their own, though. The doctrine of *parens patriae*—the sovereign power of guardianship—includes protection of children.[26]

Has the state's protection now weakened? You might think so, given the Supreme Court's 1973 decision recognizing that women have a limited right to abort fetuses. It has led to a climate in which some families may think they can discard defective babies as well. Any such impression is mistaken, because an unborn fetus is legally different from a born child.

Justice Harry A. Blackmun, who wrote the abortion decision, stated that wherever the Constitution protects a "person," it refers to a *born* being.[27] Abortion was legal during much of America's history, most states not outlawing it until after the Civil War. When our forebears therefore protected "persons" in the Constitution, they didn't mean to refer to the unborn.

You might counter with the argument that a bald eagle isn't a "person" either, but, if you kill one, the government may prosecute you.[28] Ah, but you have no constitutional right that authorizes you to kill bald eagles. In the case of abortion, a mother has a right of privacy, which enables her to control her own body, and no compelling state interest overrides it.

The Supreme Court view that a fetus isn't legally a "person" explains why some proposed constitutional amendments that would ban abortion don't actually forbid it in so many words. Usually, they merely state that every human being is a "person" from the moment of fertilization.[29]

But a born baby is protected without the necessity for a new amendment. The Constitution settles about the shoulders of a baby emerging into the world, regardless of its defects. It cannot now be deprived of life without due process of law.[30]

Doctors, other members of the medical team, and parents are vulnerable in theory (but, so far, not in practice) to criminal prosecution if they deliberately allow such a baby to die.[31] Prosecutors could accuse them of crimes stemming from child-abuse and neglect statutes. For example, a prosecutor could use the "misdemeanor-manslaughter" rule against a doctor as follows: the doctor's misdemeanor of not reporting child abuse led to a baby's death, and that constituted involuntary manslaughter. Or, against both parents and doctors, the prosecutor could use another legal theory: they omitted their legal duty to take care of the baby, the omission was intentional or grossly negligent, and the lack of medical care caused death.

For such a crime of omission to exist, the law must have set down a positive duty.[32] For example, physicians have no duty to stop at accident scenes, though they might save bleeding victims. A physician who drives on will be guilty of no crime. But a special relationship springs into being when a doctor accepts a patient.

Oliver Wendell Holmes, in his famous book *The Common Law*, told how the duty arises:

> Although a man has a perfect right to stand by and see his neighbor's property destroyed, or, for the matter of that, to watch his neighbor perish for want of his help, yet if he once intermeddles he has no longer the same freedom. He cannot withdraw at will. To give a more specific example, if a surgeon from benevolence cuts the umbilical cord of a newly-born child, he cannot stop there and watch the patient bleed to death. It would be murder wilfully to allow death to come to pass that way . . .[33]

Parents obviously have such a special relationship with their children. Their neglect, or a doctor's neglect, of their child could lead to a homicide charge.

No parent and no doctor, nurse, or other member of a medical team has been prosecuted for withholding care from a defective baby.* And even if trials took place, convictions would be doubtful. Defense lawyers would argue that, even though the parents and doctor had had that special relationship to a dead child, they had no duty actively to treat a baby who could not be cured. The lawyers would try to persuade judges to repeat the instructions that U.S. Supreme Court Justice Stephen J. Field, sitting as judge in a California case, gave a jury in 1864.

A ship captain was on trial for murder. A seaman, while furling a sail, had fallen from the yardarm into the ocean. The captain had failed to stop the ship or lower boats. At the trial, his lawyers argued that the 110-foot fall itself had killed the seaman, and, even if he had survived, it would have been impossible and dangerous to try to save him in the high seas then running.

Justice Field told the jury this:[34]

> When doubt exists as to what conduct should be pursued in a particular case, and intelligent men differ as to the proper action to be had, the law does not impute guilt to anyone, if, from omission to adopt one course instead of another, fatal consequences follow to others.

The jury acquitted the captain. His duty to save his crew had been changed by circumstances.

Intelligent men also differ on whether actively to treat defective babies.[35] The doubt as to the existence of a duty would probably lead to verdicts of not guilty. Still we can expect a prosecutor sometime in the future to bring a test case against parents and doctors who have let a baby die.[36]

Court officials do intervene informally.[37] A Nassau County, New York, prosecutor called parents and a physician and told them that unless they proceeded with an operation to unblock the intestine of a Down syndrome baby, he would see that they went to jail. They complied.[38]

Civil court actions are more likely than criminal ones. Every state has a statute authorizing judges to take control of neglected or abused children.

---

* I am omitting cases of failed abortions.

Law professor John A. Robertson and pediatrician Norman Fost suggested that, when parents try to ward off treatment for defective babies, their physicians report them to child-abuse or other state agencies. Or else, they suggested, a hospital's lawyers could initiate court action.[39] That must be an appealing course for doctors or hospital officials, who have no authority even to stick hypodermic needles in babies against the parents' wishes, and who are worried about criminal liability if they fail to treat the babies.

Voluntary advocates for babies with spina bifida may also promote court action. In the greater New York City area in the last six months, such volunteers have asked state agencies to intervene in three cases where parents were reluctant to have surgery for their open-spine children. Judges ordered treatment in all three cases. Such volunteers arrange foster care or adoption but try to persuade parents to raise the children themselves.

In a handful of other civil decisions, judges have sometimes been inclined to view continued life as the highest good. That happened in 1974 with a baby whom I'll call Dale.*

At Dale's birth, the hospital staff had seen that he had no left eye, no left ear canal, and a deformed left hand. He had an abnormal connection between his windpipe and gullet, so that his breath whistled into his stomach and stomach fluids flowed into his lungs.

Nurses fed Dale intravenously, but his father, Arthur, forbade such feeding and refused to allow a surgeon to fix that abnormal connection. So the hospital and the attending physician, Dr. Jones, took the case to court.

Further troubles developed. Dale's right eye (his only eye) wouldn't react to light. The medical staff members found that some vertebrae in his backbone weren't normal. He began to have convulsions. He developed pneumonia; doctors gave him antibiotics. He would stop breathing, and members of the staff would quickly use a "bag respirator," but the periods with no oxygen damaged his brain.

Dr. Jones now changed his mind and told the judge that Dale ought to be allowed to die. But the court moved ponderously on, with the judge stating, "At the moment of live birth there does exist a human being entitled to the fullest protection of the law." The judge continued, "The most basic right enjoyed by every human being is the right to life itself."

* All names in this case have been changed.

So Dale Smith, five days old, with an imperfect spine, partly deaf, and blind and brain-damaged, became the subject of a court order. That abnormal connection between his gullet and his windpipe must be repaired.[40]

It was. Dale died nevertheless, at thirteen days.

The judge had reflected the common-law view that life is sacred regardless of its quality.[41] But that view came into existence at a time when nature killed many afflicted babies. Since no effective medical treatment was available, their cases didn't come before courts.

Historically, judges have felt no compulsion to order useless treatment. The cases that did come before them generally involved children who could be restored to health.

As we have seen, the problem of whether to treat defective babies has been thrust upon us by advances in medical science. Thus, it is what Joseph Fletcher, visiting scholar in medical ethics at the University of Virginia, calls a "success problem." The success sometimes can be only partial, with underlying afflictions unaffected. Thus, the advances have posed problems that are both more heartening and more terrifying than when nature had control.

Here it is time for final revisions before this chapter is set in type and, except for a strong bias for continued life, I have no sweeping ethical or legal rule to pronounce. I am comforted that a professor of theological ethics took 4,000 words (more than half the length of this chapter) to explain why he believes the Baltimore baby with Down syndrome and a blocked intestine (see page 64) should have been operated on.[42] And it took a book as big as this one to record the sometimes clashing views of fifty lawyers, physicians, theologians, and others who met in 1975 at Skytop, Pennsylvania, to argue about whether open-spine babies should be treated.[43]

It's tempting to avoid the problem by silence. When I write of problems involving the possible deaths of babies, my heart seems to twist, and I awaken abruptly at night.

Others have no uncertainty. In researching this chapter, I met people who would use the courts to force treatment on every baby almost regardless of condition, and others who would give parents autonomy. People on both sides spoke with freedom from doubt. I flinched with internal guilt when they told me of their disagreement with those who would avoid sweeping rules.

But only those who would decide harsh problems with slogans would take absolutist positions. The problems are too varied for that.

The law, as always, will respond to changing social conditions. Let's imagine some future cases.

Imagine that a case came before a court involving a baby that would never be able to relate to other humans. Its parents had refused to approve treatment to correct a life-threatening defect. A judge might announce that, though life itself was still the supreme value, their baby was like others throughout our history for whom treatment was useless and whom the law had never commanded medicine to try to save.

Someday, therefore, a learned state supreme court justice who is also a capable writer may acknowledge for the court that tragedy does exist among some newborns, and that occasionally we must acknowledge that we are helpless to alter it. That writer may continue that the mere existence of a medical capability doesn't mean it inevitably should be employed. The justice might express the court's ruling like this: "There can be no simple 'right' or 'wrong' solution to the problem we have before us. Since the parents cannot be wrong, let them decide."[44]

And yet, it is incomplete to say that some parents should be given autonomy. Parents of a slightly imperfect baby might adopt the attitude, reflecting their view that the population should be limited to avoid overcrowding the world, that those who are chosen to occupy it should be specimens of good health and beauty.

A judge might well respond, "Your baby has three parents: its mother, its father, and the state. And the last of these refuses to share your view that a baby should be either perfect or dead."

I've given you "A" and "Z" examples above—one case in which a baby was so afflicted that it could never relate to others and, in contrast, another in which a baby lacked merely a little beauty or brains. A famous medical journal editor, Franz J. Ingelfinger, once remarked that As and Zs in any spectrum are easy to select, but it's deciding between the Ms and Ns that is difficult.

People resort to the law, according to bioethicist John Fletcher, when technology presents them with new options or new problems—or new opportunities to hurt others. "That is a primitive response, but it is logical," Dr. Fletcher said.

He thinks wisdom will come gradually. "The courts will act as a brake and as a teacher," he said. "And in twenty to twenty-five years, we

80 MAKING YOUR MEDICAL DECISIONS

will have administrative and organizational guidelines and an accumulated body of experience that can be taught."

And, by then, medical science will have marched on, too. Doctors will be able to remedy some of the underlying defects of babies with double trouble, perhaps through genetic engineering or other treatments while fetuses are still in the wombs. They also will extend the lives of babies who today die quickly after birth. Yet, those advances will create new problems that today I can foresee in part. I expect that they will cause anguish for those who succeed us as decision makers for babies in trouble.

5
THE CHAD GREEN STORY

IN February 1978, a blizzard buried Boston in snow. Genevieve ("Gen") V. Foley, a pediatric nurse clinician who worked with children stricken with cancer, was trapped at the Massachusetts General Hospital, unable for days to go home. Most parents were unable to bring their children for the treatment—usually chemotherapy—that they needed.

Still, families did straggle in or telephone, and within a few days the Mass General medical team had heard from all except the family composed of Gerald ("Jerry") and Diana Green and their son Chad.

Chad was twenty-five months old. He had leukemia, a form of cancer that causes a runaway growth of white blood cells. Using chemotherapy, doctors in Omaha, Nebraska, had put him in remission four months before.

The Greens were now staying with Jerry's father and stepmother, Hollis and Vera Green, in Scituate, a town on the Atlantic coast south of Boston. Ordinarily, it would have taken an hour for them to drive to the hospital, but now snow and flooding had slowed traffic in the Scituate area. It was therefore understandable that Jerry and Diana had not yet tried the trip.

Chad nevertheless needed a checkup. The month before, the Mass General staff had found that his white-blood-cell count was elevated. Chad's physician, Dr. John T. Truman, had therefore increased the dosage of two chemicals that he had prescribed to be given at home. These included a daily 6–mercaptopurine (6–MP) tablet and four weekly methotrexate tablets. He had asked Diana Green if she needed another prescription and had written out another one when she indicated she did.

After the February blizzard, nurse Gen Foley telephoned Jerry Green and discovered something even more worrisome. Jerry said that Chad had a cold and was running a high fever. Encouraged to bring Chad to the giant hospital center, the Greens arrived on February 17.

On previous visits, Chad had asked that a toy house be dragged out of a toy chest or used make-believe syringes to give his mother or nurse Foley shots in the wrist. Or occasionally he had toddled alongside Gen into what the staff called an echo chamber. This is a hallway where voices bounce off the walls. He would shout funny noises, laughing together with the nurse. He particularly liked Monica Corrigan, another nurse there, and, when he first had been able to say that long name, "Monica," everyone had clapped hands.

Now, he was pale and lethargic. Dr. Truman pressed his fingers into Chad's abdomen and could feel two swollen organs—his liver and his spleen. That pointed not to a mere cold but to a recurrence of his leukemia. A technician smeared a sample of his blood on a slide and put it under a microscope's lens. Some cells that Dr. Truman described as "primitive" appeared.

That seemed to be a tragic development. Chad's doctors had used all their weapons, but they were helpless if leukemic cells had survived in the bone marrow despite chemotherapy. Apparently, that had happened.

Thus, Dr. Truman had a sad duty—to ask the Greens whether they wanted chemotherapy continued. If so, he would agree. If not, he would stop. In either case—assuming that, despite chemotherapy, the leukemia had returned—Chad was doomed.

But a faint hope remained. Perhaps Chad's new illness was due, not to leukemia, but rather to a viral infection. That, though unlikely, was worth exploring. Dr. Truman would push a needle into a hipbone and withdraw some drops of marrow. If they showed no leukemic cells, Chad's illness was an infection.

Dr. Truman asked permission to perform the bone-marrow test—and the Greens refused.

Now suspicious, because that was a rejection of the only test that could determine whether Chad would live or die, Dr. Truman asked point-blank, "Has he been taking his pills?"

The answer was no. In fact, the Greens had stopped the daily pills three months before, and at some point had also stopped the weekly ones.

That changed Dr. Truman's assumptions. Even if the leukemia had recurred, the cells might still be vulnerable to attack.

But now the Greens had their coats on. The doctor asked that the chemotherapy be resumed, and they refused, and left.

Dr. Truman called them each day over the following weekend. After four days of such calls, when presumably the number of leukemic cells had doubled in Chad's body, he talked with the hospital's lawyer.

A decision of the state's supreme judicial court had apparently required that such life-death medical decisions be made by the state probate courts.[1] So the lawyer turned to that court. The judge there named a temporary guardian to consent to treatment.

As dusk came on in Scituate on February 22, 1978, a local police detective, with a representative of the state's Department of Public Welfare and a lawyer, whom the probate-court judge had appointed to represent Chad's interests, knocked on the Greens' door. Now Chad, with his mother for company, was admitted to Mass General for the bone-marrow test.

Children such as Chad Green are unlike the ones with double trouble that you read about in the last chapter. Those with double trouble can often be saved from death, but doctors cannot cure their underlying ailments. The most anyone can hope for them is an in-between status. In contrast, a Chad Green, if saved from death, will have no residual troubles. "There will be one of two outcomes," Dr. Truman told me. "One is complete cure, and the other is failure and death. There is no middle way."

Dr. Truman had treated more than a hundred children with leukemia, and the Greens were the first to reject chemotherapy. But other parents elsewhere have done the same. We want to find out whether judges should order parents, first, to accept conventional therapy and, second, to stop using their own treatments.

Chad Green wouldn't have been in the Massachusetts courts' jurisdiction, except that his parents had brought him to that state for the medical treatment that they later rejected. It was in Hastings, Nebraska, his mother's hometown, where his father worked as a welder, that Chad had awakened on August 30, 1977, with a fever of 106 degrees. He had been twenty months old then, the only child of the young couple.

A family doctor had referred them to a medical center in Omaha. A bone-marrow test showed he had null-cell acute lymphocytic leukemia.

In a way, that was lucky. Acute lymphocytic leukemia, the most common form of the disease in children, is the most curable. Also, the survival rate for the null-cell type is higher than for another type, known as T-cell.

In four weeks of intensive chemotherapy, the Omaha doctors had put Chad in remission. They had wanted to proceed to the next step—radiation of his brain. The parents had objected and moved to Massachusetts. It was another lucky thing that Jerry Green's father and stepmother lived in Scituate, near one of the world's foremost hospitals, Mass General.

Dr. Truman is an assistant professor at Harvard Medical School and the chief of the Pediatric Hematology-Oncology Unit at Mass General. He is so renowned for his treatment of leukemia that a layman's guide lists him as one of the nation's best doctors.

Jerry and Diana Green had had no previous experience with leukemia, but they had seen the ravages of other types of cancer. As a teenager in Hastings, Diana had seen her grandmother brought from a hospital to the family home to die. The grandmother had undergone radiation and chemotherapy. She had lost her hair and was in pain and had radiation sores all over her body. Jerry Green's grandfather had died of cancer of the spine.

And, while no blood relative had experienced leukemia, it had affected the family of Jerry's stepmother, Vera Green, of Scituate. Her brother's son had had leukemia fourteen years before, in the mid-1960s. He had gotten bald and swollen and almost skinless, Vera Green later told me. He had died after twenty-one months, "following the use of all 'orthodox' treatments with all the painful, distorting side effects."

Vera Green added in a letter, "Chad's medication (orthodox) was the SAME assortment as [my nephew's]. How can we support cancer research, per se, when the treatment is static, progressively speaking, and the 'Industry' employs a higher number of people than there are patients!!!"

Vera Green also warned me about chemotherapy. "Don't forget, chemotherapy includes nitrogen mustard," she said over the telephone. She was stating that anticancer chemicals are poisons.

Cancer specialists also sometimes use the word "poisons" to describe the chemicals. They kill bad cells, but they also kill some of the good ones. Columnist Stewart Alsop, who suffered from leukemia (though a different type than Chad had), wrote that it was like trying to kill the crabgrass without killing the grass.[2]

Vera Green was also calling up memories of the mustard gas used in World War I to cause blistering when it touched soldiers' skins. It's true that cancer specialists use nitrogen mustard.[3] In fact, it's one of the oldest anticancer drugs, having been in use for more than thirty years. Doctors now don't use it against leukemia, but rather primarily, in combination with other drugs, to treat Hodgkin's disease. They must be careful not to allow undiluted nitrogen mustard to contact a patient's skin.

Jerry and Diana Green already had misgivings about chemotherapy when they moved to Scituate. Back in Omaha, medical people had handed them a pamphlet describing how it worked and its side effects. "We had questions about whether chemotherapy was really going to do him any good," Jerry said later.

Once in Massachusetts, Jerry inquired about Vera Green's nephew, the one who had died of leukemia. Jerry learned that chemotherapy had had "devastating side effects," as he put it, on the boy. He mentioned the earlier death to the Mass General staff.

But, to the medical people there, that earlier death didn't mean chemotherapy would be useless for Chad. During the 1960s, two major advances had been made against leukemia. First, doctors learned to use drugs in combination, several at a time, to try to kill all the leukemic cells. That was only part of the battle, however, because leukemic cells might escape from the bloodstream and slip into the spinal fluid or invade the tissues surrounding the brain. Chemicals infused into the blood wouldn't touch the cells in those protected places, and the children would die of leukemic meningitis. Then, in the late 1960s and early 1970s, came the second advance. Scientists learned to irradiate the brain or inject drugs into the spinal fluid, and therefore the leukemia no longer had a haven in those places.

Also, Jerry's and Diana's grandparents' earlier deaths from cancer had little relevance to Chad's treatment for acute leukemia. It responds to chemotherapy better than many of the other 100 types of cancer.

Still, Chad's parents concluded that treatment other than chemotherapy was desirable, although none of this meant they opposed the practice of medicine. They had taken Chad for his routine vaccinations, for example.

They believed that prayer would help. As Diana Green put it, they believe the Lord works through people in everyday life. It was the Man Upstairs, not the doctors, who would, in Jerry Green's view, finally decide Chad's fate.

Earlier, when Chad was first diagnosed in Nebraska, they had put him on a diet that excluded meats, white sugar, and white flour. He ate fresh vegetables and fruits, drank goat's milk, and took vitamins and mineral supplements. The hospital staff in Omaha helped them obtain the foods, Diana told me.

Later, in Massachusetts, they talked with Dr. Truman about giving Chad the vegetarian diet, and he told them it wouldn't cure leukemia but that it was unobjectionable. They were reluctant to authorize a spinal injection (which Dr. Truman planned instead of brain irradiation), but nurse Gen Foley put them in touch with another Scituate couple, whose son had had the same treatment and had been cured of leukemia. Then they agreed to the injection.

However, they decided that chemotherapy was torturing Chad. The spinal injections were painful, Jerry later told me, and once caused Chad to collapse after coming home from the hospital. The drugs caused nausea, he said. Chad would be eating and would suddenly throw up. He had body tremors, so bad that once he would have fallen from his high chair if Jerry hadn't caught him.

Also, Chad acted like a wild animal, according to the Greens. "My wife or I would pick Chad up and hold him, and all of a sudden he'd become wild and start scratching and tearing at your face, trying to bite you," Jerry said. "And, of course, you'd have to put him down. And then he would throw himself up against the wall. And, after he calmed down, he would come back to you and say, 'I'm sorry. I'm sorry.'"

Members of the Mass General staff treating Chad thought those actions were typical of normal, two-year-old children. Later, in superior court, Judge Guy Volterra discounted the Greens' assertions of harm. He described the effects as mere "short term behavioral changes" and as "minimal." The Greens told me that the judge had observed their son for only a few minutes. They insisted the harm was significant. (The Mass General medical team did have a chance to observe Chad continuously and disagreed with the Greens on the extent of the side effects, as we shall learn.)

On November 7, 1977, Diana and Jerry asked Dr. Truman what would happen if they stopped chemotherapy. He told them that there was a 100-percent chance that the leukemia would recur. Three days later, the Greens stopped giving Chad his big, white 6–MP tablet each day, and three months later, during the Boston blizzard, Chad came down with what his parents believed to be a cold.

Now, in February 1978, under temporary court order, Chad was an inpatient at Mass General. That was the first time nurse Gen Foley had seen him truly ill. He failed to run for the toy chest. A bone-marrow test, quickly performed, showed that leukemia had recurred. Leukemic cells had crowded out the normal cells in the marrow. He therefore had no defense against bacteria. Even the bacteria that everyone carries in the intestines were dangerous. If they should find an entry into his bloodstream, he might be dead in twenty-four hours.

Dr. Truman and his staff began the three-year treatment program all over. They injected a drug called vincristine into a vein on the back of Chad's hand once a week. They gave him a daily hormone pill, prednisone. The hospitalization lasted sixteen days, and then he was released in his mother's care. The renewed treatment put him back in remission.

Chad's fame began. Mass General's news director, Martin Bander, would receive telephone calls from the hospital lobby; television cameramen were there to shoot scenes of Chad receiving chemotherapy. Hospital officials didn't want the cameramen on the ward, upsetting treatment schedules and intruding on the privacy of young cancer patients and their families. For the newsmen, though, it was a natural story. Should parents play God? Should establishment doctors tell mothers and fathers how to raise their children? Should judges interfere?

The First Superior Court Hearing

Judges were already deeply involved in Chad's case. A probate court judge had given authority for his treatment to be resumed in the hospital. The judge also suggested that a "care and protection" proceeding was wise, because of the hospital's evidence that with standard treatment, Chad had a chance of cure, but without it would die. So Dr. Truman, through Mass General's lawyer, now asked the court to find that Chad was in need of care and protection, as provided for in a state law.

The dispute was soon transferred to superior court. It holds sessions in the small Plymouth courthouse, a block from Plymouth Rock, down the coast from Scituate.

Diana Green, contesting the idea that Chad should be under state authority for his medical care, testified that chemotherapy was more detrimental than no chemotherapy. "We would love for Chad to have a full and long life," she told Judge Guy Volterra. "But it is more important to us that his life be full instead of long, if that is the way it has to be."

She and her husband remained unconvinced that Chad's leukemia had recurred in February. They would rely on prayer and diet rather than chemotherapy to control Chad's leukemia.

But Judge Volterra decided that chemotherapy could save Chad's life. Further, in his opinion, it wasn't torturing the boy.

The judge was impressed by the testimony of the Mass General medical people. They had observed Chad while he was in the hospital under court order in February. He had been under their care around the clock for sixteen days. They had given him such intensive chemotherapy to return him to a state of remission that his abdomen was temporarily distended. Still, members of the hospital staff had failed to see the distressing behavioral changes that the Greens had complained of.

The medical people had also observed Chad during outpatient visits. Aside from transient pain from shots, he had had only constipation and some stomach cramps from the chemotherapy. The staff could control those by varying the dosages.

And now, still being given regular doses of chemotherapy, Chad appeared to Judge Volterra, who viewed him in the courtroom, to be a normal, happy, two-year-old.

"I find that the side effects produced by the chemotherapy on the minor was minimal," the judge wrote. "There was no credible evidence of any serious or painful intrusions on the minor's body."

The judge decided that the state's Department of Public Welfare would have legal custody of Chad, although he could stay with his parents. A visiting nurse would make sure he took the chemotherapy pills at home.[4]

Judge Volterra predicted that Chad would "be able to attend school and to play and engage in the activities of other children his age." That was a long-range prediction, because Chad was still only two years old.

Later, the state's highest court unanimously affirmed the ruling. The justices pointed out that the Greens could come back to court every six months to try to get the order changed.

"We emphatically point out that this is not a case where there is any evidence that the parents wished their child any harm," Chief Justice Edward F. Hennessey wrote for the court. "On the contrary, the mother testified that she did not want her son to die, and that she only wanted what was best for him."[5]

Chad's fame was growing. In supermarkets, women shoppers would spy him, so small that his knit cap, topped with a pompom, was scarcely as high as his mother's waist, and say, "I bet you're Chad Green." His picture would appear in the paper, and he would point to it, saying delightedly, "Oh, that's me." He would kiss the images of his mother and himself on the TV screen. His mother would say tolerantly, "He's a ham," and his grandmother, Vera Green, later told me on the telephone, "He was an imp."

The newspaper photos showed him as pale and a little gaunt, with big, dark eyes, and shaggy hair. (Chemotherapy never caused him to lose it.) Early on, when photographers took his picture, he would say, "Cheese." Later, when the fame had lasted a third of his life, he was solemn when a camera pointed at him, or else he wore a reserved smile, barely lifting the corners of his mouth. His big eyes made him appear wise, as if he could make better decisions about his future than adults could.

The Second Court Hearing

In January 1979, Diana and Jerry Green went back to court, asking that they again have legal control over Chad. They added a new request, that they be permitted to give him metabolic treatment. They now also accepted the necessity for continuing chemotherapy, they said.

Actually, they had begun the metabolic treatment eight months earlier. Jerry later told me that they had studied books that discussed alternative therapies. Diana said that they had consulted by telephone doctors in both the United States and Europe, and those reinforced their decision to give metabolic therapy along with the chemotherapy. Jerry said three physicians had devised Chad's treatment. "We couldn't at the time give their names," he said, "but it was not a homemade program."

In addition to the chemotherapy, here is the treatment that the Greens now gave Chad: a diet of goat's milk, fresh vegetables, and raw fruit; calcium lactate and a mineral supplement; 45,000 units of Vitamin A a day (roughly twenty times the Recommended Daily Allowance for a child one to three years old); one milligram a day of folic acid (a member of the Vitamin B complex); 3,500 to 4,000 milligrams of Vitamin C a day (about 100 times the RDA); a daily enema, containing enzymes that would digest protein; one 500-milligram tablet of laetrile* daily.

Judge Volterra refused to give up state control over Chad's treatment. In a three-page preliminary order, he wrote that the Greens must refrain from giving some parts of the metabolic treatment, including the laetrile, and submit to doctors' instructions on other aspects. The Greens were to obtain a diet plan from the doctor, prepared by a dietician, which would be nutritionally sound and reflect their preference for natural foods.[6]

The parents then fled with Chad to exile in Tijuana, Mexico, where, with no court interference, he could receive both chemotherapy and their own treatment as well. They left behind a note, saying, "Chad must be protected from any further ignorance and pride, greed and violence."[7]

The Greens were bitter that the judge ordered them to get a diet plan from the doctor. A lawyer acquaintance of theirs thought they might have stayed in the state if the judge had refrained from issuing that part of the order. "I don't think anybody knows, not even they, whether they would have fled or not," the lawyer told me, "but it would have been a lot less likely."

Almost two years after the event, I asked Jerry and Diana Green about that. They replied, "Judge Volterra's order was so severe, it completely ruled out all of the nutritional supplements of vitamins, minerals, laetrile, enzymes, and everything we had seen Chad improve on, with God's help—yes, even to negate the wholesome, healthy foods he could eat. This was too much."

Diana Green later insisted that the diet order was the main reason they fled. If so, it's a shame they left in January 1979, immediately after the judge issued his order. It was an interlocutory—a temporary— order. When he put it in final form in April, he omitted his earlier instructions for the Greens to get a diet plan from the doctor. Also in his temporary order, he had forbidden them to give calcium lactate or mineral supplements to Chad without the doctor's permission, and in his final order he changed that too. "There was no evidence to suggest

---

*I am using "laetrile" in a generic sense, because most people know it by that name. Massachusetts judges used the more correct generic word "amygdalin." Other names for the drug are Kemdalin and Vitamin B-17.

that . . . calcium lactate and mineral supplements—or the vegetarian diet administered by the parents was interfering with the chemotherapy or otherwise impairing or endangering the child's health," Judge Volterra stated.[8] But by then, the Greens had been in Mexico three months.

Those aspects of the judge's temporary order were unfortunate. But consider the pressures when, at night after two weeks of hearings, he wrote it. Reporters had been excluded, as they and the public had to be for hearings involving a child. Now the reporters were pressing for information on the significant issue of how much the state should control parents' remedies for an ill child. Experts had testified that Jerry and Diana were using harmful substances, and so it seemed urgent to protect Chad at once. Also, advice from a dietician might help him gain strength. Later, Judge Volterra would receive the transcript of testimony and could study it exhaustively for his final order. He thought he had time for that. The Greens had seemed impressed by testimony about dangers in their remedies, and the judge was astonished when, later, they fled.

Judge Volterra also limited the amount of Vitamin C that Chad could receive. The judge concluded that high doses—100 times the RDA—could cause toxic effects in Chad's kidneys and possibly cause cancer. The order concerning Vitamin C nevertheless irritated the Greens because of what they felt was a lack of supporting testimony. Due to the complexity of the test, the level of Vitamin C in Chad's body had not been measured.[9]

But other evidence of damage was convincing. Dr. Truman had tested Chad's blood for poisons and had found high levels of Vitamin A and, perhaps as a result, an impairment of liver function. Too much Vitamin A can destroy the liver and damage the central nervous system. Jerry and Diana Green agreed to stoping giving the massive doses to Chad even while the court hearing was in progress. Judge Volterra was also convincing in his reason for forbidding folic acid. It could interfere with chemotherapy's effectiveness.

The enzyme enemas that Chad was receiving could digest proteins. One ingredient used in them—papain—is also used in a meat tenderizer. Such substances could have eaten small holes in Chad's intestines. The mere insertion of a hose into his colon to give him an enema was dangerous. Patients on chemotherapy are vulnerable to infection. Doctors advise parents of leukemic children not to take temperatures with a rectal thermometer. If the glass tube scratched the colon's wall, bacteria that are always present there could quickly invade the bloodstream. Similarly, they could enter if an enema hose scratched the wall or the enzymes ate holes for them to use. The judge therefore properly forbade further enzyme enemas.

A controversial part of the Green's treatment for Chad was their giving him laetrile. That drug has been shown in a clinical trial supported by the National Cancer Institute to be ineffective against several types of cancer, such as those of the lung, breast, and colon. It has not been tested against leukemia but is probably as useless as laughing gas against that disease. Four experts that Chad Green's parents invited to the court hearing in Plymouth testified that laetrile and metabolic therapy have no observable effect in curing acute lymphocytic leukemia. The best they could say for it was that it could make chemotherapy more tolerable, and increase appetite and energy levels.[10] The witnesses included Dr. Ernesto Contreras, who since 1963 has run the Del Mar Cancer Clinic, in Tijuana, Mexico. Chad was later to be treated at that clinic, as we shall see.

Laetrile can form hydrogen cyanide in the body. Dr. Truman had found a byproduct of that poison in Chad's blood and urine. The levels in Chad's body were comparable to those in African natives who eat cassava root. After long periods on the diet, some of the natives become blind or deaf and cannot walk.

It can kill, too. Chad was taking one 500-milligram tablet a day. In Buffalo, New York, an eleven-month-old girl accidentally swallowed one to five of her father's 500-milligram tablets. She fell into a coma and, fourteen hours after taking the tablet(s), stopped breathing. Doctors put her on a respirator, but she died. (They might have saved her if they had known earlier what she had taken.)[11] Judge Volterra's order forbidding laetrile, at least in the amount Chad was getting, was justified.

In Mexico

Regardless of Judge Volterra's findings, Chad was now in Mexico, outside his reach. The Plymouth court held Jerry and Diana Green in civil contempt and also found probable cause for criminal contempt. But Massachusetts officials made no attempt to extradite the Greens.

Television pictures taken in Mexico and shown in the States revealed a happy Chad, lurching about a Tijuana square with other children. Or he would laugh at squirrels, toddling after them, while the hot Mexican sun made his blond hair glint. But he seemed old for his three years. Once his parents told him they would all be taking a trip, and he asked, "Will the police be there?"

A cloud no bigger than a man's hand had followed the Greens to Mexico too—the chance that Chad's leukemia might recur. At this stage in his treatment, assuming effective chemotherapy was continued, he had a fifty-fifty chance of cure. Thus it could go either way.[12]

To his parents the threat seemed remote. In late July, 1979, in Mexico, a blood test showed Chad's blood to be normal, Jerry Green told me. A bone-marrow test was also done. "The test showed that his body was producing 100-percent normal cells," Jerry said.

Chad was receiving the vegetarian diet, chemotherapy, and metabolic treatment that he had before the court ruled in Massachusetts, except that his parents now gave him enzymes by mouth instead of by enemas. They had resumed the Vitamin A. Jerry was convinced that testimony about its dangers had been misleading. "This is nothing but a ploy to get us to stop giving Chad those things that are helping him so much," he had told Diana. In Mexico, therefore, he and Diana had samples of Chad's blood and urine sent to specialists in the States. When the counts came back normal, they started giving him the Vitamin A again. They were also giving him laetrile, in the same daily amount as before.

In early August, 1979, the Massachusetts Supreme Judicial Court announced its approval of Judge Volterra's order.[13] In Mexico, Diana Green told reporters, "God is the healer, and Chad is healthy now."[14]

At about the same time, back in Boston, Dr. John Truman was uneasy because of the possibility that Chad's leukemia would recur. A worried nonphysician, who had been connected with aspects of the case, had obtained slides from Tijuana containing smears of Chad's blood. He asked Dr. Truman to look at them under a microscope.

The cells had what the Boston doctor called "soft signs"—ominous to an expert. The red cells didn't appear to be as big as they would have been, and the white cells didn't have as many lobes as they would have, if Chad had been receiving effective chemotherapy.

"There was no sign of leukemia at that point," Dr. Truman later told me, "but of course by the time leukemia is visible in the blood, the end is very closely in sight."

Having no direct communication with the Greens, and perhaps hoping the message would reach Mexico, Dr. Truman told the newspapers about the soft signs. A physicians' magazine picked up the story, interpreting Dr. Truman's remarks as a prediction that Chad would have a relapse between August 15, 1979 and April 15, 1980.

On August 17, 1979, Dr. Ernesto Contreras, founder of the Del Mar

Cancer Clinic in Tijuana, where Chad was being treated, announced to news people that the Greens had told him Chad had been off chemotherapy for a month. "I am sorry they are putting him at risk unnecessarily," Dr. Contreras said. A Mexican blood specialist who had been treating Chad said the lack of chemotherapy might lead to a fatal relapse.[15]

The Greens saw accounts of Dr. Contreras's and the blood specialist's statements in the newspaper and on television, Jerry later told me. They were puzzled, he said, because they thought they had medical permission to taper off the chemotherapy.

Chad was off chemotherapy from July 1979 on. Jerry stressed that they had him under constant medical supervision. "Chad went to the clinic every day for his examinations," Jerry told me. "He went in every two weeks for blood tests. If a blood count came out poorer than we expected, just to be on the safe side, we would take him to another doctor and have another blood test taken, and check out the results from both of them. So we kept a very, very constant and close watch."

Until September, Chad was his usual bright self. In that month, he became depressed and listless. "He didn't want to do much of anything," Jerry Green said later.

A Friday Afternoon in October

The Greens gave the following account of the events of a Friday afternoon in October 1979.

The three members of the family were in their Tijuana apartment. The parents were watching the five o'clock news. Chad lay on the couch, looking out their picture window. Diana was beside him. Jerry sat on the floor, holding Chad's hand.

Chad, looking through the window, said, "I want to go out there."

Diana and Jerry showed interest. Perhaps he was coming out of his lassitude. "You want to go outside and play?" Jerry asked.

"No, no, no," Chad said, apparently displeased at their failure to understand. He continued to lie on the couch.

A few seconds later, he said, "I want to go out there. Let me go. Help me, Dad." He clutched Jerry's hand.

He sighed, and stopping breathing.

Jerry tried CPR, breathing into Chad's mouth, and then ran out to the car (they had no telephone) to go for a doctor.

At my home near Washington, D.C., I failed to turn off my bedside radio that night. I had been following the Chad Green story for a year, clipping newspaper stories, watching for Chad on television, and sending to Massachusetts for court decisions concerning him, but hadn't yet tried to communicate with his parents. At 2:30 Saturday morning, I was awakened by Diana Green's voice, originating in Tijuana. The voice kept breaking up in grief. She said she and Jerry would be reunited with Chad someday.

Chad was three years and ten months old when he died. A California pathologist conducted a private autopsy at the request of the Greens. It was hampered by the fact that the body had been embalmed, which would inhibit the detection of cyanide.[16] Mexican doctors also conducted an autopsy.

Within ten days of Chad's death, Dr. Contreras announced that he had had a relapse of his leukemia and had died of it.[17] At about the same time, the American pathologist was quoted in a physicians' magazine as saying: "The kid definitely had leukemic infiltrates in several organs, including spleen, liver, kidneys, and bone marrow. It wasn't an overwhelming terminal leukemia, but there definitely was a recurrence." The magazine said that at the same time tests hadn't yet been completed in an effort to find evidence of any cyanide poisoning from laetrile.

Almost a year and a half later, Jerry Green told me on the telephone that the American pathologist had been unable to find a cause for Chad's death—that neither cyanide nor Vitamin A poisoning had caused it. "He did have some leukemia in some of his organs," Jerry said, "but there was not enough to have caused death." The Greens believe Chad just gave up, from loneliness and homesickness.

I was unsuccessful, however, in my efforts to get definitive information from the final, written autopsy report itself. And Jerry Green told me that, because that formal autopsy report was a private document, it had been up to him and Diana whether to allow its release. He had instructed that it be withheld from requestors, he said.

The Final Court Appearance

Jerry and Diana took Chad's body back to Hastings, Nebraska, for burial. Just over a year later, on December 8, 1980, they appeared again in the small Plymouth, Massachusetts, courthouse. This time, before a different judge, they apologized for affronting the court when they had disregarded its orders and fled with Chad to Mexico. The judge found them guilty of criminal contempt but passed no sentence.

He ordered that the case be closed. "This court does not make light of their affront," he said, "but any further punishment would certainly be unfair."[18] He commended Dr. Truman and the Massachusetts General Hospital for the interest they had taken in Chad and his proper care.

Chad would have been five years old that same month. The state prosecutor told the judge, "There is no doubt in my mind that Chad would be alive and well and about to celebrate his fifth birthday," if the Greens had remained in Massachusetts. Outside the courthouse, Diana Green told reporters, "Only God knows that."[19]

And then she and Jerry settled in California, all the way across the country.

Before going to court that final time, the Greens wrote to me, "We had been found in each court to be intelligent and loving parents." That was true. And I could not doubt Diana and Jerry Green's devotion to their son.

After moving to California, Diana said in another letter that it could not be known whether Chad would have lived if he had continued on chemotherapy, because children die of leukemia, even in prestigious institutions. "Chad died peacefully, but at home, no bleeding, no indication of pain," she wrote. She raised the question of whether, if Chad had lived, it would have been worth the "horrors" of chemotherapy's side effects. "We won't know that," she wrote and then repeated what she had said outside the Plymouth courthouse, "Only God knows that."

The Chad Green case wasn't the only one in which parents have rejected conventional treatment for their children's cancer.[20] Orthodox doctors are galled or saddened by parents' refusal of what seems to them to be the best treatment. A cancer specialist who read a draft of this section said that such cases were aberrations that got the headlines and added, "There will always be faith healers."

Before you dismiss that specialist as biased, consider how he and his colleagues have brought hope to the formerly hopeless. Acute leukemia in children was galloping death until, in the late 1940s, scientists found a drug that could temporarily extend life. They then found others and, at first, used them one at a time. When the leukemic cells developed resistance to one drug, they would switch to another.

Children would appear to be cured. They were beautiful to me when, in the 1960s, I came to work as a writer at the Clinical Center, the research hospital for the National Institutes of Health. I wanted to send newspapers full-face pictures of them. They would be photographed in a Christmas scene, one that seemed to symbolize a hope of rebirth for the ill.

Compose such a picture in your mind. On a dais sits Santa Claus, smiling and making Santa noises, stretching out his arms. Flanking him are elves—two high-school girls. Each is dressed, as is a female elf's wont, in a skirt that scarcely covers her rump, baring legs that reach all the way from her hips to the floor. The elves are smiling, and one has crooked her arm to receive Santa's visitor.

The visitor is a little girl in a wheelchair. She wears an expectant and shy grin. She probably also wears a wig to hide a scalp that is temporarily bald from chemotherapy, but if so it is undetectable. Fastened to the wheelchair is an upright steel rod, like a hatrack, and atop it is a bottle dripping fluid through a tube into the girl's arm.

The hope symbolized by such a Christmas scene was unfounded. I mentioned to a hospital administrator my plan to send such pictures to the newspapers. He looked out the window to a darkening winter scene. "They're nearly all going to die," he said. Such children were merely in remission. Their leukemia was waiting, regrouping for a killing attack. And so I abandoned my plan. Christmas is a time to tell about beginnings, not about doomed children.

At about the same time, a mother whose child had died of leukemia asked the hospital's public information office for advice on a proposed magazine article that she had written called, "The Day They Close Two-East." Two-East was the ward where doctors conducted research on treating leukemic children. The title implied that someday they would so succeed in curing children that research could end, and the ward therefore could be closed. I don't know whether the article was published.

That was more than fifteen years ago. Scientists were then learning to use combinations of drugs, and later they irradiated the brain (that was the procedure objected to by Chad Green's parents in Omaha) or used spinal injections to ward off leukemic invasion of the central nervous system.

Two-East is still open, but what a difference—there and across the country. In early 1979, specialists at one major center reported that over the preceding several years the cure rate was about 40 percent of all children with both types of acute lymphocytic leukemia.[21] Survival for young children with Chad Green's type (null-cell) is higher than that, with girls doing somewhat better than boys. The cure rate for such children of both sexes now under treatment at leading centers will probably reach the 60-percent range.

What's a Judge to Do?

As discussed earlier in this chapter, we want to decide whether judges should order parents, first, to accept conventional treatment and, second, to stop using their own remedies. In considering both questions, we must remember that the law presumes parents have the competence and the right to raise their children free of state interference.

Does that traditional independence and the right of the family to privacy confer legal authority on the parents to reject medical treatment for their children?[22] The answer cannot be a simple yes or no.

One consideration is whether the ailment threatens the child's life or will cause irreparable harm if untreated. If the lack of a standard treatment led only to the continuation of a nondangerous disease, a judge could well respect the privacy of a family and therefore let the parents run their own affairs.

A second consideration is whether a child can be restored to a life worth living. We learned in the last chapter that a child may have such problems that the extra life a treatment yielded would fail to be worth the living. For example, the most conservative judge wouldn't order further treatment for the exhausted child with kidney problems discussed on pages 71–72.

A third consideration is whether the proposed treatment is proven. Parents should be able to reject experimental treatment. A time may come, however, when specialists agree on a treatment of choice for a disease in which the treatment has until then been experimental. When, as with leukemia, it is the only treatment that can cure the disease, parents no longer should be allowed to ignore it. Those who would do so would in effect ask that they be permitted to remove their children from the present time and return them to an earlier one when doctors were helpless.

The U.S. Supreme Court has correctly pointed out that parents have no right to make martyrs of their children.[23] For example, adult Jehovah's Witnesses usually can refuse blood transfusions for themselves, but their right of free exercise of religion isn't unqualified when their children's lives are at stake.[24]

The difference was illustrated when a judge was called to a Washington, D.C., hospital at 1:30 on a November morning in 1974. He was asked to decide whether a newborn baby, whom I'll call "Debbie," should be given blood transfusions over her parents' objections. Both were Jehovah's Witnesses.

Debbie had rising levels of a pigment, bilirubin, in her blood. That might damage her brain or kill her. Blood transfusions help with that problem. Her parents refused to permit them.

While the judge was listening to a presentation of facts concerning Debbie's need for blood, the mother, "Margaret," suddenly began hemorrhaging. Doctors at the hospital concluded that she needed an emergency hysterectomy to stop the bleeding. She also needed transfusions to replace the lost blood, but both she and her husband had forbidden transfusions earlier and now her husband refused to give permission.

The judge ordered transfusions for little Debbie. At last report, she was doing fine. He refused to order transfusions for the mother, Margaret. She bled to death.[25]

If, therefore, the proposed treatment is proven, can restore the child to a life worth living, and the child might be seriously harmed or die without it, parents should have no authority to reject it. Thus, the Washington, D.C., judge correctly ordered blood transfused to little Debbie, and Judge Guy Volterra in Massachusetts correctly commanded that chemotherapy be continued for Chad Green. In both cases, the medical treatment proposed by orthodox doctors had all three of the essential elements listed above.

But that's only half the problem. What are judges to do when parents insist on using their own remedies, some of them fads, as well?[26] That may be a more difficult decision than the other one. The following picture is drawn from several cases, not just the Chad Green one.

Desperate themselves when their children are desperately ill, parents may seek advice everywhere. They listen eagerly to those who hold irrelevant academic degrees or who, though being physicians, are not specialists in the disease that afflicts a child and are naive about scientific methods for investigating remedies.

Many of the partisans who write or broadcast advice about curing cancer have a characteristic that appeals to parents: they display confidence, even blind faith, in the remedies they advocate. Now and then, a cancer patient being treated with one of those remedies goes into a remission. Partisans hail that as proof of efficacy. More judicious scientists describe the report of such an event as "anecdotal evidence." In their minds, the treatment merely coincided with the remission, which might well have happened regardless.

In other cases, reports of miraculous cures would be found to be incomplete or inaccurate if investigated. The parents are in no position to check all the aspects and may mistakenly believe that whatever appears in print or on the air must be accurate, because otherwise it couldn't legally be given media space.[27]

The partisans who write or broadcast such reports are persuasive in part because patients and their families today reach for autonomy. That is bolstered by a traditional family opposition to outside interference.

Those outside advisers are also persuasive because many people already distrust experts in general and orthodox medicine in particular. Some of that distrust is justified, as we learned in Chapter 1.

But the child's parents add to such an underlying distrust, by believing that establishment doctors and the government are in on a conspiracy to deny them commonsense, natural remedies. The other partners in the conspiracy, in the parents' view, are drug houses that are more interested in profits than in health. The parents may believe that the companies suppress truly effective medicines—that they take nature's own remedies and contaminate them with chemicals for no other reason than to be able to patent them.

Judges who interfere with parental treatment therefore can expect resentment. Parents may dislike doctors and nurses who touch their child with a judge's permission but not theirs. Where once they would have smiled when a nurse restrained their child to give a shot, they now accuse her of cruelly holding the child down. They speak of "my son," stressing the *my*, instead of using his given name. Thus, they imply that medical people are trying to overturn the natural order of things.

Such implications alienate the medical people. They may tell each other that the parents don't want their own child to live. Whenever the family arrives at the hospital, staff members may make it clear that they would rather not have obstreperous parents around. That interferes with communication, which may already be poor.

As I shall discuss in Chapter 9 (and as you undoubtedly already know), doctors often fail to communicate well with patients and their families. In addition, they have deeply ingrained inhibitions on self-promotion. So, when parents oppose them, perhaps taking the protest to the media, they may retreat into silence. At that time, when they need communication skills the most, either to persuade the public or the parents, they tend to use such skills the least.

That failure of orthodox medical people to communicate—so striking in its contrast to the facility with which outside partisans get across their message—is probably a major reason that some parents opt for unconventional treatment.

For judges to take a detached view in such circumstances is difficult. They could start with the realization that parents are usually motivated by love for their children. That they lack scientific knowledge doesn't mean that they are unprincipled. Their remedies are not necessarily all bad. They may instead range from beneficial to useless to dangerous.

Judges will also be influenced, and properly so, by a respect for the traditional privacy of the family. They may well remember that their goal is protection of the child but with minimum intrusion on parents' autonomy. They will wisely be cautious, reluctant to intervene hastily or to issue sweeping orders that would ban the parents from having any say.

They will examine each element of the parents' treatment. They should, of course, forbid those aspects that, as shown by clear and convincing evidence, would seriously harm the child.

On the other hand, they will either ignore or approve those parts of the parents' treatment that are merely useless or for which experts can point to no evidence of harm. They will wisely try to preserve parents' freedom of action, hoping that compromises will emerge and seeking out and permitting elements of the parents' treatment that can be accepted without danger.

6
TEENAGERS: ON DECIDING FOR ONE'S OWN SELF

TEENAGERS today have more of an appearance of adulthood than ever before. They are healthier and taller than their ancestors. Sexually, they mature earlier.

In 1840, girls on the average reached puberty at seventeen. Then the age began to drop, about six months every decade, mainly because of improving nutrition. On average, American girls today have their first menstrual periods at age twelve and a half and some as early as eleven.[1]

That in turn has led to the phenomenon of children having children of their own. Obviously a twelve-year-old mother is capable of making some important decisions—has, in fact, made one already.

American teenagers are making other decisions concerning their bodies, too. They are—with legal authority—deciding their own treatment for sex- and drug-related problems. Should they be allowed to make medical decisions for other medical problems at, say, twelve, thirteen, or fourteen? Should they be able to refuse treatment? For example, should they have the same right that adults have, to decline arbitrary confinement in mental institutions?

The New Age of Majority

During an unpopular war—Vietnam—U.S. lawmakers decided to show more respect for the young voices that denounced the fighting.[2] They wanted to give teenagers a say in electing people who ran the country, so Congress passed the Voting Rights Act of 1970, lowering the voting age to eighteen. When Supreme Court justices ruled that the act couldn't apply to state and local elections,[3] Congress proposed the Twenty-Sixth Amendment. Three-fourths of the states ratified it within a year.

Thus, eighteen-year-olds today can vote in any election. "They are mature enough in every way . . . " said the Senate report proposing the amendment.[4]

That failed to give them other rights, but that was soon remedied, too. Under the common law that America had inherited from England, children were minors until twenty-one. But now states began lowering that age. By 1980, forty-three states had made children adults at eighteen.[5]

Granted, some lawmakers may have been vengeful. Teenagers' protests against U.S. involvement in Vietnam, with their sit-ins, marches, and escape-the-draft flights to Canada, struck many Americans as unpatriotic. Children who took drugs and sex but not baths disgusted older Americans.

Some divorced fathers turned on children who no longer lived with them. They had signed to support such children until they reached the age of majority. At the time they signed, that age had been twenty-one. Such support therefore would ordinarily carry children through the first three years of college.

Should divorced fathers be the beneficiaries of the new laws? Yes, ruled judges in Virginia, North Carolina, and New Mexico. They need pay only until their children were eighteen, unless they had specifically promised to pay until twenty-one.[6]

Thus, parents could now thrust eighteen-year-olds out into the world. In compensation, those newly-minted adults could buy cars or houses if their credit was okay. They could draw their own wills. They could marry or join the armed forces without their parents' consent.[7] And they could consent to their own medical care.

The Risk in Treating Minors without Parents' Consent

Adolescents under eighteen (or who are still minors at other ages in a few states) are under the control of their parents. In theory, they have no power to consent to medical care. Doctors who treat them without their parents' consent commit a technical battery. The parents might sue for damages if the treatment turns out badly.

Also, until about the 1970s, doctors who gave controversial advice or treatment to youngsters—such as fitting them with intrauterine devices—risked violating the criminal law. Prosecutors might accuse them of contributing to the delinquency of minors.[8]

Still, the proposition that doctors cannot treat minors without parents' consent is riddled with exceptions. They can treat them in emergencies, for example. The common law has always authorized such treatment, and now lawmakers in more than a third of the states have passed statutes to that effect.[9] And children who are free of ties to their parents can legally consent, as we shall see.

Also, state lawmakers have concluded that in some instances both teenagers' and the general public's health could be harmed if parents must be asked for consent. The lawmakers therefore have enacted statutes letting teenagers get medical treatment on their own for sex-related and drug problems.

Adolescent Health Problems

Measured by their death rates, teenagers are healthy. They are past the infections of babyhood and don't yet suffer from the chronic diseases of adulthood. About 70 percent of their deaths are caused, not by disease, but by motor vehicle accidents and violence. Cancer accounts for only 8 percent of their deaths and heart disease for only 5 percent.

Still, a survey of twelve to seventeen year olds revealed problems. One out of twenty had a cardiovascular problem, such as a heart murmur or high blood pressure. Forty percent couldn't see well enough to read at the twenty/twenty level, and two-thirds needed dental care.[10]

Half of all adolescents visit doctors at least once a year. A subspecialty of adolescent medicine is springing up. At least eight clinics in New York City specialize in teenagers' problems, such as menstrual difficulties, acne, infectious mononucleosis, sports injuries, and overweight. Physicians say every illness takes on a psychological aspect during that age of upheavals.[11]

The main reasons teenagers enter hospitals are, in the case of boys, injuries, and, in the case of girls, pregnancies. Teenage birthrates fell during the 1970s because of contraception and abortion. The rate peaked in 1972 at about 40 births per 1,000 girls fifteen to seventeen years old. It fell to about 33 per 1,000 in 1978.[12] Even after the decline, girls in that age range bore more than 200,000 babies a year.

Gonorrhea among teenagers fifteen to nineteen tripled in the two decades between 1955 and 1975, then leveled off. Among 1977 high-school graduates, more than 90 percent had tried alcohol, and nearly a quarter had experimented with psychoactive drugs.[13]

Thus, teenagers, despite their relative health, do have medical problems. Lawmakers have realized that to insist on parents' permission for treating some of these could in itself lead to more problems.

Treatment for VD, Drug Abuse, and Pregnancy

Teenagers usually want to conceal VD from their parents. Consider the dilemmas of the various parties if the parents had to give permission before a doctor could treat a teenager's gonorrhea.

Physician: "Left untreated, Marcie might infect others. A shot of penicillin or a dose of tetracycline would probably cure her in a week. But, if I stuck a needle in her arm without her parents' consent, I'd be committing a battery. Her parents might take out their anger on me, because they'd be unable to restore Marcie's virginity or to punish the boys involved."

Parents: "We'd be left in the dark if we weren't asked to consent to her treatment. We need to know about her sleeping with boys so we can stop it."

Marcie: "My parents just want to punish me. I'll skip the treatment if they have to approve it."

State lawmakers in the late 1960s decided that the central issue when youngsters had VD wasn't whether they should have sexual relations. That had already been resolved. The real question was whether society was to be punished by discouraging the youths from getting treatment. By the end of the 1970s, therefore, lawmakers in every state had given minors the right to consent to diagnosis and treatment of venereal disease.[14]

Many of the states that allow minors to consent to VD treatment also provide that the doctors can tell the parents about it. The excuse is that parents may need to know when a youngster has complications or must go to the hospital. Some also provide that the doctor can go to the parents to be sure of getting paid.[15]

Still, many doctors who practice adolescent medicine know that, without trust, youngsters might not come for treatment. Thus, they ask the teenagers before informing parents and, without permission, don't tell.

State lawmakers also provided that youngsters could consent to drug-abuse treatment on their own. And it made equally good sense to authorize minors to consent to care during pregnancy. More than half the babies born to girls fifteen through seventeen in 1978 were illegitimate.[16] Teenage moms often bear low-birth-weight babies. Such babies have a high death rate. They are more likely than others to go blind or deaf. To refuse pregnant girls the right to consent to medical care on their own might mean they would delay it until late in pregnancy and thus risk even more health problems for their babies. Today, therefore, laws in most states say doctors needn't get parents' permission when giving care to pregnant girls.[17]

Also, youngsters, whether married or not, can buy condoms or other contraceptive devices. New York State lawmakers prohibited distribution to those under sixteen, but the U.S. Supreme Court threw out the law.

Supreme Court Justice William J. Brennan, Jr., pointed out for the Court that a lack of contraceptives had never stopped sexual activity. Anyway, he continued, the punishment for fornication shouldn't be the birth of an unwanted child. Because a teenager has the same constitutional right to privacy as an adult, a majority of the justices ruled the New York law unconstitutional.[18]

Now we move on to an even more sensitive question. Should teenage girls be able to get abortions on their own? The answer, according to lawmakers in several states, should be no, but, according to the Supreme Court, is yes.

Among the state antiabortion laws that the courts had thrown out in 1973 was one in Missouri.[19] The next year, Missouri's General Assembly had passed a law salvaging some of the state's control over women's bodies.[20] They had labeled it an emergency act, so it could go into effect when the governor signed it. Among the emergencies was the possibility that unmarried girls under eighteen might get abortions without parents' permission. The lawmakers forbade that, unless a teenage mother needed an abortion to save her life.

In 1976, a majority of justices in the Supreme Court threw out the new act.[21] Justice Harry A. Blackmun explained that an underage girl has the same right of privacy that adults do. "Constitutional rights do not mature and come into being magically only when one attains the state-defined age of majority," he wrote.[22]

That was a fragmented decision, with disagreement among the justices. It was the arbitrariness of the Missouri law—the veto power that it gave parents—that caused it to be struck down.

The justices have been worried, though, about girls' having abortions with no advice from parents. "At least when the parents are together and the pregnant minor is living at home, both the father and mother have an interest—one normally supportive—in helping to determine the course that is in the best interest of a daughter," Justice Lewis F. Powell, Jr., wrote in another case.[23] So, in still another case, the justices approved a Utah law that required doctors to notify parents when such girls wanted abortions.[24]

Three states had such parent-notification statutes, and antiabortionists could be expected to push for them in other states after the Supreme Court decision.[25] Still, the ruling didn't affect under-eighteen girls who were free of family ties. The justices didn't rule on whether a doctor must notify the parents when an underage girl seemed mature enough to make her own decisions.

And parents continue to have no legal power to veto an underage girl's abortion decision. So jokes circulate about inconsistencies in teenagers' legal powers. "I'm planning to go downtown to get an abortion," a high school girl tells a friend, "but I need my parents' permission to get excused from school."

To sum up, laws and court decisions now allow youngsters to be treated for several problems without their parents' consent. On the teenagers' say-so alone, doctors can give them contraceptive advice, treat them for venereal disease or drug abuse, advise them during pregnancy, deliver their babies, or give them abortions.

As we have learned, doctors may inform parents, and so teenagers may view family doctors with suspicion. They crowd into places such as "The Door: A Center for Alternatives," a few blocks north of Greenwich Village. The name means its counselors try to show teenagers doors, other than drugs, pregnancy, or idleness, when they have problems.

Other centers give free care without telling parents. "They include family-planning centers, public VD clinics with their promise of free and anonymous care, mental-health centers, and a network of community social agencies that reach out to help," a writer commented in a physicians' magazine.[26]

Runaways, Throwaways, and Emancipation

Aside from the sex-related and other illnesses discussed above, underage youngsters still need parents' consent for treatment. But they can consent for themselves, regardless of the nature of a disease, if they are free of family ties. The legal word for such freedom is "emancipation."

I want to tell you about a newer concept too, one that enables mature minors to consent to medical care regardless of whether they are free of their families. The problem with both concepts—emancipation and maturity—is that their boundaries are so uncertain.

Many children are unwilling to wait to be declared adults legally. By 1974, a million children were running away from home each year. In New York City, 43 percent of those leaving home were between the ages of eleven and fourteen.[27] Throwaway children make up another group—those whom parents beat, or sexually abuse, or tell to get out and make it on their own.[28]

Many of the runaways and throwaways, as well as teenagers who leave with the friendly consent of their parents, are emancipated. Being free of family ties, they can legally handle their own affairs.

Emancipation came into its own when the Industrial Revolution brought a demand for child labor and a belief that all persons, even children, could make their own way.[29] Today, a youngster who has married or joined the military service has good evidence of freedom from family ties. But what measure can be used for others? A judge might ask a teenager the following questions:

Do you live away from home or, if you are still at home, do you pay room and board?

Do you work for someone other than your parents? If so, do you spend your pay as you like?

Do you pay your own bills?

Have your parents taken your name off their tax forms as a dependent?

A "yes" answer to all those questions would indicate that the teenager is emancipated, but judges have occasionally ruled that even stronger evidence is needed.

The Mature Minor Concept

Today, a maturity test is taking its place alongside emancipation. The test is whether the teenager understands the nature and consequences of the medical treatment. Those who do are "mature minors"—not old enough to be adults, but mature enough to make their own medical decisions.

A theme has run through the law since ancient times that children who understood what was going on were mature enough to be responsible. Thus, in 1629, an English executioner hanged an eight-year-old boy named Dean, who had burned two barns. The trial judge had concluded that Dean had had "malice, revenge, craft, and cunning," and therefore had the necessary maturity to be executed.[30]

In America today, juvenile court judges usually look at youngsters' ages, criminal records, and seriousness of their crimes when deciding whether to send them to trial as adults. In Boston, in 1978, a judge in an adult court sentenced a fifteen-year-old boy to life after he pleaded guilty to the holdup-murder of a sixty-four-year-old oil dealer who had been making emergency deliveries in a blizzard.[31]

People who are hurt by children can sue them for damages. In 1951, a five-year-old boy in Washington State snatched a lawn chair from under an arthritic woman who was seating herself. She tumbled and broke her hip. Instead of treating that as a prank, she sued the boy, whom I'll call Bobby.

Justices on the Washington Supreme Court said it was not Bobby's age that would govern whether he was responsible. It was rather his "experience, capacity, and understanding." These determined that he had known what would happen when he jerked the chair aside. The woman won a judgment for $11,000.[32] (Perhaps Bobby's family had insurance that covered his acts.)

Some state laws say that children ten to fourteen years old can name their own guardians after their parents have died. Judges settling custody battles must ask even younger children which parent they want to live with. A Texas judge who failed to ask an eight-year-old's opinion on that question was told by appeals judges to hear the case all over again.[33]

Similarly, in scattered instances, responsible teenagers make their own decisions about medical care.

That makes sense. Youngsters' IQs stabilize, and their ability to think for themselves develops, earlier than their late teens.[34] By the age of fourteen or so, their moral and intellectual capacities approach those of adults, stated Justice William O. Douglas in another context.[35]

For example, a sixteen-year-old kidney patient, "Karen," on the adolescent ward of the Yale-New Haven Hospital, decided to forgo further treatment. That meant she would die.

Surgeons had removed her kidneys because of nephritis. Treated on an artifical kidney machine, she had chills, nausea, headaches, and weakness. Surgeons then transplanted a kidney from her father, but her body defeated it. She went back on the machine, lonely, uncomfortable, and weak.

When a surgeon took the transplanted kidney out, it had the same appearance as her own had. It was therefore clear that her body would defeat any transplant.

A week after the kidney was removed, the shunt on her arm became infected. A shunt is a device that is left attached to the arm's blood vessels, for repeated connection to an artificial kidney machine. Doctors worked on the shunt, cutting away part of a vein.

Three days later, the shunt clotted closed. Karen refused to have any more work done on it. She declined any further dialysis. Her parents agreed with her.

She made out a will, picked a burial spot near her favorite horseback-riding trail, and told her father, "Daddy, I will be happy there, if there is no machine, and they don't work on me anymore."

Nurses and doctors spent sleepless nights. Tempers flared. Hospital staff morale went down. Still, Karen's physicians felt they had no choice except to make her comfortable and tell her every day she could change her mind. She didn't. She died in nine days.

Had Karen been old enough to understand what she was doing? Had she understood the concept of death? A pediatrician, Dr. John E. Schowalter, a child psychiatrist, Dr. Julian B. Ferholt, and a social worker, Nancy M. Mann, thought she had. "Older adolescents, like [Karen], can appreciate their suffering and fatigue and can comprehend when it is likely that life will never offer any more than continued disability, doubt, and suffering," they wrote.[36]

No judge was involved in that case. But judges have ruled that mature minors could consent to their own medical treatment.

For example, a seventeen-year-old Kansas girl, Nancy Younts, allowed a doctor to transplant some skin from her wrist to her finger. Her mother later sued in Nancy's behalf, pointing out that Nancy was a minor.

The mother had gone to the hospital for major surgery. After the operation, nurses wheeled her on a surgical cart to her room. Nancy followed, but a nurse asked her to step out into the hall while they transferred her mother to a bed. She did so, a nurse closed the door, and Nancy screamed with pain. She had placed her right ring finger in the space between the door and the jamb. When the door closed, it had acted like scissors, cutting off her fingertip, which fell to the floor.

Nancy was taken to the hospital's emergency room, and a doctor there thought it best to graft some skin over the raw place. Consider the legal situation. Nancy's mother was still recovering from her own major surgery. To wait until she could consent would have meant that Nancy would have had to wait, in pain, for hours. Nancy's father was divorced and living apart, 200 miles from the hospital.

So the emergency room doctor called Nancy's family doctor, got his agreement, and went ahead. He cut an elliptical piece of skin from the wrist and then stitched that wound shut. He cut the fat off the back side of the piece of skin, trimmed it to the proper shape, and stitched it to the end of her finger.

When Nancy's mother recovered, she sued the hospital in behalf of her daughter. She complained that the nurse had been negligent in causing the injury, and that the doctor had done the transplant without getting proper consent.

She lost on both counts. We are interested only in the consent question. Justices on the Kansas Supreme Court ruled that Nancy's own consent was enough. "She was of sufficient age and maturity to know and understand the nature and consequences of the 'pinch graft' utilized in the repair of her finger," commented Justice Alex M. Fromme.[37]

Notice that Nancy, at seventeen, was close to the age of majority. Eve W. Paul, a lawyer active in population planning, wrote, "The author knows of no case holding a physician liable in damages for supplying any medical service to a minor without parental consent where the minor was older than fifteen and the treatment was for the minor's benefit and performed with the minor's consent."[38]

Teenagers' cooperation is sometimes essential for the success of medical treatment. That furnishes an additional reason for allowing them to decide on medical care. In 1955, the highest New York state court ruled that a fourteen-year-old boy, whom I'll call Erik, could turn down a harelip operation, because his cooperation would be needed for the speech therapy that must follow.

Erik's upper lip was split vertically, as if someone had cut it with a knife. The split continued through to the roof of his mouth, which opened into his nasal cavity. County health department officials proposed that doctors close the lip and the split at the back part of the roof of his mouth. The doctors would then fashion a dental appliance to cover the split at the front part of the roof of his mouth.

Erik's father believed that forces of the universe healed the body. His son took on his hostility to an operation. A majority of the New York court's judges ruled that the health department shouldn't be allowed to force the operation on Erik. They saw less harm in letting him wait until he was an adult and then make the choice.[39]

But Erik had made his decision once and for all. He learned upholstery in a vocational high school. He was elected head of the student council and graduated at the head of his class. He set up his own interior decorator business. And, once again, after he reached adulthood, he chose not to have the operation done. He was nevertheless active and successful.[40]

The mature minor concept is so enticing that, in 1975, the board of trustees of the National Association of Children's Hospitals and Related Institutions endorsed a Pediatric Bill of Rights. It provided that people, regardless of age, could consent to medical care if they were "of sufficient intelligence to appreciate the nature and the consequences" of the treatment.[41]

No state passed the Pediatric Bill of Rights as proposed. Still, Arkansas and Mississippi provided that a youngster who understood the nature and consequences of treatment could consent to medical treatment.[42]

The mature minor approach makes sense but doesn't give doctors objective guidelines. The physicians must ask questions of themselves, the answers to which vary according to subjective impressions. "Is she mature?" a physician might ask about a teenager who wanted treatment. "Does she have the intelligence and ability to understand the medical concepts and the consequences involved in treatment?" Physicians could be forgiven for telling themselves they were not judges and insisting on getting consent from parents before starting treatment. State statutes that named definite ages or particular medical problems, or combined the two, would instead be preferable in designating which minors could consent to medical care.

In the early 1970s, lawmakers or administrators in several places spelled out such ages. In Alabama, for example, lawmakers set the age at fourteen. "The consent of no other person shall be necessary," their statute said. Children even younger could consent if they were married, divorced, or pregnant, or had VD or drug or alcohol problems.

In Oregon, the age of consent for medical treatment was set at fifteen and in South Carolina at sixteen. In Quebec, it was set at fourteen (parents must be notified if treatment is extended) and in Ontario at sixteen for hospital patients. In the United Kingdom, it was set at sixteen.[43]

So we have a hodgepodge of laws. What's to be done to give minors the power to consent to medical treatment, and yet to preserve safeguards against their making irreversible decisions that could be harmful?

First, the category of illnesses in which youngsters have power to consent could well be extended to include psychiatric troubles. They should be able to seek mental help at any age.

Second, teenagers should be permitted to consent to medical care in their early teens. That is especially needed in cases in which care is necessary and is uncontroversial. The age of consent might well be set as low as fourteen.[44] Lawmakers could also consider new provisions for payment to doctors—whether family medical policies could be used, for example.

Third, protection could well be retained for risky operations and elective procedures that promised paradise. It's dangerous to allow a fourteen-year-old to make a snap decision to remodel a nose, or have breasts enlarged, or have a sex-change operation. Safeguards are needed to check on competency of doctors and guard against quackery. Medical groups could define or list the controversial treatments for which parental consent would be required.[45] Teenagers close to the age of majority could well be permitted to make even controversial decisions for themselves.

Finally, children should be able to refuse treatment, subject to court review. Because teenagers have a right of privacy, they should hear explanations about medical treatment.

A fourteen-year-old girl gave a compelling reason why she herself should be consulted. She had leukemia, and doctors needed a liver biopsy. They asked her mother for permission, but not her.

"It's my liver," the girl said angrily at a group meeting. "What am I, some sort of rat or something?"[46]

Refusing to Be Confined to Mental Institutions

Teenagers should also have a right to reject arbitrary confinement in mental institutions, just as adults do. Unfortunately, parents in several states still have a legal right to place children in mental institutions without a sufficient check on their decisions.

Granted, parents are usually motivated by an interest in the well-being of their children. Still, they often send to mental institutions children who merely have trouble adjusting to the norms of society.[47]

Teenage patients in Pennsylvania mental hospitals in 1975 included those whom parents had committed for running away, chasing and striking a girl, truancy, and physical ailments, such as colitis and weight loss. A mother and father committed their Down syndrome son to Pennsylvania's Polk State Hospital so they could go away on vacation.[48]

Pennsylvania law provided that parents could commit their children through the age of eighteen to state mental hospitals. When abuses were brought to the attention of Federal judges, they issued a stinging opinion requiring the state to erect safeguards. Before the U.S. Supreme Court could hear the case, state lawmakers passed new legislation. Now, parents could commit only those children thirteen and younger, and any person could ask a juvenile court to decide whether such a child would be as well off in a less restrictive place. Those children fourteen and older could commit themselves or withdraw.[49]

The change of heart in Pennsylvania has been duplicated in some other states.[50] But, in most, parents have been able to commit their children to mental institutions by merely applying. Such children are "volunteer" patients, though they themselves have failed to volunteer and cannot leave at will, as adult volunteer patients can.

Children have been about as well-protected against arbitrary confinement as was the famous Mrs. Dorothy Packard in the 1860s. She was the wife of a Calvinist minister, the Reverend Theophilus Packard. She publicly disagreed with her husband's theological views. Divorce would have cost him his pulpit.

A state law provided that a husband could commit his wife "without the evidence of insanity required in other cases." So the Reverend Mr. Packard silenced his wife (or so he mistakenly thought) by putting her in the Illinois State Asylum.

Mrs. Packard came home after three years, but her husband shut her away in her bedroom. She got out through filing a writ of habeas corpus (which is normally used to get out of jail). Then she managed to change the laws in four states, so that adults could contest their involuntary confinement.[51]

The story of mental institutions since then has been one of adult patients winning rights gradually. Today, you must go through a formal commitment proceeding to put a balky relative in a mental institution. You must show by clear and convincing evidence that the relative is insane.[52]

In contrast, children have had little legal protection against commitment by their parents. But the youngsters began suing to get out, and winning.

In Connecticut in 1972, the parents of a fifteen-year-old boy whom I'll call Russell put him in a private psychiatric institution merely by signing an application. A year-and-a-half later, Russell applied for a writ of habeas corpus. He wanted to be treated as an outpatient only.

Russell won in an appellate court. Connecticut had enacted a Patient's Bill of Rights. Judge Robert I. Berdon pointed out that youths sixteen and older had the right under that law to admit themselves to mental hospitals. It followed that they could sign themselves out.[53] Thus, Russell could leave the institution, unless a court committed him involuntarily.

Though youngsters won in some state courts, they failed in the U.S. Supreme Court. Consider the short life of "J.L." In 1950, when he was six, his mother and stepfather brought him to the Central State Regional Hospital in Milledgeville, Georgia. They told an admitting physician that J.L. had been aggressive. School authorities had expelled him because he was uncontrollable.

A doctor diagnosed J.L. as having a "hyperkinetic reaction to childhood." Such children have too much energy, are emotionally unstable, and have a short attention span.

After J.L. had been in that mental hospital for two years, doctors sent him home on furlough. In only two months, his mother and stepfather brought him back, saying they could not control him. Two years later, they surrendered him to the county.

Hospital employees recommended that J.L. be placed with a "warm, truly involved" foster family. That never came to pass.

Later, at the age of eleven, J.L. found himself at the center of a lawsuit contesting Georgia's commitment procedure. The state's law provided that parents or guardians could apply to send children under eighteen to mental hospitals. The children could be detained indefinitely if they had treatable mental illnesses.

J.L. died while justices on the U.S. Supreme Court were considering the lawsuit. But the suit continued, because all the children under the age of eighteen in state mental hospitals had been named as plaintiffs. The Georgia Legal Services Program and the Southern Poverty Law Center provided lawyers for them.

They lost. A majority of the justices agreed that Georgia's rules satisfied the Constitution's requirement that due process be used before taking away anybody's liberty.[54]

"Most children, even in adolescence, simply are not able to make sound judgments concerning many decisions, including their need for medical care or treatment," Chief Justice Warren Burger wrote in announcing the majority's decision. "Parents can and must make these judgments."

The chief justice stated that parents possess what a child lacks in maturity, experience, and capacity for judgment in making life's difficult decisions. The court nevertheless recognized that parents do make errors. So a neutral factfinder was needed, and a staff physician at a mental hospital could fill that role. Georgia's commitment procedure allowed for such review, and that was acceptable, in the view of the court's majority.

They rejected the argument that the factfinder ought to be a judge or lawyer. Medical decisions ought to be made by medical people, they ruled. Besides, parents shouldn't have to fight their own children in court.

The justices would have been well advised to give weight to the influences that may sway psychiatrists. Granted, such physicians are trained to discover subconscious influences within themselves as well as others.[55] Yet, they are not immune to being taken unawares by such influences. The psychiatrists identify more with parents than with children, because they themselves are adults and may have children of their own. They may tend to think that there is something mentally wrong with children whose families reject them. Subconsciously, they may think that it is better to declare people mentally ill and be wrong than to declare them mentally fit and be wrong.

An economic interest may influence officials at mental institutions. That interest is obvious at private institutions. At those controlled by the state, the patient census can be kept at a constant level, either by keeping patients longer or relaxing admission rules. That is not a generalized pratice. Psychiatrists have reduced the number of inmates at many state institutions. But venal people exist in every profession.

In contrast to the ease with which youngsters can be sent to mental institutions, they are entitled to protections before they can be sent to juvenile detention homes. That came about because of a Supreme Court ruling in the case of an Arizona teenager, Jerry Gault.

On a Monday morning in June 1964, the sheriff in Gila, Arizona, took fifteen-year-old Jerry into custody after a neighbor woman complained about some sexual remarks telephoned to her. At a hearing a few days later, a juvenile court judge committed him to the State Industrial School "for the period of his minority [that is, until the age of twenty-one], unless sooner discharged by due process of law."

The judge had a vague impression that Jerry had earlier stolen a baseball glove and then lied to police about it. Thus, he viewed Jerry as being "habitually involved in immoral matters." Actually, Jerry had no such record. The woman who had received the "dirty" telephone call never appeared in court. Jerry was not represented by a lawyer.

The deficiencies of the hearing were a logical outgrowth of the ideal of protecting juveniles. In theory, Jerry was not on trial. The state of Arizona, through the juvenile court judge, was merely guiding him on the right path. Thus, with love, the state was going to send him to the detention home for as long as six years. If he had been an adult, he couldn't have been sentenced to longer than two months for the offense that he was charged with.

In the Supreme Court, Justice Abe Fortas pointed out that safeguards that were customary for adults had been discarded for Jerry. "Under our Constitution," he wrote for the Court, "the condition of being a boy does not justify a kangaroo court."[56] A majority of the justices agreed that Jerry had been deprived of his liberty without due process of law.

Today, therefore, a juvenile court judge must tell a youngster in such a situation that he and his parents have a right to hire a lawyer. If they can't afford it, one must be appointed by the state. But no such general protection exists for youngsters who are "volunteered" by their parents into mental institutions.

Granted, the goal of confining juvenile delinquents is different from that of juvenile mental patients. Yet, the liberty of a youngster is at stake in both instances.[57] Safeguards can cut the chance of mistakes. As they do now in juvenile court proceedings, lawyers could take an active role in the mental institution commitment process.[58]

It might be urgent in emergencies for parents to send children to treatment centers without hearings. Even so, juvenile court judges could hold postcommitment hearings.[59] Children could well be asked to express opinions about incarceration.[60]

Michigan has provided for that, so that children thirteen years and older can invoke court hearings to protest their parents' placement decisions. Lawmakers there made a mistake, though, when they designated treatment personnel to warn the teenagers of their rights. Doctors who warn them may seem to be colluding with them against their parents.[61]

Lawyers could instead be the ones to tell teenagers their rights and help them discover facts about incarceration and the institutions. If a teenager were opposed to staying, the lawyer could negotiate with the parents for alternative arrangements. Or the lawyer could represent the teenager at a postcommitment hearing and call in outside psychiatrists.[62]

Though that would seem to pit families against children in court, a family has already been disrupted once the mother and father have sent a youngster to a mental institution. A victory for the teenager wouldn't be Pyrrhic, therefore, contrary to what one law-and-psychiatry professor contended.[63]

Granted, it seems illogical to allow a teenager who is thought to have mental troubles to make mature decisions about treatment. But the commitment process has been abused often enough that authorities ought to listen with respect to a teenager's objections, even though parents believe the reasons are crazy. Parents' claims that institutional treatment is needed ought to be supported by clear and convincing evidence.

7
DECIDING FOR PATIENTS WHO CAN'T DECIDE FOR THEMSELVES

THE suggestion, on a spring night in 1975, that Karen Ann Quinlan took drugs shocked her parents. Twenty-one years earlier, a nun had placed Karen as an adoptive baby in Joseph and Julia Quinlan's hands and said, "A gift of God." After she was grown, the only fault they had admitted to was that she drove too fast in her Volkswagen among the hills and cliffs surrounding Landing, New Jersey, where they lived.[1]

Now, following a birthday party for another girl at a highway tavern, Karen was unconscious, and a doctor at Newton Memorial Hospital was asking if she took drugs.

Her parents said no. And when technologists later checked her blood and urine, they found only traces—not an overdose—of two tranquilizers, Valium and Librium, and, in a normal range, barbiturates.[2]

The technologists also found quinine. That was to be expected. Tonic water contains quinine, and her friends said she had drunk gin-and-tonics at the party.

Tranquilizers, barbiturates, alcohol—all are depressants. When they are combined, one plus one equals ten, and they can deliver a blow that stuns the person who took them.[3]

At the roadside tavern, Karen had seemed about to pass out, so her friends had taken her to the cottage at Cranberry Lake, New Jersey, where she was then living. They had put her in her bed, gone downstairs, and when they returned found she had stopped breathing. They had used mouth-to-mouth resuscitation and frantically called police and a rescue squad. She had stopped breathing again, and police used a respirator.

Her brain had been starved for oxygen at least a half hour. That had destroyed her higher mental functions.

At the hospital, doctors ran a tube from a respirator through a mouthpiece to help her breathe. The next morning, her father signed permission for a surgeon to cut a hole in her windpipe and run a tube from a respirator through the incision. As it turned out, it would take him a year to rescind that permission.

She was transferred to St. Clare's Hospital in Danville, New Jersey. She became famous, and artists drew pictures of her as a sleeping beauty. They were inspired by her high school graduation photograph. In it, Karen's hair falls over her shoulders and breasts. She has dark eyes, a straight nose, a full face and lips, and a cleft chin.

In contrast, the Karen in the hospital bed was short-haired. Her forearms were drawn in against her chest, her hands pointed downwards, like a praying mantis. Her knees pressed against her abdomen, and her feet were pulled against her buttocks, with toes extended in a frozen ballet pose. She lost weight—from 115 pounds down to 80.

Her entire brain was not dead. Rather, the deeper parts, those that control breathing, chewing, swallowing, sleeping, still worked. She lacked the higher functions. "We have a more highly developed brain," said a specialist, Dr. Fred Plum, in court, "which controls our relation to the outside world, our capacity to talk, to see, to feel, to sing, to think."[4] Karen no longer had that capacity.

The respirator was a gray box, standing as high as a nurse's waist. It heated and humidified air and sent a preset volume to Karen's lungs with each breath. If she tried to fight off the breaths, an alarm would sound. Now and then, the machine sent a sigh to her lungs. Those deep breaths kept tiny air sacs in shape.[5]

When doctors would remove her briefly from the respirator, she would sometimes breathe twice as fast as normal, but would take in only half the air she needed.

It seemed apparent that, if they kept her off it, she would die. On the other hand, a New York neurologist, Dr. Julius Korein, told the family not to be surprised if she breathed successfully on her own.[6]

Karen's mother, Julia, and her brother and sister, John and Mary Ellen, decided that Karen should be removed from the respirator. Karen's father, Joseph, also gradually came to the same conclusion. If it were God's will to take her, he said, she could go on to life after death.

The local parish priest, Father Thomas A. Trapasso, supported the family's conclusion. He advised that the use of the respirator in Karen's case could be regarded as "extraordinary" medical treatment, and it would be no sin to discontinue it.

Two-and-a-half months after Karen fell ill, her parents signed a statement directing her physician to discontinue the respirator. But the physician concluded that to comply would be to deviate from medical tradition and would involve measuring Karen's quality of life. So he refused.[7]

Joseph Quinlan asked the New Jersey Superior Court to appoint him Karen's guardian with the power to tell doctors they could stop life-sustaining measures. The Quinlans lost in superior court,[8] and the case went to the New Jersey Supreme Court. There, for the first time, a state's highest court ruled that life-support measures could be ended for an incompetent person who had no hope of returning to a knowing existence.[9]

The justices decided that Karen's constitutional right of privacy meant that she herself could refuse the respirator. Since she was incompetent, her father could act for her.

The justices ruled that New Jersey had no compelling interests that overrode Karen's right of privacy. The state did have an interest in maintaining her life, according to Chief Justice (formerly Governor) Richard J. Hughes. But that interest had weakened, because her medical outlook had dimmed and the medical invasion of her body was great.

Medical custom could not control the decision, Justice Hughes wrote. Doctors were too often conservative in such cases, too frightened of malpractice suits or criminal prosecution.

The New Jersey justices pulled out and reused an ancient legal doctrine—substituted judgment. Since then, as we shall see, other courts have used the same doctrine. So I want to examine it.

Also, we need to know who should make life-death treatment decisions for incompetent patients who are hopelessly ill. Should it be the doctors, the family members, or the courts?

The New Jersey justices instructed that an ethics committee be consulted. Would such committees help in other cases too?

And what criteria should be used in making decisions?

The Doctrine of Substituted Judgment

In 1816, the Court of Chancery in England ordered that a "lunatic" named Hinde be allowed 2,000 pounds a year from his own money for upkeep, and that several relatives also share in his funds. But a niece named Whitbread protested that she was not getting enough money. So Lord Chancellor John Scott Eldon said the court would look "at what it is likely the Lunatic himself would do, if he were in a capacity to act." A rich lunatic, for example, wouldn't want his relatives to disgrace him as beggars.[10]

The niece may have clapped her hands on learning about those words, but I found nothing in the court's opinion to show that she received any extra money. Lord Eldon could hold off decisions for years. Still, law writers cite his words today as if he had announced a crisp decision.

Judges now use "substituted judgment" to decide whether an incompetent person should help a relative whose kidneys have failed. If the veil were lifted for a moment, the incompetent person might be willing to give up one kidney for transplantation.[11]

Now, in New Jersey, justices decided that the substituted judgment doctrine was to be used for Karen Ann Quinlan. She was in imagination to stand before her father as she once had, five-feet, two-inches tall, clear-eyed, so that she could tell him her decision. Joseph would place his one good arm about her shoulders (his left arm had been lost to artillery fire in World War II) and say, "Look, honey, let's say that on the night of April 15 last year, you went at least a half-hour without breathing. You now lie pinned at the throat by the connection from a respirator. You are deformed and shrunken and have none of the ability to reason or communicate that makes humans human. A respirator keeps you breathing. Should it be disconnected?"

Everyone knew what her decision would be. When a relative and two friends had died of cancer and a brain tumor, she had said she would never want to be kept alive by extraordinary means.[12]

Joseph Quinlan was ready to enforce her presumed decision. So physicians began weaning Karen off the respirator—two hours a day at first, then longer. Soon, to the surprise of many, she was breathing on her own.

She no longer needed hospital care. Twenty-two New Jersey institutions now refused her before Morris View Nursing Home—a county institution that was required to accept her—allowed her admittance. In

June 1976, fourteen months after she first fell unconscious, she was moved there, her withered body lying on a water bed in a yellow room.

Today, she lives on. Joseph and Julia Quinlan visit Karen twice a day. They bring flowers on her birthday, each March 29.[13]

Patients Who Have No Track Record

Let's consider the substituted judgment doctrine further. What's a judge to do if an incompetent patient has never had an adult's reasoning power?

In 1976, justices on the top Massachusetts state court mistakenly thought they knew the answer for a patient who had a mental age of a child two years and eight months old and the body of an adult sixty-seven years old. His name was Joseph Saikewicz ("You pronounce it Sah-KEH-vitz," a doctor of Polish ancestry told me), and he lived in the Belchertown State School.

He had acute myeloblastic monocytic leukemia, a cancer of the blood. The question for Massachusetts justices was whether doctors should treat him with chemotherapy. The school's officials asked the courts to decide.

Joseph Saikewicz had no ability to talk. He could merely gesture and grunt. He had been in state institutions for fifty-three years.

The justices decided that, if he were given the reasoning power of a normal, sixty-seven-year-old brain, he would refuse the treatment. They therefore declined to order doctors to give it.[14]

The justices saw Saikewicz as analyzing his problem like this (I have paraphrased their version):

"The chance for chemotherapy to help me would be lower than for a young person. Also, chemotherapy might cause numbness and tingling of my hands and feet, bladder irritation, and nausea.

"Given my feeble comprehension, I would fail to understand that the pain was for a good purpose. When I tried to fight off needles, doctors would tie me down. That would compound my pain and fear and weaken my resistance to the chemotherapy's toxic effects."

Actually, if the veil of incompetency had been lifted, Joseph Saikewicz might well have come to precisely the opposite conclusion, like this:

"Granted, like anybody else who had a three-year-old mind, I wouldn't understand why doctors would stick needles in me. I might even cry. But adults soothe three-year-olds. For fifty-three years, my friends in institutions have been telling me what to do, and I would obey them now as always. Anyway, intravenous needles don't hurt once they are in place, so I wouldn't try to tear them loose."

Actually, it's uncertain whether "substituted judgment" is appropriate for such a case. People who have no track record of deciding things for themselves have given no clues as to what they would decide.

In such a case, judges could use a "best interest" test instead. And the best interest of Joseph Saikewicz might have been served by giving him chemotherapy.[15] Never receiving it, he died five months after falling ill. Bronchial pneumonia, a byproduct of leukemia, caused his death.

What Is Competency?

Competent patients have the legal right to make their own medical decisions. But which patients are competent?

In California, two sisters, ages sixty-eight and seventy, were burned over more than 90 percent of their bodies. While they were waiting at a stoplight in their car, a construction machine hit a gasoline line nearby, setting off an explosion that leveled a city block. Their husbands, in the car with them, were also burned. Ambulances took the husbands to one burn center and the sisters to another—the one at the Los Angeles County-University of Southern California Medical Center.

A physician and other medical team members entered the room of the younger sister. She asked if she were going to die. The staff members answered that, to their knowledge, no one her age with such extensive and severe burns had ever survived.

This woman decided she did not want heroic measures used to prolong her dying. "I'd like to go quietly and comfortably," she said in a matter-of-fact voice.

The older sister doubted she was dying. "Wouldn't I be hurting terribly?" she asked. The staff explained that deep burns destroy nerve endings, and thus she failed to feel pain. She too refused full treatment.

The burn-center staff tried to arrange a telephone call with the husbands, but they were receiving emergency treatment. The sisters' beds were moved next to each other. They joked about the damage the fire had done to their hair, talked about funeral arrangements, and prayed with a chaplain. The younger sister died in a few hours, the older the next day.[16]

The staff at the burn center had decided that truth was kindness. When patients refused full treatment, they would stop transfusing fluids such as blood plasma or solutions containing electrolytes, but would give pain medications or other treatment to keep them comfortable.

At a later medical conference, attendees pointed out that stopping fluids makes death come quicker and makes it certain beyond doubt. They questioned whether such patients were emotionally competent to make this last decision of their lives.[17]

On the other hand, the burn center's director, Dr. Bruce E. Zawacki, told me that the sisters had been "very competent." They had been given the information about themselves in as sensitive and loving a manner as he was capable of. There's a lot of touching in such a situation, he said.

"It is exceedingly difficult to remain objective, to remain in control, to remain professional, and yet be a friend," he said. "When I go in [to the patient's room], I must have a nurse and a chaplain to support me. These are terrifying decisions. I have to have some very honest people with me who won't let me manipulate. I want them to be there to keep me honest. By 'honest,' I mean saying the truth as clearly as I can so that the patient understands it."

A patient who understands is a legally competent patient, as I shall outline below.

Emotional upsets don't necessarily make a person incompetent. A Seattle man whom I'll call Johnny had a scuffle with his son and then went to the hospital with a suspected heart attack. He was given four drugs, including morphine and Librium. Nurses often found him weeping.

The suspected heart attack turned out to be only a muscle strain. But, while in the hospital, Johnny agreed that a specialist could operate on his nose, to open a nostril. That turned out badly, and Johnny later claimed in court that he had been in such a state, as affected by drugs, that he had been unable to make an intelligent choice about the operation. If he could show that he had been incompetent, then he hadn't truly consented to the operation, and the doctor had assaulted him in performing it.

A judge threw the case out. The law presumed that Johnny had been competent. He had merely shown that he had been depressed.[18]

A legally competent patient is one who is able to understand the illness, to grasp the nature and effect of the proposed treatment, and to know the risk in either accepting it or refusing it.[19]

That's the formal definition in several states. In practice, judges, doctors, and families put a "competent" tag on a patient who has made what they regard as the right medical decision. They use a risk-benefit measurement, as follows:

A female patient refuses to take an antibiotic to fight a bacterial infection. The low-risk treatment would almost surely cure her. Nearly everyone thinks she has made the wrong decision, and they therefore try to show that she is legally incompetent. "Look at how forgetful she is," they might say.

Now, imagine the same woman as old. She turns down a risky abdominal operation that has little chance of halting a cancer. Her family and doctor view this decision as correct, so they point to her normal aspects to show she is competent. "Look at how composed she is," they say.[20]

Relatives Giving Proxy Consent Has Little Legal Foundation

Spouses, parents, siblings, or adult children usually have not been appointed as the legal guardians of patients. In only a few states, therefore, do they have explicit legal authority to consent in place of the patients.[21] Still, doctors and hospital staffs in all states accept their signatures on consent forms or their oral permission to change treatment.[22] That is sensible. They are the natural ones to turn to. Judges would probably name them as legal guardians if asked.

Ethics Committees

When the justices of the New Jersey Supreme Court decided that Karen Ann Quinlan could be taken off the respirator, they added that her doctors should consult an ethics committee.[23] A Texas pediatrician, Dr. Karen Teel, had pointed out in a 1975 law review article that physicians were making life-death judgments that they were not trained to make, and for which they could be sued or put in jail. Hospitals could get more input, she said, by putting doctors, social workers, lawyers, and theologians on ethics committees. Such "God Squads"—as Dr. Teel said they had been irreverently called—would be advisers to patients and their doctors on ethical dilemmas.[24]

When Karen Ann Quinlan was moved to Morris View Nursing Home, administrators there set up an ethics committee with the membership that Dr. Teel had recommended. The members held three long meetings. There was no need for them to decide whether Karen would be connected to a respirator at Morris View, because, like most nursing homes, it had none. They decided that, if she ever needed resuscitation, the staff would forgo transferring her to a hospital. Instead, she would be allowed to die.

The committee's chairman, the Reverend Dale H. Forsman, told me that other patient-care aspects were considered as well. "It has and continues to be our decision, for example, to continue to feed Karen Ann Quinlan, using the nasal-gastric tube methodology," he commented. "Not to do so, it has been decided, would be unethical."

The ethics committee meets about twice a year at Morris View Nursing Home. Debate continues on ethical questions of the type that Mr. Forsman described.

It seemed to me, on the other hand, that the New Jersey justices were confused on what they expected such a committee to do. Although they endorsed a committee with the composition that Dr. Teel had recommended—which the one at Morris View Nursing Home later had—the justices seemed also to want such a committee to give a medical opinion on whether Karen Ann Quinlan would return to a knowing state.

But social workers, lawyers, and theologians have no training in making prognoses. Nor do doctors need their help with such questions. They can call in consultants for that. Thus, although a few hospitals have set up ethics committees, none has been a prognosis committee.

Officials of the American Medical Association have opposed such committees because they fear they would nose their way between doctors and patients.[25] Some bedside physicians have echoed the objection. "These committees would be just another form of oppression," the late Dr. Acors W. Thompson, a Virginia internist, told me.

One of the nation's finest hospitals, Massachusetts General, in Boston, has a group known as an Optimum Care Committee.[26] It came into being because families complained that their dying relatives were being given medical treatment uselessly. Its members facilitate communication between patients' families and doctors. Unfortunately, only doctors are permitted to bring problems before the committee, although relatives are then invited for discussions.

The committee chairman is a psychiatrist and Catholic priest, Dr. Ned H. Cassem. Other members include a cancer specialist, a surgeon, the nursing supervisor of all Mass General's intensive care units, the hospital's lawyer, and a former cancer patient who is also a physical therapist.

"One of our major functions is to provide a climate in which physicians will say what they honestly believe," Dr. Cassem told me. "In our early work, we found that families yearned for that sort of honesty."

Physicians often hesitated to be frank. One reason was their reluctance to admit defeat, to acknowledge that their efforts could not make some patients well. Another was their fear of criticism, or even malpractice suits, if they gave less than the maximum effort.

In a typical problem, a patient has lung or heart trouble and, associated with it, such poor circulation in the feet that gangrene sets in. Surgeons would have to amputate the feet for the patient to survive. But the family might object: "If you cannot make his heart better, and he will therefore die regardless of what you do, why put him through the pain and expense of an amputation?"

Dr. Cassem pointed out that in medical ethics life is not the absolute good and death not the absolute evil. Thus the job of medicine is not just to preserve life. "Our job is to restore health and relieve suffering. And our predicament in the modern era comes when, the more we try to restore health, the more suffering we inflict."

Questions about treatment arise in intensive care units more than other places in a hospital because patients are in worse condition there and medical machinery is omnipresent. In Dr. Cassem's view, the committee must point out the limits of technology. "It is only cockeyed thinking to say, 'The machine is here; therefore, we have to use it.' When you say that, the machine uses you, not you the machine."

On the other hand, the physician on a case may feel that, though the chance of a treatment's succeeding is only one in ten, it is justified. Perhaps better communication alone is needed, so the family will understand the reasoning that led to the continued treatment.

The committee at Mass General has been criticized for focusing mainly on the relationship between the physician and the hospital staff.[27] I felt that the criticism was unjustified, because of Dr. Cassem's sympathetic attitude toward patients and their families, and that he had chosen respected and nonthreatening professionals as the other members of the committee. Still, in that giant hospital, doctors ask for the committee's help only six or seven times a year.

Other hospitals have largely failed to follow Mass General's lead. If they do so, they must either appoint commanding figures or else risk their committees becoming mouthpieces for chiefs of hospital departments.[28]

Another type of committee is a bioethics study group. Members of one at Montefiore Hospital, New York City, and another at Saint Joseph Hospital, Orange, California, decline to make recommendations on ending active treatment for patients but do discuss how such decisions should be made.[29]

When you or a relative face a question of whether life should be prolonged, you'll be lucky if a committee like the one at Massachusetts General Hospital is available. The odds are against that happening, however.

Bioethical Counselors

You'll probably ask advice of your own informal committee, composed of the doctor, relatives, friends, and your spiritual adviser. None of these is likely to have training in bioethics, but a new type of specialist—a bioethical counselor—may be available.

One of these is Dr. John Fletcher, a former Texan whose accent has been modified during his years as a Fulbright scholar at the University of Heidelberg and while researching the ethics of medical research at Union Theological Seminary, New York.

Dr. Fletcher has "one foot in, one foot out" at the Clinical Center, the research hospital for the National Institutes of Health. He spends about 80 percent of his time there and the rest at the Alban Institute, which counsels ministers and congregations. He believes his independence from the hospital is essential.

A minister himself, Dr. Fletcher says most ministers don't have the experience or training to function well in highly charged hospital situations, where decisions must be made fast. And it is a "hokey democratic" solution for a family to call in persons who bill themselves as thanatologists or who have had sketchy training in human relations.

"To learn slowly—it's going to be painful, but I don't see any other way out," he said. "To be economically responsible, to be humanly responsible—we've got to learn to make decisions about quality of life, and it's the hardest thing in the world. It's good to be conservative and to err on the side of the life of the patient."

Courts as Decision Makers

Discussions about treatment for incompetent patients often center on *who* should make medical decisions for them. Doctors have often taken charge. Families, on the other hand, are better qualified to use the substituted judgment method of making decisions. Courts are too clumsy and too few in number to do other than give occasional guidance.

In some ways, court decisions are superior to others: they are arrived at in the open. Also, the incompetent patient for whom the decision is made will have a guardian *ad litem* (meaning "for the suit")—usually a lawyer—for protection. And court opinions are available to everybody for guidance, or to criticize.

Yet court intervention ought to be rare. A court hearing can further upset families whose relatives are ill, and the expense of lawyers would be added to that of doctors and hospitals.

In Massachusetts, the Supreme Judicial Court once stated that only courts should decide such matters but later had to back off. The case, one that I discussed earlier (page 123), was that of Joseph Saikewicz, a sixty-seven-year-old state school inmate with a mental age of less than three years, who had leukemia. You'll recall that the court ruled chemotherapy could be withheld, and then Mr. Saikewicz died.

By making this decision, the Massachusetts justices, in effect, told doctors and families to stay out of decisions that required "detached but passionate" qualities.[30] In their view, apparently, only judges had those.

In fury or confusion, doctors began uselessly saving people. In one hospital in one day, they used electric paddles seventy times on a dying woman.[31]

The reaction impelled the justice who had written the opinion, Paul J. Liacos, to retreat. In a public speech, he said hospital lawyers ought to refrain from asking courts to decide self-evident matters, such as whether to resuscitate a dying patient. Still, he continued lamely, "the judiciary must be involved in such matters from time to time."[32] Such a public explanation of a court decision is extraordinary for a judge.

And when a similar case came before the Massachusetts justices in 1980, they softened their earlier language. Granted, they held to the view that the *ultimate* decision on treatment of incompetent patients rested with the courts. But only a certain combination of circumstances would make court approval necessary. The justices didn't spell out the circumstances, because, they said, medical practice and opinion are moving too fast.[33]

It seems evident that, when family members and doctors agree on treatment for an incompetent patient, courts aren't usually needed. That's especially true when the patient has expressed a view beforehand on the very affliction and treatment at issue.

That happened with an eighty-four-year-old Marist brother, Joseph Charles Fox. During an operation for a hernia, his heart stopped and he went into a coma. That damaged his brain, and doctors put him on a respirator.

Brother Fox had lived in retirement, almost blind, spending much time gardening, in the Chaminade religious community in Mineola, New York. When he had heard of the Karen Ann Quinlan case, he said he "would not want any of this extraordinary business"—meaning useless, burdensome treatment.

Now he himself was in a vegetative state. His religious superiors requested that he be removed from the respirator, but hospital officials refused. The specter of a malpractice suit or of criminal prosecution was raised.

The Reverend Philip K. Eichner had had a close relationship with Brother Fox since his own novitiate a quarter-century before. Now, as director of the community, he went to court to ask that his old companion be allowed to die.[34] Brother Fox's twelve nieces and nephews agreed. "Our position has always been that the family or guardian, in concert with the doctor, is the appropriate place for a decision to terminate medically useless life support systems," Father Eichner wrote to me later.

Before an appeals court could decide, Brother Fox, after 114 days on the respirator, died. Still, the difficult issue had not died with him.

More than a year after his death, therefore, the highest court in New York State issued a significant decision. A majority of the justices gave strong weight to opinions that people express before falling ill. In this case, they had before them clear and convincing evidence that, if Brother Fox had been able to decide, he would have rejected the respirator. In their opinion, that was enough evidence for the courts to do the same.[35]

While the law that justices announce in such a case is effective only as far as the state line, the New York court is influential. Other state supreme courts often follow its lead. Thus, the Brother Fox decision is important for people who want to sign a Living Will. When they do so, they forbid useless treatment (see Chapter 8). The Brother Fox decision therefore gives extra influence to such a document.

The Illogic of Physicians' Taking Exclusive Control

Physicians have often believed they had exclusive responsibility for decision-making about life-prolonging treatment for incompetent patients. That belief is unjustified. Though doctors are experts in diagnosis, prognosis, and other technical aspects, they are unlikely to know a patient's wishes and, at least in the past, have had little formal training in how to handle such cases. Relatives of a patient should have the paramount say about life-extending treatment.

Granted, the physician's decision has in the past often gone unquestioned. "The decision to prolong life by artificial or other unusual means in the face of what obviously appears to be a fatal illness is one of a physician's most difficult and lonely tasks," Dr. Howard P. Lewis, of the Oregon University Medical School told members of the American Medical Association at their convention in 1968. Dr. Lewis continued that, although the doctor might consult others, he alone must decide such an issue. "At such a time, he draws deeply upon his own sense of compassion, knowledge, clarity of thought, and moral strength," he said.[36]

A physician may possess most of those characteristics to no greater extent than members of a patient's family. Still, mistaken impressions cause families to surrender full control or physicians to seize it.[37]

One is that patients and their relatives cannot understand the facts about illnesses. Granted, if they are not told the facts, they will fail to comprehend them. Thus, a doctor's prophecy that they won't be able to understand can be self-fulfilling.

Actually, the family has little need for technical medical details. No special knowledge is needed to comprehend that a patient is in a persistent vegetative state, for example.[38] The family needs to know the certainty of a doctor's prognosis but not every technical element that led to it.

Another false impression is that most dying old people will be attended by physicians who have known them all their lives and that they have told those doctors their views on intimate subjects. But many old people don't communicate well with younger doctors. Also, old people, like other Americans, move often. They are more likely than younger ones to move long distances—oftentimes for retirement to different states.[39] Thus, to be treated by one doctor for a lifetime is rare, and doctors often have no idea of incompetent patients' private views on life-prolongation treatment.

Another mistaken impression is that practice alone makes perfect. Thus, a family may decide to place a decision in the doctor's hands on the reasoning that the doctor has faced similar problems before. But doctors' life-prolongation decisions may be erratic. Law professor Charles H. Baron worked alongside medical personnel. He noticed that they failed to work out explicit or consistent standards for such decisions and therefore used standards of the moment.[40]

What guidelines do doctors use? One physician said that to resolve problems of prolonging life, he needed only "the universal rule of 'Love thy neighbor'."[41] That meant he was using a personal Golden Rule—to treat the patient as he himself would wish to be treated. But doctors are different from patients. A doctor therefore might fail to treat the patient as the *patient* would wish to be treated.

Formal Training in Medical Ethics

Still, that doctor's statement about the Golden Rule illustrates that medical students do come to the study of the profession with an aim of helping people. And, in regular medical school courses, professors mix in doses of moral decision-making. Medical students are thus taught that ethics are part of every aspect of medicine that they will deal with in professional life.

On the other hand, when teaching a subject is every faculty member's responsibility, it may turn out to be no one's. Also, the teaching of ethics demands a grounding in the subject. Instructors need training in both medicine and moral philosophy and, perhaps, some acquaintance with the law.

Deans at half the nation's medical schools have now set up separate ethics courses.[42] Professors have built their classes about case studies—whether to allow an open-spine baby to die, whether to treat an old man who has been burned.

Some philosophers scorn that method as being "dilemma ethics" and say the students ought to start with ethical theory. Yet the future doctors learn to reason about cases similar to those they will run across in professional life, and so the method is a good one.

It would take forty years to give formal ethics training to all physicians. But some physicians attend short courses, such as those at the Kennedy Institute of Ethics at Georgetown University.[43] Others (too few so far) discuss ethical problems in meetings at their hospitals.

The training means that doctors of the future will be able to provide more consistently logical advice to families. But they should not supplant them in making life-prolonging decisions.

Prognosis Is the Doctor's Business

Whether an illness can be reversed is a medical decision.[44] But many writers on medical ethics mistakenly assume that a confident prognosis is always at hand. Doctors, in contrast, know they can be fallible in making prognoses.

Physicians sent a woman who had cancer at the lower part of her uterus off to die in a Catholic home in Cambridge, Massachusetts. She was wasted, anemic, and had a bloody vaginal discharge. The house officer wrote in her medical records that she'd probably die in a day.

Twelve years later, she was still waiting for death, working as a nurse's aide at the home. Her pelvis showed the signs of the radiation that technicians had used on her, but a specialist found no signs of cancer. She was in excellent health.[45]

Because of uncertainties in prognosis, doctors can sometimes confirm that a treatment will be useless only by trying it.[46] Patients or family members who imagine that recommendations about treatment are based on 100-percent-certain prognoses have not been able to listen to hospital debates on whether to keep intravenous lines going, whether to keep an oxygen mask applied, whether to continue the patient on a respirator, whether to call a crash cart if the patient arrests, and whether to fight infections with antibiotics. A half-dozen physicians and nurses may give views. The physicians will include the intern, the chief resident, the "attending" (the private physician who sent the patient to the hospital), and a specialist, such as an oncologist.

Dr. Fred Finkelman, Associate Professor of Medicine at the Uniformed Services University of the Health Sciences, Bethesda, Maryland, says the intern may argue that active treatment should be discontinued. "He's the one who's being kept up nights taking care of the patient. He's the one who gets complaints that the patient is suffering. Sometimes he's wrong in his recommendation, because he's too sleepy or too stressed. But he represents one important viewpoint, since he has the most direct contact with the patient."

The chief resident and the attending will opt for continued treatment if they have ever seen a patient in a similar condition recover. "Physicians in chemotherapy—oncologists—tend to be particularly aggressive," Dr. Finkelman said. "They will say, 'There's one more new drug that hasn't been tried yet.'"

Doctors rarely move with complete assurance in such situations. Yet you will see that the discussions Dr. Finkelman mentioned center on prognoses. Questions are raised that only physicians can answer. He feels that it is wise to continue treatment when the outcome is in doubt and there is a reasonable chance that the benefits of such treatment will outweigh its risks and demands upon the patient.

"The doctor has to make a judgment," Dr. Ned H. Cassem, of the Massachusetts General Hospital, told me. "Consider a patient in whom bladder cancer has recurred for the third time. What will be involved in a fourth surgical procedure? What are the costs? How much tumor can the surgeon remove? How much bleeding will it entail? What are the risks of infection? How much time will be spent in the hospital recuperating?"

The doctor has to be honest about the technology and its limits, according to Dr. Cassem. If doctors really think it'll help, it's their obligation to say so. And if they really think it will not help, then the obligation is also there to make that plain.

"And if [incompetent] patients could only talk for themselves, they would listen to the possibility of benefit and what they have to pay to get the benefit," Dr. Cassem said. Then it would be their job to say, 'I won't buy that price. That's not worth it.' Or, in contrast, they might say, 'It's worth the risk. I'll give it a shot.'"

The families of incompetent patients must speak for them. But, first, they must have the clinical judgment of the physician. That is a technological judgment. It is the doctor's business.

The Complex Motivations of Families

Families of incompetent patients are usually motivated by love. Still, they may be swayed by other motivations.

A philosopher-minister who worked in hospitals told me that, when a family member says, "Don't do anything for Grandma; I can't bear to see her suffer," it may mean, "We want to get rid of Grandma." Or family members may insist on prolonging Grandma's dying from feelings of guilt, having mocked her when she forgot things and ignored her when she gave her opinions.

Staff members at a western hospital still puzzle over one wife's actions.* She had been neglected by her workaholic husband. Then one day at work, he suffered a heart stoppage. A rescue squad saved him with CPR, but a lack of oxygen had damaged his brain. Helped to breathe by a respirator, he existed at the hospital in a vegetative state.

Neurologists said he would never again have a knowing existence. His wife insisted, "You've got to do everything." She bitterly protested their failure to restore his upper brain, but it could not be done. Physicians would not ask that he be removed from the respirator, but it was obvious that, if he had another heart attack, he should be allowed to die.

After eight months, he had another attack. His heart was quivering and twitching, meaning that death, in its kindness, was near.

His wife demanded that electric paddles be used. A resident physician refused. She then started a panicky effort to restore his regular heartbeat herself.

She worked away, kneading his chest.

Time passed.

The resident said, "Excuse me, he's dead."

She stopped.

Afterward she was serene.

Thus, influences that the relatives themselves may not understand, and that it would take a psychiatrist to uncover, come into play. These include hatred, fear, or denial—or, perhaps, love.

Whether to Continue Treatment Is an Ethical Decision

Instances such as that wife's trying to return her husband to a life that wasn't worth living fail to negate the usual rule that a family should control treatment for a terminally ill relative.

Still, when a patient is beyond hope of recovery, a cessation of active treatment doesn't automatically follow. Rather, family members may well consider the patient's social situation, desires, and quality of life.[47] The decision is ethical, rather than medical, in nature.

---

* I have altered some aspects to conceal identities.

Some judges have criticized the use of quality of life. They meant you shouldn't consider the value of a person's life to society. The judges were correct. That is the interpersonal measurement. It is too utilitarian.

But not every life is of equal value to the person concerned.[48] Families could therefore consider the value of life *to that person*. This intrapersonal measurement is a valid consideration.[49]

On Deciding Treatment to Be Withheld: The Use of Code Words; Religious Perspectives

Should antibiotics be withheld from a patient whose illness cannot be reversed?[50] Should feeding tubes be used? In Chapter 8, I'll tell you about a physician who has forbidden his own doctor to use such tubes if he should lose his mental capacity. He'd rather starve.

Many persons single out the respirator, so that the phrase "pulling the plug" has become the usual term for the withdrawal of life-extending treatment. But Dr. Julius Korein, Professor of Neurology at New York University Medical School, says a respirator doesn't constitute special care more than other treatment. Intravenous infusions, nasogastric feeding, and use of antibiotics are also life-support measures. "To the point where they can do something for patients—where they help them—fine," he said. "If it becomes clear as time goes on that the probability of helping them approaches zero, then stop."

Dr. Korein is world-renowned for his studies on persistent vegetative states and brain death. He examined Karen Ann Quinlan and was called as an expert witness in the court case concerning her. A lawyer asked him whether Karen could recover her mental functions. Although Dr. Korein stressed that Karen is not brain-dead (many persons think she is), he said the chance of her recovering her awareness could be compared to the chance that a fountain pen would rise when he released it. The subsequent course of her illness proved him to be correct.

Some of the Quinlan court testimony centered on the Catholic teaching of the nonnecessity of "extraordinary" treatment. "The definition of 'extraordinary' has to be looked at in context," Dr. Korein told me. "Turning Miss Quinlan every two hours is extraordinary care. If they stopped turning her, she'd soon be dead of pneumonia."

Communicating knowledge to the patient's family is the first, and sometimes neglected, stage in the decision-making process, according to Dr. Korein. It should be a group decision, he thinks, with the family taking a leading role.

The words "ordinary" and "extraordinary," so important in the Karen Ann Quinlan case, have guided Catholic philosophers for many years. Ethicists and others who are not Catholic have adopted the reasoning behind them. The words are, however, giving way to new, more precise ones.

"Ordinary" means medicines, treatments, and operations that offer a reasonable hope of benefit and that can be used without excessive expense, pain, or other inconvenience. Thus, whether a treatment is "ordinary" or "extraordinary" is related to the condition of the patient. For example, doctors often tell nurses to infuse a solution of a simple sugar, glucose, into patients' veins as a food. Also, they use digitalis, from the foxglove plant, to treat congestive heart failure. Those are ordinary uses. But it would be extraordinary for them to force glucose and digitalis on a ninety-year-old dying man who was in a coma with heart and kidney problems.[51]

Still, those words cause confusion. Some doctors have mistakenly thought of "ordinary" as usual medical practice and "extraordinary" as bizarre treatment, or else that the words relate only to the use of machines, such as respirators.

In 1980, the Vatican abandoned "ordinary" and "extraordinary," while affirming that the principle reflected by those words was still correct. Instead, the Congregation for the Doctrine of the Faith said, some people prefer to speak of "proportionate" and "disproportionate" means.

"When inevitable death is imminent," it said, patients need not be given "forms of treatment that would only secure a precarious and burdensome prolongation of life." In giving advice to patients and families, doctors can judge whether "the investment in instruments and personnel is disproportionate to the results foreseen." They may also advise against use of techniques that would "impose on the patient strain or suffering out of proportion with the benefits which he or she may gain from such techniques."[52]

From the orthodox Jewish perspective, on the other hand, treatment may be withdrawn only from a *goses*—one who is in the death throes. A professor of Talmudic and Jewish law at Yeshiva University, Rabbi J. David Bleich, discovered that doctors were omitting aggressive treatment for an elderly woman relative of his. She had kidney failure, was in a coma, and her doctors unanimously predicted death. Rabbi Bleich nevertheless insisted that the doctors use every possible treatment. That each instant of life has value was shown when, after thirty-six hours of unresponsiveness, she answered Rabbi Bleich's Sabbath greeting with a weak but clear, "*Gut Shabbos.*" Thus, she had lived long enough to respond one more time to the divine commandment to keep the day holy.[53]

Now to turn to another pair of words—"reasonable" and "unreasonable"—that physicians and ethicists sometimes use in discussing whether treatment should be withdrawn.[54] The words come from the "reasonable man of ordinary prudence" formula that judges announce in damage suits.

A man who has acted reasonably needn't pay damages even though he hurt someone and will collect if someone hurt him. British humorist A. P. Herbert described the reasonable man: "He is the one . . . who neither star-gazes nor is lost in meditation when approaching trapdoors . . . , who . . . will inform himself of the history and habits of a dog before administering a caress . . ."[55]

The phrase would change to "reasonable person" today, to make it clear that reasonable women exist as well as men.

It's tempting to transfer the formula to an incompetent patient and say, "We'll use the treatment that a reasonable person would want. Would a sick person be unreasonable?"

That particular sick person might, and the unreasonableness ought to be respected. The question of whether to continue treatment is different from a negligence problem in a courtroom, where antagonists are arguing over the caution that people ought to observe in their relations with each other.

On the other hand, doctors, nurses, and others can use the reasonable person test for a check on the decision.[56] If a family insisted on treatment that only a stupid person would accept, the medical team might think the problem best put in the hands of a judge.

Code words such as "extraordinary," "disproportionate," or "unreasonable" will continue to be used by philosophers and others. Still, only persons with identical training can say such words to each other with confidence of being understood. Also, code words should not be dictators. They can help mainly in orienting general thinking. It is therefore appropriate for a family to refuse to idolize them, instead remembering and perhaps using the wise reasoning that led to them.

Deciding as the Patient Would

It is the patient, with human imperfections in reasoning, whose presumed decision should be respected. Relatives have seen that person in crises. They know of hopes for the future, of a sense of a life completed. Perhaps, as with Karen Ann Quinlan or Brother Fox, opinions will have been expressed beforehand.

Family members will have had such intimate physical contact with the patient that they will almost automatically choose the treatment that the patient would if competent. A son or daughter who says, "Daddy wouldn't want to live like this," is expressing a view shaped by a lifetime of living with Daddy.

Thus the technique a family may use is one that has been used by courts for so many years—that is, substituted judgment.

8
LIVING WILLS AND NATURAL DEATH LAWS

YOU would think, because physicians are not so likely as before to prolong life at any cost, that Living Wills—documents forbidding useless medical treatment—wouldn't be necessary. Yet doctors themselves advocate such documents. For example, Dr. Milton D. Heifetz, Clinical Professor of Neurosurgery, University of Southern California, recommended a "Directive to My Physician" in a book that he published in 1975. People signing the Directive forbid any life-prolonging treatment in the event of unconsciousness or mental incompetency from which they will not recover.[1]

Those instructions illustrate the importance with which physicians view mental acuity. For example, they know that a lack of oxygen for four or five minutes might irreparably damage the brain. Some of them instruct their own doctors that in such an event they aren't to be treated at all.[2]

In 1970, a distinguished professor of medicine at Duke University, Eugene A. Stead, Jr., sent such instructions to his doctor. Among other things, he wrote that, if he suffered major brain damage, his doctor was to forgo the tube feedings that might preserve his life.

Dr. Stead's letter is printed on page 142. (A cerebral accident, mentioned in it, includes strokes and also hemorrhages in the brain area. A subarachnoid hemorrhage is a sudden bleeding in the space under one of the membranes covering the brain; it kills about half its victims and leaves some others brain-damaged.)

In 1980, Dr. Stead told me he would not change those instructions.

"I do not wish my assets to be dissipated on the chance that I might be restored to good health after the periods defined in my letter have passed," he wrote me. He felt the chance of full recovery from the illnesses he described was only one in one hundred. "The odds are too great for me to want to play," he commented.

A LETTER FROM EUGENE A. STEAD, JR., M.D., TO HIS PHYSICIAN

If I become ill and unable to manage my own affairs, I want you to be responsible for my care. To make matters as simple as possible, I will leave certain specific instructions with you.

In event of unconsciousness from an automobile accident, I do not wish to remain in a hospital for longer than two weeks without full recovery of my mental faculties. While I realize that recovery might still be possible, the risk of living without recovery is still greater. At home, I want only one practical nurse. I do not wish to be tube-fed or given intravenous fluids at home.

In the event of a cerebral accident, other than a subarachnoid hemorrhage, I want no treatment of any kind until it is clear that I will be able to think effectively. This means no stomach tube and no intravenous fluids.

In the event of a subarachnoid hemorrhage, use your own judgment in the acute stage. If there is considerable brain damage, send me home with one practical nurse.

If, in spite of the above care, I become mentally incapacitated and have remained in good physical condition, I do not want money spent on private care. I prefer to be institutionalized, preferably in a state hospital.

If any other things happen, this will serve as a guide to my own thinking.

Go ahead with an autopsy with as little worry to Ev as possible. The Anatomy crematory seems a good final solution.

Medical Times 98 (1970): 191. Reprinted by permission of Dr. Stead.

If it's important for physicians to tell other physicians to withhold treatment under certain conditions, it must be important for lay people as well. Still, laymen don't know the terms to use, and many have simply signed form documents.

In the first part of this chapter, I'll tell you about two such form documents—the Living Will and the Christian Affirmation of Life—and then compose an alternative—a Medical Care Directive—in an attempt to avoid their defects.

In the late 1960s, Luis Kutner, a Chicago lawyer and committee chairman in the World Peace Through Law Center, predicted that such documents would be useful. He noted that doctors often assumed that patients wanted all-out treatment, even when they were practically vegetables. People could avoid that, according to Mr. Kutner, by signing a document beforehand, to provide that surgery, radiation, drugs, resuscitation, or use of lifesaving treatment would stop in such extreme cases.[3]

The Living Will has become well-known since then, but the document isn't a will at all, as the word is usually understood. I explained the difference to a Navy captain and his wife when I was drawing their wills.

"Can you include a Living Will in mine?" the wife asked me.

"This is the wrong document for that," I said. "A regular will, which is what I am drawing, tells how you want your property distributed after you die. A Living Will tells how you want your body treated medically while you are still alive."

I added that the Living Will had only a moral effect in Virginia, where they lived, not a legal one. (Since 1977, as we shall learn, lawmakers in ten states have legalized similar documents.)

Concern for Dying's Living Will, and the Christian Affirmation of Life

When people speak of a Living Will, they usually mean the one issued by Concern for Dying, a New York organization. That document became popular in the early 1970s. "Dear Abby" mentioned it in a column, and 50,000 persons wrote to ask for copies. Then the Karen Ann Quinlan case broke into the news, and the number of requestors jumped to a million. By 1981, four million persons had requested copies.

Concern for Dying's version of the Living Will is reproduced below, and optional provisions are on pages 144–45. In its brevity, the document is appealing, but it is vague. Its key sentence is this: "If . . . the situation should arise in which there is no reasonable expectation of my recovery from extreme physical or mental disability, I direct that I be allowed to die and not be kept alive by medications, artificial means or 'heroic measures.'"

A LIVING WILL
(*Prepared by Concern for Dying*)

To My Family, My Physician, My Lawyer and All Others Whom It May Concern

Death is as much a reality as birth, growth, maturity and old age—it is the one certainty of life. If the time comes when I can no longer take part in decisions for my own future, let this statement stand as an expression of my wishes and directions, while I am still of sound mind.

If at such a time the situation should arise in which there is no reasonable expectation of my recovery from extreme physical or mental disability, I direct that I be allowed to die and not be kept alive by medications, artificial means or "heroic measures." I do, however, ask that medication be mercifully administered to me to alleviate suffering even though this may shorten my remaining life.

This statement is made after careful consideration and is in accordance with my strong convictions and beliefs. I want the wishes and directions here expressed carried out to the extent permitted by law. Insofar as they are not legally enforceable, I hope that those to whom this Will is addressed will regard themselves as morally bound by these provisions.

Signed_____
Date_____
Witness_____
Witness_____
Copies of this request have been given to_____

Reprinted with permission from Concern for Dying, 250 West 57th Street, New York, New York 10019.

OPTIONAL PROVISIONS FOR THE LIVING WILL

People signing the Living Will may want to insert extra provisions above their signatures. Concern for Dying suggests the following provisions as optional:

1. (a) I appoint _____ to make binding decisions concerning my medical treatment.

OR

(b) I have discussed my views as to life-sustaining measures with the following who understand my wishes

_____,
_____,
_____.

2. Measures of artificial life support in the face of impending death that are especially abhorrent to me are:

(a) Electrical or mechanical resuscitation of my heart when it has stopped beating.

(b) Nasogastric tube feedings when I am paralyzed and no longer able to swallow.

(c) Mechanical respiration by machine when my brain can no longer sustain my own breathing.
(d) ──────────────────────────────

3. If it does not jeopardize the chance of my recovery to a meaningful and sentient life or impose an undue burden on my family, I would like to live out my last days at home rather than in a hospital.

4. If any of my tissues are sound and would be of value as transplants to help other people, I freely give my permission for such donation.

Those words could apply to almost any illness or treatment. Let's say a heart attack has left a scar, as if a shoemaker had cut out a piece of your heart muscle and had sewn leather in its place. That patch of leather would refuse to squeeze and therefore wouldn't help pump blood. You could be so handicapped that you consider the 10:00 P.M. news as the late, late show. As for sex, you wouldn't be able to take yes for an answer. You would have an "extreme physical disability," as the Living Will puts it, but you wouldn't want the doctor to forgo efforts to keep you alive.

On the other hand, you could recover from the attack to vigorous health. A heart attack almost killed Lyndon Johnson long before the day that he took the oath as president in an airplane in Dallas. Later, in an auditorium at the National Institutes of Health, President Johnson told an audience of 500 about the vigor with which he intended to promote health research. He reached out as if to embrace us in the audience and gave us a grin so big that it crowded his eyes and forced them to squint.

When he ended his talk, the audience stayed in place for security reasons. The president was scheduled to leave by a side door, near the stage. I had freedom to roam because I was helping reporters and television crews, so I left my aisle seat and walked fast toward the rear of the auditorium.

There was a noise behind me, and I looked around. President Johnson was striding up the center aisle, almost atop me, grabbing hands of people seated to his left and right, outwalking his Secret Service escort. I, who had once had a heart attack myself, jumped aside to get out of his way.

There was a man who still had no "reasonable expectation of recovery," which is the language of the Living Will. He undoubtedly had a leather scar on his heart that could not be repaired. Yet, if another heart attack had felled him there, he undoubtedly would have wanted one of the several hundred doctors in the audience to use every possible method to save him.

The document is also vague in identifying the treatment that it would forbid. The words "medications," "artificial means," and "heroic measures" are sweeping. "Artificial," for example, could include a wooden tongue depressor. And "heroic" could vary in meaning according to which hero applied the treatment.

The original version of the Living Will was so criticized for its vagueness that Concern for Dying in the current version invites you to add provisions, if desired (see page 144). You should include at least the first optional provision—the one in which you designate someone to make binding decisions or else name people with whom you have discussed your views. When you sign a vague document, you need to identify someone who understands what you really mean.

I also object to the Living Will's instructions on painkillers, reading, "I do, however, ask that medication be mercifully administered to me to alleviate suffering even though this may shorten my remaining life."

When I wrote a newspaper column about the Living Will, I advised readers to line through those words. Granted, they reflect an ethical principle called "double effect." According to the principle, a doctor does not intend to cause death in such a situation. Instead, it is the easing of pain that is overriding. Death, if it occurs, is only incidental.

Yet, the sentence in the Living Will has too permissive an air, as if inviting an overdose. Also, it implies that medications alone should be used. Having heard about control of pain from Drs. Cicely Saunders, Sylvia A. Lack, and Josefina B. Magno—pioneers in the hospice movement—I have learned that it is complex. It often consists of regular doses adequate to control pain before it begins, thus forestalling anticipatory dread. Feelings of security and trust in others—these being essential features of hospices—can also lessen pain. The Living Will is therefore out-of-date when it invites a stunning of the patient with drugs alone.

Some people may also object to the Living Will because it is impersonal. Officials of Concern for Dying obviously wanted a document that would fit everybody, including those who feel no compulsion to invite love or frank communication, or to profess a religious faith.

The Reverend Kevin D. O'Rourke preferred instead a document of reflection and reverence. He composed a "Christian Affirmation of

Life," which is available from the Catholic Hospital Association, National Office, 4455 Woodson Road, St. Louis, MO 63134. In its instruction on life-prolonging treatment, it is as vague as the Living Will.

Still, Father O'Rourke uses improved instructions on controlling pain. The Affirmation states: "I request . . . that my pain, if unbearable, be alleviated." That language makes room for new methods that scientists are discovering and for the efficient loving care that, as hospice workers have found, can reduce pain.

Naming People to Make Decisions for You

Two philosophers, Sissela Bok and Robert M. Veatch, have felt so strongly about naming people to make decisions that they suggested in the mid-1970s that you draw up a sort of power-of-attorney. You would name a trusted friend or other person who would control treatment when you were incompetent.[4] Dr. Veatch recommended that the person go to court if medical people refused to follow instructions.

"I and many others fear that physicians who presume to be in charge of terminal care may not carry out our wishes," he wrote in a letter to me. "It is for that reason that we want our directives to be legally enforceable rather than simply moral guidance."

I prefer giving such a person an advisory role rather than trying to confer legal authority. In some states, a power-of-attorney document would be ineffective once you became incompetent. And in one state, Michigan, where a lawmaker tried to confer sure legality on such a power-of-attorney, it never got out of committee.[5]

As we have learned, however, the idea of naming someone to make decisions is a good one, especially if the provisions in the document are vague. Otherwise, you would leave it to strangers to interpret words that have no sure meaning. Nevertheless, because you may outlive the persons who are close to you emotionally, or because you may move away from their area, you need a document that will be effective regardless of whether you name them or whether they will be available when needed.

The Medical Care Directive

I have tried to avoid the objections that arise in connection with other documents, and have included a paragraph naming someone to make decisions for you, in the Medical Care Directive, pages 149–51. It is copyrighted, but I authorize you to make a copy for your personal use.

This Directive forbids life-prolonging treatment in two situations that seem to worry people most—first, when they are in a terminal condition and, second, when they are in a persistent vegetative state (paragraphs 4 and 5).

But I recognize that in other situations, which I can describe only vaguely, you also might not want life-prolonging treatment. Only a person who knows you and your philosophy of life can accurately make the decisions that you yourself would make in such vaguely defined situations. So, in paragraph 6 of the Directive, you can name people to make decisions based on the imprecise expressions of wishes given there.

You could add other provisions to the Medical Care Directive. You could ask to be cared for at home or in a hospice when dying. You could express a religious belief. Or you could reinforce your conviction that certain treatments are divinely forbidden, such as blood transfusions for a Jehovah's Witness.

The following comments are keyed to paragraphs of the Medical Care Directive:

Paragraph 1: A call for love. It is a truism, but should be a falsism, that everyone dies alone. Dr. Cicely Saunders, of London's St. Christopher's Hospice, and others teach that a patient needs love at the time of dying. Perhaps you will impel people to display it by calling for it.

Paragraph 2: A call for knowledge. Many people want to know all about their illness and outlook. If you don't want to be told, line through the first sentence in the paragraph. This paragraph also states that you intend to retain control over your own medical care so long as you are competent. Of course, that doesn't preclude your deferring to the advice of others. It only means that you retain authority.

Paragraph 3: A definition of incompetence. This paragraph makes it clear that your instructions on life-prolonging treatment are applicable if you yourself are unable to make rational decisions. The definition of incompetence is one that is used by judges in some states.

Paragraphs 4 and 5: Directions on medical care. These forbid life-sustaining procedures when they would merely prolong the dying process or when you were in a state like Karen Ann Quinlan. I have used the words "persistent vegetative state" to describe the latter.[6] I have added the protection of requiring that two physicians concur in such determinations.

MEDICAL CARE DIRECTIVE

To my family and those who attend me in an illness:

1. If I should suffer a serious injury, disease, or illness, I desire that those who love me touch me and tell me so, demonstrating that I am precious to them. I ask that those involved in my medical care conduct themselves so that it is apparent that I am included in their love for all humanity, trying to make me aware of that love through any of my senses, regardless of my condition. I particularly desire that I not be walled off with silence when dying.

2. I request that I be informed of my condition and prognosis so long as I am able to comprehend them. So long as I am competent, I intend to control my own medical care.

3. I shall express below my wishes concerning my medical treatment if I should become incompetent. I would consider myself incompetent if I were unable to understand my illness, to grasp the nature and effect of proposed treatment, and to know the risk in either accepting it or refusing it.

4. I ask that life-sustaining procedures be withheld or withdrawn if I should have an incurable injury, disease, or illness stated to be a terminal condition by two physicians, one of whom is my attending physician, and these physicians
    a. have determined that my death from that injury, disease, or illness will occur regardless of whether or not life-sustaining procedures are used, and
    b. have determined that the application of life-sustaining procedures would serve only to prolong the dying process.

5. I also ask that life-sustaining procedures be withheld or withdrawn
    a. if I should be in a persistent vegetative state, and
    b. if two physicians, one of them being my attending physician, have determined with reasonable certainty that I will never regain the higher functions of my brain. The two physicians shall include an appropriate specialist.

6. (Optional—This paragraph is ineffective if crossed out or not filled in. Fill in either a or b, not both.)
    a. If I should become incompetent, I appoint _____ to make binding medical decisions in my behalf.
                                        OR
    b. If I should become incompetent, I ask that the advice of one of the following persons concerning my medical treatment be sought. I am ranking them in order of priority. If any person ahead of another on the

list is unavailable or should fail for any reason to serve, I ask that the next person be consulted.

_____,
_____,
_____.

In addition to making decisions or providing advice in the situations described in paragraphs 4 and 5 above, the person(s) named above are hereby directed to make decisions or provide advice in other situations that I can describe only in general terms, as follows. I would, if competent, reject treatments that imposed on me suffering or strain out of proportion with the benefits expected to be gained by the use of such treatment. I would reject life-prolonging treatment when I had irrevocably lost the ability to interact knowingly and effectively with others. When inevitable death was imminent, I would refuse forms of treatment that would secure only a precarious and burdensome prolongation of life. I realize that the situations described in the above three sentences are subject to various interpretations, and I am confident that the person(s) named in this paragraph will exercise the judgment that I myself would exercise if competent. If the persons(s) named are unavailable or should fail for any reason to serve, I nevertheless request that my instructions in paragraphs 4 and 5 be observed.

7. As examples of the treatment that I desire to be withheld under the circumstances described in paragraphs 4, 5, and 6 above, I ask, for example, that mechanical ventilators, artificial kidney machines, administration of blood products or antibiotics, and resuscitation be withheld or withdrawn. I ask that I be given only such medical and surgical care as will keep me comfortable. Food should not be withheld. Pain should be alleviated, if possible, but no method to control pain should be used with the intention of shortening my life.

Signed _____ Date _____

The person who signed above is either known to me or has shown me such identification that I know the signature correctly identifies that person. I am not related to that person by blood or marriage. I will not inherit anything from that person either by provisions of a will or by operation of law. I am not financially responsible for that person's medical care. I am not named in paragraph 6 above.

Witness _____ Date _____
Witness _____ Date _____

Directions: Draw a line through and initial undesired sentences or words. You and the witnesses should all be together when signing. After signing, hand copies to those who may be involved in your medical care. Ask that a copy be placed in your medical record.

To revoke the Directive after signing: Deface it, mark through its words, tear it to pieces or burn it. If you cannot retrieve all copies, write on a paper, "I revoke the Medical Care Directive that I signed on (date) _____," and sign and date it. Send the revocation to persons to whom you sent the Directive. Ask that the fact of revocation be entered in your medical record.

Copyright © 1981 Bowen Hosford

Paragraph 6: This is a combination of a description of your philosophy[7] and the designation of people to make decisions or give advice. As we have learned, when you give imprecise guidelines, you must either explain them with volumes of additional text or else name someone who will understand what you mean. Hence the two are linked in this paragraph. As to whether the people that you name should make binding decisions or merely give advice, I prefer the latter, that is, "b."

Paragraph 7: Examples of treatment that could be withheld.[8] The list is not meant to be exclusive. I used the language in the Christian Affirmation of Life in the call for alleviation of pain.

Statement for witnesses: This statement, above the witnesses' signatures, is intended to make sure the witnesses are independent of you and have nothing to gain by your death.[9]

Natural Death Statutes

A weakness of many such documents is that they have no legal power to excuse doctors from liability or to force doctors to follow their instructions. Doctors might fear that, if they withheld treatment from dying patients, relatives would sue or else prosecutors would bring manslaughter charges against them. While the chance of legal action's being taken against the physician is remote (none has been taken against any physician for withholding treatment from a dying patient), the fear might influence them. Consequently, legislators have advocated laws that would give such documents legal force.

Twenty-five state legislatures considered such bills—and failed to pass them—before California became the first to make such a document legal. The California Natural Death Act went into effect in 1977.

Lawmakers in nine other states followed the California lead. They are Arkansas, Idaho, Kansas, Nevada, New Mexico, North Carolina, Oregon, Texas, and Washington. In eight of the ten states, they prescribed forms like Living Wills for their residents to sign.

I want to tell you why the movement to pass such laws has slowed. Then I shall tell you more about California's law, because it was first, about Arkansas's, because it is strikingly permissive, and about Kansas's, because it is one of the best.

Such laws have been introduced in more than four-fifths of the states. In the first enthusiasm, lawmakers passed bills. Then opposition hardened. Some people saw the laws as being a step onto a slippery slope of moral values—that they might lead to killing off helpless sick people.[10] Opponents spoke of Naziism and its murders of weak and useless Germans.

In Maryland, State Senator John Carroll Byrnes said of a proposed death-with-dignity bill: "What's at stake is whether this state will take the first, perhaps small, timid, and tentative steps toward recognizing a philosophy we know as euthanasia."[11] Catholic and right-to-life groups fought the bill.[12] It was defeated.

The Society for the Right to Die, based in New York City, encourages the passage of state laws. Until about 1980, the Society was allied with the Euthanasia Educational Council. That aroused suspicion among opponents.[13] The organizations are now separate, and the Euthanasia Educational Council has changed its name to Concern for Dying.

Given the protections that are built into most state laws, the fear that the laws will lead to mercy killings is unjustified. Nearly all of them disavow such an intention, and, in several states, people who are relatives of, or who will inherit anything from, persons who sign forms authorized by the laws cannot act as witnesses.

Some physicians, too, have opposed such bills on the grounds that they were already allowing patients to die naturally. Thus, in their view, the laws would surround the doctor-patient relationship with an undesired atmosphere of legality.

My own doctor, the late Acors W. Thompson, said of such laws: "The law is interfering in a private, personal matter among the doctor, the patient, and the patient's family. If the doctor and the family cannot agree, then the proper solution is for the family to obtain the services of another doctor."

And in the view of the editor of the *New England Journal of Medicine*, Dr. Arnold S. Relman, legislation puts pressure on physicians to let incurable patients die prematurely. Thus, a doctor who would normally still be trying to decide whether it was the time to end life-prolonging treatment might be rushed into it.[14]

Doctors' statements that they will allow patients to die naturally are disputed by Alice V. Mehling, executive director of the Society for the

Right to Die. "Without legislation," she wrote me, "a physician is often reluctant to halt or withdraw treatment for several reasons: his own training to preserve life, the medical armamentarium at his disposal, the hospital setting, geared to treatment."

Mrs. Mehling believes that, although a person has a right to reject medical treatment, a dying patient is often unable to exercise that right. "The monster is not the physician but rather medical technology," she commented.

And Dr. R. H. Kampmeier, writing in *Southern Medicine*, noted that, in the "goldfish bowl of a city hospital," the resident staff fights to keep patients alive. He cited the case of a seventy-seven-year-old woman on his ward. An unsuccessful bypass operation on a blood vessel in her foot was followed by midnight amputation, her heart stopping, implantation of a pacemaker, and tube-feeding. At the end of all this, she had a chronic brain syndrome. When Dr. Kampmeier wrote the article, after almost a year, she was still oblivious to her surroundings but still existing, because of the pacemaker.

Dr. Kampmeier noted that California had passed a natural-death statute, and indicated that it was justified. "Society and we of the medical profession face a problem we ourselves created in the name of scientific progress," he wrote.[15]

Despite controversy preceding the adoption of natural-death legislation, the laws have gone into effect smoothly.[16] "What seems most evident months after the enactment of these laws is the lack of problems," wrote Emily Friedman, field editor of *Hospitals*, the journal of the American Hospital Association, in 1978. State hospital associations had reported minor troubles or none at all. And now, four years after the California natural-death law went into effect, there have been no cries that it has led to mercy killings or euthanasia.

Defects of the California Statute

Indeed, the main criticism in California is that opponents forced too much pruning of the bill before passing it. So many compromises were necessary that now few people can qualify to make binding the directives that they sign under authority of the law.

The California statute contains a form directive. In signing it, you direct a doctor to withhold or withdraw life-sustaining procedures if you had an incurable condition and death was near. If you signed a directive before you were in a terminal condition, it would have an advisory effect only. But, fourteen or more days after a doctor told you that you were dying, you could make the directive binding by filling in the name of the physician who made the grave prognosis. After that, a *second* doctor could withhold the life-sustaining procedures. A doctor who didn't want to do so would have to transfer you to another physician.

Do you understand all that? A survey in Santa Clara County showed that most doctors didn't. They didn't know the difference between an advisory directive and a binding one.

In any event, the requirements for making a directive binding are too strict. Most directives signed by Californians probably don't meet the requirements and therefore have no legal effect.

The California Medical Association distributed 100,000 copies of the natural-death directive to its doctor-members.[17] After the act had been in effect almost a year, the Association's staff asked physicians about their experiences. Of the 112 who responded, half reported that it had improved their relationships with patients and their families. In 67 instances, patients who had signed directives had been in terminal condition, and the doctors had withheld treatment that might have extended their lives.[18]

Apparently, the act made a difference in physicians' attitudes. After fourteen months' experience with the new act, a sample of physicians in Santa Clara County were queried by three law students. Two-thirds of those responding said that, when a patient signed a directive, it would make a difference in whether to withhold or withdraw treatment.[19]

Nevertheless, the directives are not in wide use. And it is apparent that the California Natural Death Act has thrown a false air of legality over writing a directive. Californians would be as well off signing one of the documents discussed earlier, such as the Living Will, the Christian Affirmation of Life, or my own Medical Care Directive.

The Arkansas Statute—Vaguest of All

In contrast, the Arkansas statute is permissive. It allows people to forbid treatment but doesn't specify when the document they sign will take effect.[20]

The Arkansas law also provides that people can draw up such documents for their relatives who are too young to sign or are incompetent. That's a good idea, but the lawmakers created potential conflicts. For example, a husband might insist that life-support mechanisms be withdrawn from his unconscious and incurably ill wife, while her father insisted on the opposite. Both would be on legally sound grounds, under the Arkansas statute. Thus, it promotes court fights.

And some Arkansas lawmaker decided that, if people were going to be given the right to forbid treatment, they should be given the opposite right as well. So the lawmaker added a provision that people could legally require that every possible means must be used to *prolong* their lives.

Such a command is unnecessary. Also, lawmakers may have added to the state's financial burden with that provision. When a state law gives a patient the right to demand every conceivable treatment, the patient could logically expect the state to pay for it. So far, luckily, no judge has interpreted the Arkansas statute to that effect.

The Kansas Statute—the Best So Far

After lawmakers in some states passed defective statutes, Yale Law School students, members of Yale Legislative Services, drafted a model act. The Society for the Right to Die requested the project. The next two states to pass such statutes, Washington and Kansas, based them on the model act. Their statutes are similar, with Kansas having a slight edge in quality.[21]

Each of the two statutes contains a form document, but residents can personalize them. They can add specific provisions of their own. For example, they could add provisions from my Medical Care Directive on pages 149–51.

Both of the statutes provide for safeguards. They require that two physicians certify a patient is in a terminal condition before life-sustaining procedures can be withdrawn.

The Kansas statute is slightly superior to Washington's because it omits a provision that "imminent death" must be at hand before such procedures can be stopped. In other states, "imminent" has been defined as being from a week to six months. Statutes ought to avoid such vague words or else define them.

The declaration authorized by the Kansas statute is printed below. Only Kansas residents should use it, and they should check to make sure it is the current form.

DECLARATION

Declaration made this ——————————— day of ———— (month, year). I, ———————————————————, being of sound mind, willfully and voluntarily make known my desires that my dying shall not be artificially prolonged under the circumstances set forth below, do hereby declare:

If at any time I should have an incurable injury, disease, or illness certified to be a terminal condition by two physicians who have personally examined me, one of whom shall be my attending physician, and the physicians have determined that my death will occur whether or not life-sustaining procedures are utilized and where the application of life-sustaining procedures would serve only to artificially prolong the dying process, I direct that such procedures be withheld or withdrawn, and that I be permitted to die naturally with only the administration of medication or the performance of any medical procedure deemed necessary to provide me with comfort care.

In the absence of my ability to give directions regarding the use of such life-sustaining procedures, it is my intention that this declaration shall be honored by my family and physician(s) as the final expression of my legal right to refuse medical or surgical treatment and accept the consequences from such refusal.

I understand the full import of this declaration and I am emotionally and mentally competent to make this declaration.

Signed _____
City, County and State of Residence _____

The declarant has been personally known to me and I believe him or her to be of sound mind. I did not sign the declarant's signature above for or at the direction of the declarant. I am not related to the declarant by blood or marriage, entitled to any portion of the estate of the declarant according to the laws of intestate succession or under any will of declarant or codicil thereto, or directly financially responsible for declarant's medical care.

Witness _____
Witness _____

Although the movement to enact natural-death laws has slowed, legislators are considering them in additional states. You can find out whether your state has enacted such a law by writing The Society for the Right to Die, 250 W. 57th Street, New York, N.Y. 10019.

Of the ten natural-death laws that have been enacted, eight contain form directives for people to sign. You may get a form from your doctor or hospital, or ask The Society for the Right to Die to send one for your state.

LIVING WILLS AND NATURAL DEATH LAWS

Although two of the state statutes, those of Arkansas and New Mexico, contain no form, the state hospital associations have drafted forms and distributed them to hospitals. If your hospital has none, you might query the associations, at the following addresses:

Arkansas Hospital Association, 1501 North University Avenue, Suite 400, Little Rock, Arkansas 72207.

New Mexico Hospital Association, 3010 Monte Vista Boulevard, N.E., Albuquerque, New Mexico 87106.

9
YOUR SEARCH FOR MEDICAL INFORMATION

PATIENTS tend to be more dissatisified with the information their physicians give them than with any other aspect of medical care.[1] Doctors themselves sometimes realize the lack when they reverse roles and become patients.

A surgeon, Dr. Harold Lear, dying of heart trouble in New York, fought a years-long, largely losing battle to get information and break through his doctors' avoidance of him.[2] A pediatrician, Dr. Elliott Podoll, dying of cancer in Miami, complained that his doctors would announce treatment decisions without explaining them. He said they ought to learn to talk to their patients. In a videotape made for a friend a few days before his death, he described a dying person's requirement. "He must be made to know that he's really being cared for," he said. "And cared about."[3]

However doctors' ability to communicate and their willingness to do so is changing. Some patients even say, paradoxically, that their doctors are telling them *too* much.

Informed consent suits by patients have sensitized doctors. The consumerism movement, with a drumbeat of criticism against taciturn and authoritarian doctors, has caused a changed attitude.

Physicians have been influenced also by a changing medical school selection process and attitude of professors. The percentage of women in medical schools tripled in the 1970s.[4] Women appear to have an inborn compassion. Students who majored in the humanities do as well in their medical studies as those who majored in science, and more of the broadly trained students probably are being admitted.[5] Some medical schools even offer humanities courses.[6]

Medical students now practice interviewing patients in front of videotape cameras. Doctors who have been through such training get patients to talk about their emotions more than others do, because they show their own concern.[7]

Communication between doctor and patient is important. One-third of a group of physicians who had been sued or threatened with suit for malpractice said that poor communication was a common factor in causing patients to elevate a complaint to a lawsuit.[8]

Good communication leads to better compliance with the doctors' orders, too. Researchers found that, when diabetics and patients with congestive heart failure knew what their drugs were intended to do, they took the right ones, on the right schedule, more than uninformed patients did.[9] And anesthesiologists found that, when they spent extra time with surgical patients, telling them how to relax the muscles under their incisions, the patients called for pain medication less often and went home sooner than other patients.[10]

Many physicians remain unconvinced that telling everything about an illness helps the patient make better decisions. We shall learn nevertheless that patients' autonomy is self-justifying.

But first, what makes a physician uncommunicative?

A Lack of Time to Talk

A lack of time works against communication between doctor and patient. A professor of speech communication at San Francisco State University, Dean C. Barnlund, wrote: "It takes time to explain, time to listen, time to dissipate fears, time to assimilate frightening facts, time to prepare for crises, time to enter the experiential world of another person."[11]

In addition, a doctor retains some aspects of a long-ago priestly role, and derives authority from it, though perhaps only twenty-six years old and treating an elder.[12] Medicine is often a substitute for religion,[13] and one must be highhanded to deal with powerful forces that cannot always be defeated by the use of reason.

Moreover, to act with authority instills confidence. A voice that expresses certainty can wipe away symptoms, in the same way that a placebo—a sugar pill—can ease pain.[14]

I told a neighbor, a General Motors executive, that my doctor had told me to lose weight and to exercise and that he charged me $15 for each monthly visit.

"I'll give you the same advice for $10 a month," my neighbor said.

It wouldn't have been the same. The doctor, by his calm assurance, was helping ward off a worsening of my heart trouble.

My doctor's fee then went to $20 and then to $25, far outpacing inflation. Unfortunately, my neighbor, with his $10 offer, had moved.

Observers also have speculated that doctors are unconsciously motivated against sharing knowledge, because that would be to reduce respect and to share power. A former psychiatric nurse, married to a physician, described, in a letter to the Washington Post, the use of medical terminology to command respect from patients. "Rare is the physician who will simply state: 'I don't know,'" she wrote. "Instead, the profession has contrived adjectives that can be used to maintain credibility. 'Nonspecific,' 'atypical,' 'undifferentiated' and 'idiopathic'— all translate into 'I don't know.'"[15]

Patients who search for knowledge may arouse anger. An internal medicine specialist, with reddening face, told me about a woman patient who studied a book to learn about her forthcoming heart catheterization.

"She's trying to be her own medical intern," he said. Finally, in anger and disgust, he canceled the test.

A researcher found that British general practitioners also were angered when their middle-class patients probed for explanations. Questions concerning minor illnesses about which the doctors could do nothing seemed especially threatening. The doctors thought the patients were trying to intrude upon their control of knowledge.[16]

It is therefore how much a patient doesn't know that may count in the power relationship with the doctor. In studies dating back to the 1960s, observers found that, when some physicians knew the defects a child would suffer from polio, and when others knew the date that tubercular patients would be discharged from the hospital, they delayed in telling the patients or their relatives. Sociologists likened that to bosses' keeping power over workmen by maintaining uncertainty about what they were going to do.[17]

Still another motive comes into play when a patient doesn't respond to treatment. A physician may unconsciously punish a dying patient by adopting an indifference that seems to be rejection.

Nurses, too, shun the dying or evade their questions.

"Am I going to die?" a patient asked a nurse.

"Well, we all go sometime," she answered.[18]

Beyond failing to communicate, doctors may lie, especially when a patient's outlook is poor. That may reflect the doctor's own fear of death, a reluctance to admit defeat, a queasiness at being the messenger for bad news, or a reluctance to destroy hope.[19]

A lie will place a mental strain on a dying patient, according to a 1969 appraisal by Dr. Laurens P. White of the University of California School of Medicine at San Francisco. "A man with abdominal cancer and intestinal obstruction, vomiting, in pain, with an enlarging belly, yet fully conscious . . . is well aware that he is getting worse; if this is denied and he is lied to, an additional burden is placed on him. Now he is not only worried about his disease; he must also fear that he is crazy."[20]

Relatives, friends, and doctors—apparently, they all lie to the dying. Author Leo Tolstoy described the fictional death of a forty-five-year-old member of the Court of Justice in Moscow:

> What tormented Ivan Ilyich most was the deception, the lie, which for some reason they all accepted, that he was not dying but was simply ill. . . . This deception tortured him—their not wishing to admit what they all knew and what he knew, but wanted to lie to him concerning his terrible condition, and wishing and forcing him to participate in that lie. . . . This falsity around him and within him did more than anything else to poison his last days.[21]

Sending Messages from One Subworld to Another

Still another problem is that communication between patient and doctor takes place in a sociocultural matrix.[22] Patients may think they and their doctors speak to each other as impersonally as computers. In fact, the subworlds within which they live color their words.

To pick examples at random, old people, patients with Spanish-American roots, or blacks, may have trouble giving and receiving information when they enter the subworld of the usually young or middle-aged, non-foreign-language-speaking, white doctor.[23]

Differences that may exist in education, income, or social standing cause trouble, too.[24] Working-class patients may receive little information from doctors, though they may desire knowledge.[25] A Boston University professor found that was true when he went to Scotland to observe lower-working-class women on a maternity ward. The eighteen doctors attending the women underestimated their comprehension. So they told him almost nothing.

Some of the women used their own techniques to learn what was happening. When a doctor came by, in company with medical students, one woman eavesdropped. "I get some information from him when he's speaking about me to the students, although he doesn't know he's giving it to me," she said.[26]

I once deceived an Augusta, Georgia, dentist by wearing a khaki shirt and pants and clod-knocker, high-top shoes. I told myself he'd charge little money for a filling if he thought I was a laborer. But the disguise only meant that the dentist asked for cash and drilled in silence.

Today I wear expensive clothes to the physician's office. The patient who rides to the hounds will get better information than one who has gone to the dogs.

The Legal Doctrine of Informed Consent

Doctors are changing, though. Some are garrulous in comparison with the old days. Lawsuits charging a lack of informed consent have influenced them.[27]

A nurse—who happens to be my wife, Frances—and a nurse's aide were changing a patient's bed linen. It took two of them, because the man was in traction. Vertebrae in his neck had been fractured in an accident. Emergency-room workers had inserted restrainers—like ice tongs—in his skull, and now, through use of ropes and pulleys, his head was being kept in alignment with his body.

An orthopedic surgeon entered, and Fran and the aide stood aside while he talked about an operation in which the neck bones would be fused. "Too bad you have a thick and short neck," he said. "It's easier to work with a neck that is thin and long."

He felt the top of the man's hipbone. "This is where we'll take bone for transplantation to the neck. We call it the iliac crest."

Then he talked about the hazards of the operation. "You could be paralyzed from the neck down," he said. "Or you could die on the operating table."

Later, walking down the hallway, the aide, wide-eyed, said to Fran, "I wouldn't have that operation."

The two had witnessed the process of informed consent. The surgeon was giving the patient information so that he could make up his own mind whether to have the operation. The patient did consent, and, though he will have a stiff neck the rest of his life, he is paralysis-free.

Such a legal ritual is well established. But, when the ritual began early in this century, it was unnecessary to tell the patient about alternatives and dangers.

Consent itself was necessary, however, because otherwise a surgeon would be committing a battery (an unauthorized touching), and the patient could collect damages under the law of assault.

For example, in 1914, a New York woman, Mary E. Schloendorff, complained that surgeons had removed a tumor without her permission. As an outgrowth of the operation, she claimed, she had developed gangrene in her left arm, and some of her fingers had had to be amputated.

Because of technical reasons, she lost her damage suit against a hospital. Yet law students today pore over the report of that case. In it, Benjamin N. Cardozo, then sitting on New York's highest state court and later destined to become a Supreme Court justice, announced a rule of law, as follows:

> Every human being of adult years and sound mind has a right to determine what shall be done with his own body; and a surgeon who performs an operation without his patient's consent, commits an assault, for which he is liable in damages.[28]

Such lawsuits, in which patients claimed they hadn't given *any* consent, contrast with today's *informed* consent cases. In the latter, patients usually acknowledge that they signed a form or otherwise gave permission. But they say they weren't given enough information so they could make their own decisions. Such lawsuits come under the general heading of malpractice.

For example, in 1960, a Kansas woman, Andrea Chand,* unwillingly made legal history.[29] A surgeon removed her left breast because of cancer and then referred her to a radiologist.

He used cobalt irradiation, which was then new. The machine was housed in a room with forty-inch-thick concrete walls. The operator stayed outside, peering through a periscope.

The effect on Andrea was disastrous. She later said in court that the

---

* Not her real name.

skin, flesh, and muscles beneath her left arm had sloughed away and her ribs were so burned that they had died.

She and her husband claimed the radiologist had failed to warn her that the new cobalt "bomb" could hurt or kill her. They sued him and the hospital where he practiced.

The doctor was uncertain as to what he had told her. He said, "I remember in a vague way that we discussed the treatment, about how long it took, the number of areas we would irradiate."[30]

In ruling on Andrea's lawsuit, Justice Alfred G. Schroeder of the Kansas Supreme Court wrote a plain-language opinion that excited lawyers. "A doctor might well believe that an operation or form of treatment is desirable or necessary, but the law does not permit him to substitute his own judgment for that of the patient," he wrote.[31]

It followed that Andrea had been entitled to enough information to make up her own mind. If she could show that if he *had* given the information, she would have refused the operation, she could collect damages.

That does not mean that patients automatically win cases when they claim the doctor didn't inform them. In the District of Columbia in 1972, a federal judge, Spottswood W. Robinson III, told a "depressing tale" of a nineteen-year-old FBI clerk-typist, Russell Devlin,* who had originally had only a back pain.

Russell claimed that a neurosurgeon never told him a back operation could result in paralysis. A day after his operation he had fallen from his hospital bed. The lower half of his body had been paralyzed, and he had had to be operated on again. He now had no control over his bladder or bowels. He hobbled into court on crutches.

Because this youth had been underage at the time of the proposed operation, his mother had had to consent. She was a widow living in West Virginia and therefore had talked to the surgeon by telephone. She said she had asked him if the operation was serious and that he had replied, "Not anymore than any other operation."[32]

Once again, the case was notable not because of how it turned out but because of the judge's careful explanation of informed consent.

Doctors have a duty to disclose enough information for patients to make an intelligent choice of treatment, the judge ruled. They needn't

---

* Not his real name.

disclose every insignificant risk. On the other hand, they ought to mention even a slight chance of death or serious disablement.

Russell could not win his case merely by showing that the neurosurgeon had failed to inform him or his mother. He had to show that, if the surgeon had told all the risks, a reasonable person would have declined the operation.[33]

Russell Devlin eventually lost his lawsuit.

Still, the cases kept coming. A Californian, Taylor Rogers,* had an ulcer in the horseshoe-shaped part of his small intestine just below his stomach. A surgeon operated and evidently injured his spleen. Taylor then went back to the operating room, where the surgeon took out the spleen. Taylor then developed stomach pains. X-rays revealed a gastric ulcer. The doctor tried to control it with antacids and a diet, but Taylor later vomited blood. So he went back to surgery, during which half his stomach was removed.

Did you know that that chain of complications can result from an operation for a duodenal ulcer? Taylor Rogers hadn't, and he claimed the doctor hadn't told him. California Supreme Court justices ruled that, if he could prove that and show that a prudent person, informed of all the hazards, would have refused the operation, he could collect.[34]

Those two 1972 lawsuits—the ones brought by Russell Devlin and Taylor Rogers at opposite sides of the continent—had further significance. In them, judges insisted patients must be told about material risks. If a reasonable patient would give significance to a risk in making a decision, the doctor had to tell the patient about it.

Although there's a trend for judges to endorse the "material risk" test, those in most states cling to an older one that gives physicians more protection. That "professional standards" test requires that doctors tell only as much as other doctors in similar communities tell. Physicians favor that test, because it allows them to set their own responsibilities.[35]

The series of informed consent cases that I've described here, and others in which judges followed the same reasoning, alarmed physicians.[36] Their lobbyists went to state legislatures, persuading lawmakers to draw up extra protection. In 1975 and 1976 alone, eighteen states passed laws defining or restricting the doctrine of informed consent. The number is now up to twenty-three.[37]

* Not his real name.

Some of the new laws rejected the "material risk" test and accepted the "professional standards" one instead. Also, some of them provided that, if a patient signed a consent form, it created a legal presumption that the doctor had actually provided the information.

Still, if physicians depend on such laws to set boundaries, it could lead to more mistrust of the medical profession.[38] Physicians are well advised to follow the rules given by judges in the most patient-oriented court decisions instead. What follows, therefore, is a rundown on what such decisions require.[39]

The threshold question is this: which treatments should physicians explain? They needn't discuss simple or common procedures. Thus, they needn't explain about a blood count or the risks of commonly used drugs. Also, an office nurse needn't tell a patient that, when she draws blood, it might cause a welling up (a hematoma) under the skin.

Also, doctors needn't explain in emergencies. As a radio station's news reporter, I once stood at the doorway of an emergency room at the Macon (Georgia) Hospital and saw blood squirting from a patient's arm so that it splashed against the wall a few feet away. I would have written a sarcastic story if the intern had said to the patient, "Before starting treatment, I want to explain its risks and alternatives."

Also, the doctor needn't talk about the risks when patients are so ill or distraught that they cannot make rational decisions, or when the explanation would cause psychological damage.[40] That is called the "therapeutic privilege."[41]

The therapeutic privilege looks like a handy loophole, but doctors who use it will be closely questioned if lawsuits ensue. Federal judges in the District of Columbia noted that a doctor can usually find patients' relatives of whom to ask permission if the patients themselves would be harmed by the conversations.[42]

On the other hand, patients do have a right, without asking, to be told information that is relevant to their intelligent decision as to whether to undergo operations or other risky treatments.

Risky diagnostic procedures fall in the must-explain category. On the one hand, a physician need not explain a simple colon inspection (a sigmoidoscopy) but on the other should explain the risks and alternatives before inserting a lighted instrument through a patient's abdominal wall (a peritoneoscopy). Also, doctors should provide enough information about new or uncommon drugs so patients can decide whether to take them.

Doctors need not tell every possible complication. A minicourse in medical science is not required.[43] But they should explain in lay terms the complications that might occur, including the potential of death or serious harm. They should also point to alternatives that the patients might choose rather than the ones that they themselves recommend.

Now here is a twist that might leave you gaping: though the law requires that doctors tell patients about their proposed treatment, it does not require that the patients understand the explanations. Judges just assume that they will understand.[44]

Doctors Are Communicating More Than Before

Influences other than legal ones are making doctors talk more today than before. The consumerism movement is partly responsible. "In this era of 'patients' rights,' an attitude of frankness feels right and, indeed, given the current disputatious atmosphere of medical practice, may be the safest one to adopt," commented a group of researchers in Rochester, New York.

The researchers revealed a shift in physicians' attitudes toward telling cancer patients about their illnesses. First, they looked back at a 1961 study at a Chicago hospital. There 88 percent of physicians who had responded to questions said they generally refrained from telling a patient about a diagnosis of cancer. Now, almost two decades later, the researchers put the same questions to physicians at a Rochester hospital. This time, 98 percent said their general policy was to tell patients.[45]

That represented a nationwide trend. Paradoxically, not all patients were delighted. A Washington, D.C., science writer, Natalie Davis Spingarn, reported, "Two hard bouts with cancer have left me with a new complaint. I suspect doctors are talking too much." She said that cancer sufferers were being asked to make decisions they were not qualified to make and that they were being robbed of hope.[46]

Another patient, a seventeen-year-old girl with leukemia, was so besieged by nurses, social workers, chaplains, medical students, and physicians who wanted to talk candidly that she locked herself in the bathroom. "If one more person asks me how I feel about my disease," she screamed through the door, "I'm going to sign myself out of here."[47]

Some physicians also feel the movement toward frankness has gone too far too fast, even causing heart attacks and suicides.[48] Thus we have arrived at the reverse—the dark side—of the placebo effect. Just as a physician's assurance can ease pain, bluntness can cause adverse reactions.[49]

It would be a shame if legal requirements caused physicians to slug patients with information. One doctor, having given no communication of the diagnosis beforehand, sent a certified letter notifying a patient he had cancer.[50] Perhaps he mistakenly believed he had to do that to satisfy the law.

Though the content of the message is important, the manner of telling it is also. A theologian, Dr. J. Michael Wilson, of the University of Birmingham, England, shared communication with his wife during her six-year losing bout with cancer. "You do not hand someone a communication on a plate as if it had come from outer space—the communicator is part of the message. . . ." Dr. Wilson commented. "It is as important to acquire skill in human relationships as in materia medica."[51]

On Not Sharing Medical Records

The medical record could be an important source of information for the patient. The record is the collection of lab slips, medication orders, nurses' reports, doctors' comments, and other material collected in a folder in the doctor's office or hospital record room.

In most states, doctors and hospital staffs regard the records as their property. A mother, whom I'll call Mary,* was frustrated by that attitude. She wanted to carry her daughter's record with her, to show to strange doctors when the daughter needed treatment.

Her daughter Eileen, now eight, has a rare disease, Ehlers-Danlos syndrome. It is a connective tissue disorder, in which the skin is elastic—you can pull a pinch of it away from its normal place like rubber, and it will then settle back. Some sufferers have displayed themselves in sideshows as India-rubber men or elastic ladies.

A mere bump against a table can tear Eileen's fragile skin. Recently, she had an open sore on her leg. "There was no skin left to sew," Mary said. Eileen's body manufactures thin, paperlike scars over places that she bumps, such as elbows, knees, and shins.

Mary's husband had the same syndrome, and in the wake of their divorce, she moved to a different town. "I wanted to hand-carry the medical records, so I could show them to another doctor if Eileen hurt

---

* Names and other identifying details have been changed.

herself," she said. "It's a rare disease, and doctors need to grasp what it's all about."

Neither the hospital nor Eileen's doctor would hand over a copy of the records. So, in her new town, Mary found a doctor who would give them to her. Then she wrote to the hospital and first doctor asking that the records be sent to the new doctor. Soon she had copies in hand.

She is frustrated, though, that she had to use that stratagem. She cannot understand why she had no legal right to demand the records. She regards them as her own.

While patients have had trouble obtaining medical records, outsiders can get them. "Confidential information is being provided to insurance companies, credit agencies, attorneys, employers, educational institutions, law enforcement agencies and others who will use it for non-patient-care purposes," said an official of the American Medical Record Association.[52]

Important decisions therefore could be based on false or misleading information in the records. Yet patients who are denied access have no method for knowing about any misinformation.

A growing minority of states have given patients the right to see their records.[53] Some of them authorize access to regular records, such as those dealing with heart attacks or kidney trouble, but deny access to those dealing with mental problems. That is reverse logic, because an error in a record that describes psychiatric treatment is more likely than other information to cost a patient a career opportunity.

Even in the few states that allow access, patients may have trouble in getting the records. As far back as 1945, lawmakers in Massachusetts gave patients an absolute right to their hospital records. In 1973, however, researchers at Boston University Law School found that nine of ten major hospitals refused to honor patients' requests for information.[54]

In contrast, people who have been patients at federal hospitals can get their records with ease. They use the Privacy Act of 1974 in asking for them. Thus, a Veterans Administration, Public Health Service, or Army, Navy, or Air Force hospital patient can see and correct the records. When a patient might be harmed by the knowledge, government Privacy Act officials send the records to a third party, such as the patient's private physician.

Members of a federal Privacy Protection Study Commission were impressed by the benefits of releasing the records to patients. Medical people had predicted a deluge of requests, but only a small percentage of patients demanded the records. Also, the commission members found, the records were improved, because doctors and nurses now omitted irrelevant material.[55]

Congressmen have proposed, without success so far, that nearly all hospitals and nursing homes be forced to let patients see and correct their records.[56] Meanwhile, one sure way to be able to see your medical records is to ask your lawyer to get them for use in a court case.

Those who do are sometimes surprised. One woman sued her doctor for malpractice and, after her lawyer obtained her medical records, found that the doctor had written this describing her: "A little nutty." She won the case, in part because those disdainful words were read out in the courtroom.[57]

The benefits of showing medical records were revealed by a study at the Royal Melbourne Hospital, Australia. Two physicians and a nurse told twenty-five patients on a research ward that they could look at their records at any time.

The patients became no more depressed or anxious than others. However, they asked so many questions that physicians complained it was taking too much time. They also told of fears that doctors hadn't suspected.

Some watched the accuracy of their records, and one pregnant woman found a serious mistake. Her record showed the wrong blood type. She had an Rh incompatability with her fetus. She protested, and doctors were alerted to give her an antibody when her baby was born. Otherwise, she could have been sensitized and harmed future fetuses.[58]

The Form That Nobody Knows

Consent forms have two purposes. One is to assist physicians in informing patients. The form therefore tells patients what is going to happen to them. The other purpose is to protect the physicians against later accusations that they didn't provide informed consent. The two purposes are related. A form that provides enough information will protect the physician.[59]

A study has shown, however, that many patients think the consent form's sole purpose is to shield physicians. Oddly enough, some physicians think the same thing, and people who draw up such forms reach for words that will protect the doctors if things go wrong.

The forms therefore may contain ludicrous sentences. A patient, about to undergo an appendectomy, was astonished to find this language in the consent form: "I understand that this operation may render me sterile." Some overcautious lawyer had put those words in there. They conjured up in the patient's mind an image of a surgeon snipping aimlessly in his abdomen. He crossed out the sentence.

Doctors are too enamored of the idea that a perfect consent form exists, according to Dr. Lonnie R. Bristow, of San Pablo, California. Dr. Bristow is an internal medicine specialist and has written articles for medical journals on, among other things, professional liability and malpractice suits. Some doctors think that, if they can find that perfect form, they will be insulated from liability, he told me.

"That's not the purpose of the form. That's not the purpose of the concept of informed consent," Dr. Bristow said. "The main point is whether a sincere effort has been made to inform the patient. If you've done that, then the form begins to lose significance. I feel the emphasis should be on 'informed' rather than on 'consent.'"

How many consent forms will a hospitalized patient be asked to sign? Perhaps none, perhaps three or more. A written consent before surgery is customary, but neither it nor any other consent form is required by law.[60] Still, as we have learned, several states now provide that patients' signatures on consent forms lead to a presumption that they were informed about risks and alternatives. It will be a rare doctor who will operate without the patient's having signed. Even so, only a simple form is needed.[61]

Hospitals and surgeons have been stung by accusations of ghost surgery, in which the patient authorized one doctor but another actually performed it. At a Virginia hospital, a neurosurgeon objected when he saw only his partner's name on a consent form for back surgery (a laminectomy). "Have the patient sign another form with my name on it," he said stiffly to the nurse.

For legal safety, that surgeon himself should be present when patients sign consent forms. The Mayo Clinic's legal counsel, Robert M. Moore, Jr., explained: "The physician is thus able to verify personally that the risks and alternatives were carefully explained, that an ample opportunity was given for the patient to ask further questions, and that the patient (or next of kin if the patient was not able) did sign the form and did appear to understand the risks."[62]

Also going out of date is the blanket consent form. A patient who signs it gives unnamed doctors permission to perform unspecified operations.

A Louisiana woman sued because she said she went into the hospital to have only her appendix removed, and surgeons took out her uterus and ovaries too. Lawyers for the defense pointed to a blanket consent form that she had signed. It merely said:

> I hereby authorize the Physician or Physicians in charge to administer such treatment and the surgeon to have administered such anesthetics as found necessary to perform this operation which is advisable in the treatment of this patient.

But an appellate court ruled that the woman hadn't really consented to the removal of her reproductive organs when she signed that pre-printed form. The court ordered two physicians and their insurance company to pay $3,500 to the woman and her husband. "We think the above so-called authorization is . . . almost completely worthless, and, certainly, since it fails to designate the nature of the operation . . . it can have no possible weight . . ." Judge George W. Hardy, Jr., wrote for the court.[63]

Blanket forms may still be in use in some hospitals. Patients are well advised not to sign them until they have written in the names of the surgeons and the types of operations involved.

Most patients probably won't follow that advice. Nine South Dakota medical students stated after a study that, "The majority of patients do, and will probably continue to, sign consent forms . . . willy-nilly, whether informed or misinformed." The students reminded themselves that, after they became doctors, it was they who must insist that patients be informed. The patients would be too meek to insist for themselves.[64]

Many observers have noted that hospitalized patients are malleable. Their clothes have been removed, their privacy and sense of dignity have been invaded, and they are confined to frightening, rushed places.[65] They obey the uniformed persons in charge—that is, they sign when they are told to.

Some forms have such long words and sentences that it is doubtful whether patients can understand them, particularly when excited and vulnerable in that strange world. A researcher measured the readability of consent forms at five major medical facilities in the Los Angeles area. Four of the five forms were written at the level of difficulty of a scientific journal. The fifth was at the level of a specialized academic magazine.[66]

Pennsylvania researchers questioned 200 patients within a day after they signed consent forms for chemotherapy, radiation treatment, or surgery. Only 60 percent knew what their treatment involved.[67]

It therefore makes sense for a patient to sign beforehand, in the doctor's office. A neurosurgeon discussed a nerve operation with a women in his office. He easily could have had her sign a consent form there, perhaps calling in her family as well to make sure everyone understood. Instead, he sent her off to the hospital, where a foreign-born resident explained the operation and handed her a consent form to sign.

The operation went badly and had to be repeated. The woman sued. Even though she had signed, she said, she hadn't understood what she was agreeing to, because of the foreigner's accent and because she was in no condition in a hospital to comprehend. A jury awarded her $15,000.[68]

Even better than having patients sign in their offices, doctors could allow them to study the forms at home. At the University of Rochester (New York) Cancer Center, researchers asked forty patients who were scheduled for radiation treatment to take their consent forms home before signing. As a result, the patients had an almost 100-percent understanding of the procedures they were to undergo, their purpose, and the discomforts and risks.[69]

Those hospitalized patients who nevertheless are handed forms to sign the night before surgery might well remember a rule of contract law. Whatever they write on the form will take precedence over the printed words.

In 1972, a woman whom I'll call Grace went into the hospital for a breast biopsy and other surgery.

It was ten o'clock the night before the operation. A nurse brought Grace a pen and a form and said, "You have to sign this."

"Does this mean that if the biopsy is positive that I authorize a mastectomy?"

"Yes," the nurse said.

"No, I'm not going to sign that."

"You have to."

"It's my breast, and they're not going to take it off if I don't say so." Grace took the form and wrote in the margin, "No mastectomy."

The nurse then summoned a female doctor. Grace said placatingly, "I want to compliment you [a woman] on being the hospital resident."

But the doctor was disgruntled that a patient wanted the form changed. "It's a routine thing," she said.

Grace said, "It's not routine to me."

The doctor said it would be easier on Grace for a mastectomy, if it turned out to be necessary, to be performed while she was still on the operating table after the biopsy. "You'd have to undergo anesthesia only once," she said. "The operating room might not be available next time when you needed it."

Grace persisted. The nurse then called her personal doctor, and finally surrendered. A clerk typed Grace's changes on a fresh form, and Grace, after marking through some words, signed it.

She would not have refused a mastectomy if the biopsy had shown a malignancy. "I only knew that it was my body, and before they cut my breast off, I was going to have to say so."

Grace didn't have to say so. The lump, as with most lumps in women's breasts, was benign.

Getting Information from the Doctor

How do you get doctors to communicate? First, you should be as careful in choosing your personal physician as in choosing your spouse, according to Dr. Isadore Rosenfeld.

"How awful to have to confide your personal problems to some cold, disinterested fish," he wrote.[70]

A professor of speech communications in North Carolina, Harry E. Munn, says you can sense a doctor's negative attitude during your first contact. "If the doctor seems anxious to get the communication over with or appears to be impatient with his . . . patient, this attitude will place an insurmountable barrier between them in future," Dr. Munn wrote.[71]

You may even judge your physician's attitude by his or her uniform. "I don't know whether you've noticed," the late Dr. Acors W. Thompson, of Falls Church, Virginia, told me, "but most of the time I don't wear a white coat. [I had noticed.] I want patients to feel that I too am a human being and don't have to wear a badge to denote what I am."

The physician who always stands while you are seated or lying in bed is telling you, "I'm in charge here." The one who pulls a chair to your bedside is telling you, "Let's communicate about your illness and you as a person."[72]

Even with a friendly doctor, you will often feel hurried. How do you make sure you remember all the things you meant to ask? "Make a list," advises my wife, Frances, a nurse on a surgical ward.

A female physician told me, "I take a list when I see my own doctor." She also suggested that you write additional questions while talking to the doctor. "I believe in husbands and wives, or friends, going together to the doctor. The second person can take notes, or help ask questions."

Rose Kushner, whose role in the breast cancer controversy is told later in this chapter, says, "You should make a list with all your questions. And go in to the doctor, and never look at him. Don't make eye contact. Just take out the list and say, 'Doctor, I've got some questions.' Then read down the list."

Patients want something they can hold in their hands, or listen to, after they leave the doctors' offices. Thus, parents of children with heart defects have shown that, while they wanted cardiologists to draw pictures of the heart, they wanted to have such pictures and other materials, such as pamphlets, to take home to study. Most of all, they wanted doctors to encourage them to ask questions.[73]

Although audiovisual aids cannot in themselves substitute for question-and-answer sessions with doctors, they can help patients remember important points.

Doctors at the Veterans Administration Hospital in Little Rock used a taped program to show patients the difference between two kinds of artificial kidney treatment. The patients were making up their minds whether to take part in a research study. Some asked for a second or third viewing.[74]

Thus, the specialist of the future may have a viewing room and a stack of videotapes or discs, each one explaining a particular illness or medical procedure. A patient will watch as such a program plays on a television set, and then will go into the doctor's office to receive personal instructions and to ask questions.

How can a patient best remember the doctor's explanations? Reporters and other writers have learned how to remember interviews. They carry cassette recorders.

In future, thoughtful doctors will record their voices as they talk to patients.[75] Doctors at Mayo Clinic, Rochester, Minnesota, recorded final interviews with outpatients, and handed them the cassettes.

At home, the patients listened to the tapes an average of three-and-a-half times each. They called in their spouses or other relatives to listen. After three months, when the doctors sent them questionnaires,

91 percent thought the tapes had helped them understand the physicians' discussions, and 86 percent believed the taped interviews had improved their health care.[76]

The Principle of Autonomy

And now we arrive at a fundamental question. Is informed consent really necessary? After all, most patients cannot understand basic biological processes.

Researchers found, for example, that when doctors explained about family planning, only 12 percent used the information in their decision-making.[77] A study of genetic counseling revealed that only half the families had a good grasp of the information given.[78]

I'm not surprised at the smallness of a figure such as 12 percent but rather at its huge size. We shall learn that some patients are "energized," but only a few have that special quality.

There are other justifications for informed consent. People may want to live their lives in their way. The British social thinker John Stuart Mill wrote:

> If a person possesses any tolerable amount of common sense and experience, his own mode of laying out his existence is the best, not because it is the best in itself, but because it is his own mode.[79]

Although Mills is too idealistic, the principle of autonomy that he identified overrides other reasons for patients' making their own decisions.[80] Doctors should offer them the opportunity even if they decide not to use it or if their choices are unwise.[81]

A forty-year-old California woman had cancer of the colon. Dr. Lonnie R. Bristow, an internal medicine specialist whom we mentioned earlier, and a surgeon recommended that the affected portion be cut away. The shortened colon would be connected to her abdomen in the procedure known as a colostomy, with a bag adhering to her skin to collect the body's waste.

Despite earnest conversations with Dr. Bristow, she rejected the surgery and chose radiation instead. She had a man friend and thought the colostomy would interfere with her sexuality.

"We talked about the fact that refusing surgery was risky," Dr. Bristow later told me. "I said, 'Whatever you do, I'm going to stick with you. I'm not going to get upset with you because you don't do what I would do. I'll stay with you.'"

In four months, it was apparent that the cancer had spread, and in another four, she was dead.

Dr. Bristow still believes, of course, that she made an unwise decision. "I couldn't see how anybody could trade the possibility of losing their life for their sexuality. But, for her, it was important." Other influences cause people to make their own choices. "The important thing is to respect their reasons, even if they don't do what you and I would do."

People have to live their lives in their own way, Dr. Bristow said. "I've come to understand that what makes people special and unique is the fact that they don't do everything like machines. That's what makes them interesting, and why I love them. But you want them to make their decisions from the basis of as much information as you can give them."

Dr. Bristow thinks that, as doctors mature, they become more understanding. "In the first part of medical training, you think, yes, by God, you know all there is to know. If I could guarantee that people would live forever, then I might be justified in insisting that they do it my way. But, since our art is imperfect, we don't have the prerogative to tell patients what they must and must not do. Give them alternatives, give them your recommendation, and then let them decide in terms of how they see their own lives."

The principle of autonomy does not mean patients reject all medical advice. They might decide to accept any instructions the doctor gave and even so would remain fully in control of their own bodies. They would have exercised their autonomy by placing themselves in the hands of a person who they believed could handle their problems better than they could.[82] On the other hand, such surrender should be consciously and logically made. Otherwise, we would return to a medical paternalism that is going out of style.

Another justification for informed consent is that full disclosure by doctors will generate respect and trust for medical practice. Also, a doctor who is forced to explain a diagnosis or a treatment automatically reexamines the problem.

Alert Health Consumers

Alert health consumers are in the minority, but their number is growing. Who are they? For one thing, they are the educated. They can see future payoffs for present behavior.

"*Years of schooling usually emerges as the most powerful correlate of good health,*" said one observer, putting the words in italics.[83] That is true no matter how health is measured—whether in death rates, amount of illness, symptoms people report, or their own evaluations of their health.

On the other hand, sociology professor Lois V. Pratt believes that an overriding factor in seeking good health is a quality of being "energized."[84] "Evidence from my research," Dr. Pratt wrote, "indicates that persons who obtain the best medical care, both preventive and restorative, are those who strive for mastery over their health needs, are experienced in dealing with professionals and formal agencies, and are ready to negotiate assertively to obtain good care."[85]

Rose Kushner, of Kensington, Maryland, is one such person. "It was Saturday night, June 15, 1974, when I found the tiny bulge on the edge of my left nipple," Rose wrote in her book *Why Me?*[86]

A few days later, she told her husband the philosophy with which she would begin her search for knowledge: "Nobody's hacking off my breast while I'm unconscious unless I'm convinced that's the only thing there is to do."

After her initial medical appointments, she stopped off at the public library and found that it had just one pertinent book—it was about the "breast cancer controversy."

"I hadn't even known, then, that there *was* a breast cancer controversy!" she later wrote. But there was. It centered on whether a surgeon should remove merely a lump from the breast or perform more extensive surgery.

The next day, she went to the National Institutes of Health library and learned about another problem—whether a woman should give permission for a biopsy and, possibly, removal of her breast, all in one operation. She learned that sometimes a one-stage operation is best. For example, a woman might be a high surgical risk, so that two operations would be dangerous, or might have a big or irregularly shaped growth in the breast.

On the other hand, there are strong arguments for a doctor's performing a biopsy, then waiting. A specialist looking at a bit of breast tissue at leisure can decide with better accuracy whether it is cancerous than when looking hurriedly while the patient is still on the operating table. Also, during that time, the physicians can more accurately "stage" the trouble, to decide how extensive the operation should be.

Finally, a woman needs to prepare herself psychologically for removal of a breast.

Rose decided that she would have a biopsy first, and then wait. If a mastectomy was indicated, she would forgo the "Halsted radical," in which the chest muscles that control the arm are removed, and would instead have a "modified radical." Her breast and affected nodes in her armpit would be removed, but the chest muscles would stay with her.

She was naive enough to believe that a surgeon would do precisely what she wanted. But Rose began with her own consent form, which she drafted with a lawyer's help, forbidding a doctor to perform more than a biopsy. Later, after the lump was found to be cancerous, she rejected a Halsted operation planned for her by a New York specialist. Finally, she found a qualified surgeon who would perform only the operation that she desired.

Afterwards, when she related in her book her fight to make her own decision, she was invited onto radio and TV talk shows. Women called her, and she started the Breast Cancer Advisory Center. She paid expenses from her book profits, hiring a nurse to help her. They answered more than 10,000 calls and letters. She often spoke before medical groups.

Although she had written that it does no harm to have a loud voice and stubbornness, I found her to be feminine, with a soft but firm voice. She once wore a low-cut dress on television, perhaps demonstrating what she had gained by controlling the extent of her breast operation. A woman listener, who had had the mutilating Halsted operation instead, telephoned her while she was on the air and, with malice in her voice, said, "I'll dance on your grave."

Surgeons began to change their procedures. "At the beginning, it might have been economic pressure," Rose told me. "Women just put on their clothes and walked out of doctors' offices. Then the data changed, and the surgeons changed to go with it. What was heretical in 1974, when I wrote my book, became adopted."

The Halsted radical operation had been designed in the 1880s. Now, in the 1970s, scientists had gained new knowledge on how malignant tumors spread. They were doing clinical studies, comparing the survival of women who had extensive surgery with those having less.

Four years after Rose Kushner's operation, a panel of nine male and one female physicians from the United States, France, and Italy gathered at the National Institutes of Health to come to a consensus on breast cancer surgery. Rose joined them—the only lay person invited into this group.

They rejected the Halsted radical mastectomy as unnecessarily extensive for early, localized breast cancer. Instead, they recommended saving the chest muscles. Also, largely at Rose Kushner's recommendation, the panel endorsed a two-step approach: a biopsy first, followed by a wait for a woman and her doctor to reflect on possible surgery.[87]

Rose Kushner is now a member of the National Cancer Advisory Board, thus helping guide the direction of government-sponsored research.

"My thesis is that a person ought to know more about disease," she told me. "You're going to get the best out of the doctor if you handle your own affairs—if you get out and try to find out some things for yourself."

Although energized persons are not necessarily hostile to their doctors, it is tantalizing to speculate that the demanding person defeats some illnesses with emotions. Researchers at Johns Hopkins Oncology Center, Baltimore, found that among thirty-five women with spreading breast cancer, those who showed signs of anxiety, depression, guilt, or hostility lived longer than placid patients.[88]

That finding needs to be supported with studies of bigger groups of patients. Still, it may well be wise to refuse to "go gentle into that good night."

Editor Norman Cousins, who laughed his way out of a crippling illness and fashioned other treatment in partnership with his doctor, believes that we underestimate the regenerative power of the human mind and body. "Protecting and cherishing that natural drive may well represent the finest exercise of human freedom," Cousins remarked.[89]

Thus, until the ultimate surrender to death, a will to live and the assertion "I'm in charge" may help summon one's life forces.

NOTES

Titles of the following medical periodicals are abbreviated in these notes:
Journal of the American Medical Association—abbreviated *JAMA*.
New England Journal of Medicine—abbreviated *NEJM*.
Standard legal abbreviations are used.

Notes to Chapter 1
THE POWER STRUGGLE BETWEEN PATIENTS AND THEIR DOCTORS

1. *Report of the Secretary's Commission on Medical Malpractice* (Washington, D.C.: DHEW, 1973), pp. 6–7.
2. Ibid., pp. 8–13.
3. American Bar Association Consortium for Professional Education, *Discussion Guide: Preventing Legal Malpractice* (Chicago: ABA, 1978), p. 1.
4. *Money*, 8 (Oct. 1979):4.
5. "A Cult of Ignorance," *Newsweek* 90 (21 Jan. 1980): 19.
6. "Public Doubts about Science," *Science* 280 (6 June 1980): editorial page.
7. Philip Shaver, "The Public Distrust," *Psychology Today* 14 (Oct. 1980): 44, 46.
8. See Catherine S. Chilman, *Adolescent Sexuality in a Changing American Society: Social and Psychological Perspectives* (Washington, D.C.: NIH Pub. No. 80–1426, 1980), pp. 69–71.
9. See generally "Lung Cancer Rises 30 Percent in Women; Cancer Increases Slightly Overall," *Washington Post*, 20 Oct. 1978, p. A–6.
10. John B. McKinlay, "The Changing Political and Economic Context of the Patient-Physician Encounter," in Eugene B. Gallagher, ed., *The Doctor-Patient Relationship in the Changing Health Scene*, (Washington, D.C.: DHEW Pub. No. (NIH) 78–183, 1978), pp. 155, 183, referred to hereafter as *The Doctor-Patient Relationship*.
11. Ellen Hume, "Cost of Unneeded Surgery Put at $4 Billion," *Los Angeles Times*, 27 Dec. 1978. Molly Bolton, "Report Raps Unnecessary Surgery, Uneven Quality in U.S. Medical Care," *Boston Globe*, 28 Dec. 1978. "AMA Calls Figures on Unneeded Surgery Exaggerated," *New York Times*, 20 Mar. 1979.
12. *Health, United States 1978* (Washington, D.C.: DHEW Pub. No. (PHS) 78–1232, 1978), p. 305.

13. Ibid., Table 109. *Health, United States 1980* (Washington, D.C.: DHHS Pub. No. (PHS) 81–1232, 1981), Table 41.
14. *Health, United States 1980*, pp. 113–17.
15. Betty Ann Williams, "Fear of Malpractice Lawsuits Found to Spur Cesarean Births," AP story in *Washington Post*, 5 Apr. 1980, p. A–4. See *Health, United States 1980*, p. 115, citing B. S. Merrill and C. E. Gibbs, "Planned Vaginal Delivery Following Cesarean Section," *Obstetrics and Gynecology* 52 (1978): 50.
16. "Third Thoughts on Second Opinions," editorial in *New York Times*, 29 Jan. 1981, p. A–18. Ronald Sullivan, "Blue Cross Study Finds 2d Opinions Increase Surgery and Hospital Costs," *New York Times*, 22 Dec. 1980, p. 1. "Second Look at Second Opinions," *Time* 117 (5 Jan. 1981): 87. Lawrence K. Altman, "The Question of Unnecessary Surgery," *New York Times*, 28 Mar. 1979.
17. Statement by Dr. Milton I. Roemer to American Public Health Association. *Washington Post*, 20 Oct. 1978, p. A–6.
18. *Medical Nemesis* (New York: Pantheon, 1976, Bantam, 1977).
19. *Omni* 2 (Feb. 1980): 44.
20. *Chicago Sun-Times*, 23 Apr. 1979.
21. *Confessions of a Medical Heretic* (Chicago: Contemporary Books, 1979, New York: Warner, 1980), p. 18.
22. See "Interview with Michael Novak, Philosopher: Power of the New Class 'Is Extraordinary,'" *U.S. News and World Report* 88 (25 Feb. 1980): 69.
23. Statement by Dr. Marian Osterweiss in *The Doctor-Patient Relationship*, p. 260.
24. United States v. Rutherford, 442 U.S. 544 (1979).
25. Robert D. McFadden, "The Drug Whose Growth Defies the U.S. Medical Law of Gravity," *New York Times*, 19 June 1979.
26. People v. Privitera, 74 Cal. App.3d 936, 141 Cal. Rptr. 764, 770 (1977), rev'd, 23 Cal.3d 697, 153 Cal. Rptr. 431, 491 P.2d 919, cert. denied, 444 U.S. 949 (1979). See James J. Kilpatrick, "Laetrile and a Cruel Law," *Washington Star*, 14 Feb. 1980, p. A–15.
27. "Holistic Health or Holistic Hoax?" *JAMA* 241 (1979): 1156.
28. See generally George Yahn, "The Impact of Holistic Medicine, Medical Groups, and Health Concepts," *JAMA* 242 (1979): 2202.
29. Michael Halberstam, "Holistic Healing: Limits of 'The New Medicine,'" *Psychology Today* 2 (1978): 26.
30. Andrea Pawlna, "Fighting for the Health Needs of Women," *Baltimore Sun*, 2 Nov. 1980.
31. Paula Span, "A New Era for Feminist Health Clinics," *New York Times Magazine*, 23 Nov. 1980, p. 108.
32. Barbara Rowland and Lawrence J. Schneiderman, "Women in Alternative Health Care: Their Influence on Traditional Medicine," *JAMA* 241 (1979): 719.
33. Walt Whitman, "When Lilacs Last in the Dooryard Bloom'd," in *Leaves of Grass*, Emory Holloway, ed. (New York: Doubleday, 1926), p. 280.
34. See photograph in "The Real Calvin Coolidge," by Grace Coolidge, *Good Housekeeping* (June 1935): 42.
35. William Allen White, *A Puritan in Babylon: The Story of Calvin Coolidge* (New York: Macmillan, 1938, reprinted, Gloucester, Mass.: Peter Smith, 1973), p. 308.
36. Thomas McKeown, "Determinants of Health," *Human Nature* (Apr. 1978): 60, 62.
37. *Special Report on Aging, 1978* (Washington, D.C.: DHEW Pub. No. (NIH) 78–1538), p. 2.
38. *Patterns of Disease Among the Aged* (Washington, D.C.: DHEW Pub. No. (NIH) 78–1407, 1978), p. 8.

39. *A National Profile of Catastrophic Illness* (Washington, D.C.: DHEW Pub. No. (PHS) 78–301. 1978), p. 9.
40. N. J. Bellergie. "Medical Technology as It Exists Today," *Baylor Law Review* 27 (1975): 31. 32.
41. British Transplantation Society, "The Shortage of Organs for Clinical Transplantation: Document for Discussion," *British Medical Journal*, no. 5952, vol. 1 (1 Feb. 1975): 253.
42. "Life or Death—Whose Decision?" *JAMA* 197 (1966): 139.
43. Nancy L. Caroline, "Dying in Academe," *New Physician* 21 (1972): 655.
44. "Statement on Measures Employed to Prolong Life in Terminal Illness," *Bulletin of the New York Academy of Medicine* 49 (1973): 349, 350.
45. *JAMA* 227 (1974): 728.
46. *American Medical News*, Jan. 1977, cited in *Wall Street Journal*, 25 Jan. 1977.
47. Norman K. Brown and Donovan J. Thompson, "Nontreatment of Fever in Extended-Care Facilities," *NEJM* 300 (1979): 1246.
48. See generally Parker Rossman, *Hospice* (New York: Association/Follett, 1977, Fawcett, 1979). For a more emotional and less useful treatment, see Sandol Stoddard, *The Hospice Movement* (New York: Stein and Day, 1978). For a technical treatment, see Kenneth P. Cohen, *Hospice: Prescription for Terminal Care* (Germantown, Md.: Aspen, 1979). For a summary, see Melvin J. Krant, "The Hospice Movement," *NEJM* 299 (1978): 546. For the story of a daughter's death in a hospice, see Victor and Rosemary Zorza, *A Way to Die* (New York: Knopf, 1980).
49. Cicely Saunders, "Hospice Care," *American Journal of Medicine* 65 (1978): 726.
50. See Sandra G. Boodman, "The Explosive Growth of Hospices," *Washington Post*, 3 July 1978.
51. See generally Terry L. Corbett and Dorothy M. Hai, "Searching for Euthanatos: The Hospice Alternative," *Hospital Progress* (Mar. 1979): 28, 41.
52. See Linda E. Demkovich, "Hospices and HEW," *National Journal* 11 (1979): 1258.
53. "Statement on a Patient's Bill of Rights," *Hospitals* 4 (16 Feb. 1973), reprinted in Tom L. Beauchamp and LeRoy Walters, eds., *Contemporary Issues in Bioethics* (Encino, Calif.: Dickenson, 1978), p. 140. See Willard Gaylin, "The Patient's Bill of Rights," *Saturday Review of the Sciences* 1 (24 Feb. 1973): 22, reprinted in *Contemporary Issues in Bioethics*, pp. 141, 142.
54. See generally George J. Annas, "How to Make the Massachusetts Patients' Bill of Rights Work," *Medicolegal News* 8 (Feb. 1980): 6; Patrick R. Carroll, "What's Right with Patients' Rights," ibid., p. 9.
55. Robert Spanier, "Perspectives on Patients' Rights," *Forum on Medicine* 3 (1980): 763, 765.
56. C. K. Allen, *Law in the Making*, 7th ed. (London: Oxford Univ. Press, 1964), chap. 1.
57. Edward H. Levi, *An Introduction to Legal Reasoning* (University of Chicago Press, 1948), pp. 103–4. See generally Benjamin N. Cardozo, *The Nature of the Judicial Process* (New Haven: Yale University Press, 1921).
58. Levi, ibid., pp. 2–4.
59. William O. Douglas, "An Intimate Memoir of the Brethren," *New York Times Magazine*, 21 Sept. 1980, pp. 38, 40 (excerpt from *The Court Years 1939–75*.)
60. Griswold v. Connecticut, 381 U.S. 479 (1965).
61. Alexander Brooks, "The Right to Refuse Medication" (Paper delivered at Staff College, National Institute of Mental Health, Rockville, Md., 27 Feb. 1981).
62. Allen, *Law in the Making*, pp. 321–46.

Notes to Chapter 2
REFUSING MEDICAL TREATMENT

1. Evan Charney, "Patient-Doctor Communication: Implications for the Clinician," *Pediatric Clinics of North America* 19 (1972): 263, 271.
2. See Robert W. Schlauch, Peter Reich, and Martin J. Kelly, "Leaving the Hospital against Medical Advice," *NEJM* 300 (1979): 22.
3. See Robert M. Byrn, "Compulsory Lifesaving Treatment for the Competent Adult," *Fordham Law Review* 44 (1975): 1, 30–3; and Note, "Statutory Recognition of the Right to Die: The California Natural Death Act," *Boston University Law Review* 57 (1977): 148, 149–57.
4. UPI dispatch in *Washington Post*, 5 July 1971, p. A–10. Palm Springs Gen. Hosp., Inc. v. Martinez, No. 71–12687, Dade County (Fla.) Cir. Ct., 2 July 1971.
5. Union Pacific Ry. v. Botsford, 141 U.S. 250 (1891).
6. Ibid., p. 251.
7. See William F. Swindler, *Court and Constitution in the 20th Century: The Old Legality, 1889–1932* (New York: Bobbs-Merrill, 1969), p. 32.
8. Professor Byrn believed that a simple right to determine what should be done with one's own body, or the right of free exercise of religion, was controlling. "Compulsory Lifesaving Treatment," pp. 3–10.
9. See generally Bill Severn, *The Right to Privacy* (New York: Ives Washburn, 1973), 18–28; Donald M. Gillmor and Jerome A. Barron, *Mass Communication Law*, 3d ed. (St. Paul: West, 1979), pp. 313–16; and William L. Prosser, *Law of Torts*, 2d ed. (St. Paul: West, 1955), 635–41.
10. Vol. 4 (1890): 193.
11. Prosser, *Law of Torts*, pp. 637–40.
12. Swindler, *Court and Constitution*, pp. 261–4.
13. Olmstead v. United States, 277 U.S. 438, 464 (1928).
14. Quoted in Alexander M. Bickel, *The Supreme Court and the Idea of Progress* (New York: Harper, 1970), p. 20.
15. *Olmstead* decision, pp. 478–9 (dissenting opinion).
16. See Judge Thomas Cooley, *Torts*, 2d ed. (1888), p. 29, for an earlier use.
17. The three concepts are discussed by P. Allan Dionisopoulos and Craig R. Ducat in *The Right to Privacy: Essays and Cases* (St. Paul: West, 1976).
18. See Thomas I. Emerson, "Nine Justices in Search of a Doctrine," *Michigan Law Review* 64 (1965): 219; and Paul G. Kauper, "Penumbras, Peripheries, Emanations, Things Fundamental and Things Forgotten," ibid., pp. 235, 280–1.
19. The right had been mentioned in other cases, in concurring or dissenting opinions, or had been used to add weight to other constitutional rights. Kauper, "Penumbras, Peripheries, Emanations," pp. 275–9.
20. Griswold v. Connecticut, 381 U.S. 479 (1965).
21. See Fred Rodell, *Nine Men* (New York: Vintage Books, 1955), pp. 274–6, for a sketch of Justice Douglas.
22. *Griswold* decision, pp. 485–6.
23. Ibid., pp. 484–5; and Robert G. Dixon, Jr., "The *Griswold* Penumbra: Constitutional Charter for an Expanded Law of Privacy?" *Michigan Law Review* 64 (1965): 197, 206–7.
24. Palko v. Connecticut, 302 U.S. 319, 325 (1937). See generally Harold W. Chase and Craig R. Ducat, *Edward S. Corwin's The Constitution and What It Means Today*, 13th ed. (Princeton: Princeton University Press, 1973), pp. 239–68.
25. Eisenstadt v. Baird, 405 U.S. 438, 453 (1972). Justice Brennan's italics.
26. Roe v. Wade, 410 U.S. 113 (1973). See also Doe v. Bolton, 410 U.S. 179 (1973).

In the latter case, the court decided that Georgia restrictions on physicians performing abortions were unconstitutional. See Laurence H. Tribe, "The Supreme Court, 1972 Term," *Harvard Law Review* 87 (1973): 75–85.

27. Appellants' brief, Roe v. Wade, in Philip B. Kurland and Gerhard Casper, eds., *Landmark Briefs and Arguments of the Supreme Court of the United States*, vol. 75, (Arlington, Va.: University Publications, 1975), p. 89.

28. Bob Woodward and Scott Armstrong, *The Brethren* (New York: Simon and Schuster, 1979), pp. 223, 239.

29. Unless a mother's health required it. Roe v. Wade, p. 195.

30. Ibid., pp. 157–64.

31. In the Matter of Quinlan, 70 N.J. 10, 355 A.2d 647, 663 (1976).

32. See generally Dionisopoulos and Ducat, *The Right to Privacy*, chapters 1 and 2.

33. See *Jehovah's Witnesses and the Question of Blood* (New York: Watchtower Bible and Tract Society of New York, Inc.; Brooklyn: International Bible Students Association, 1977).

34. "A Jehovah's Witness is Recipient of Artificial Blood," AP dispatch in *New York Times*, 22 Nov. 1979, p. D–14.

35. In re Brooks, 32 Ill.2d 361, 205 N.E.2d 435, 437 (1965).

36. Ibid., p. 442.

37. Richard E. Morgan, *The Supreme Court and Religion* (New York: Free Press, 1972), p. 158.

38. Ned H. Cassem, "When to Disconnect the Respirator," *Psychiatric Annals* 9 (1979): 84.

39. David L. Jackson and Stuart Youngner, "Patient Autonomy and 'Death with Dignity,'" *NEJM* 301 (1979): 404.

40. Jacobson v. Massachusetts, 197 U.S. 11 (1905).

41. Byrn, "Compulsory Lifesaving Treatment," p. 21. Refusal of burdensome treatment is not suicide; Vatican Congregation for the Doctrine of the Faith, *Declaration on Euthanasia* (Washington: United States Catholic Conference, 1980), pp. 9–10.

42. I am indebted to Robert M. Veatch, *Death, Dying, and the Biological Revolution*, (New Haven: Yale University Press, 1976), p. 144, for this Catch-22 formulation.

43. Application of President and Directors of Georgetown College, Inc., 331 F.2d 1000, 1007 (D.C. Cir. 1964), *cert. denied*, 337 U.S. 978 (1964).

44. *Georgetown* decision, p. 1009.

45. But see In re Osborne, 294 A.2d 372 (D.C. Ct. App. 1972), allowing a coherent Jehovah's Witness, whose children were provided for, to refuse transfusions.

46. Meeting, President's Commission for the Study of Ethical Problems in Medicine and Biomedical and Behavioral Research, Miami, 9 April 1981, p. 34.

47. Competency Interview, Perlmutter v. Florida Medical Center, No. 78-9747—Ferris, Broward County (Fla.) Cir. Ct., 30 June 1978.

48. Final Judgment, Perlmutter v. Florida Medical Center, 11 July 1978.

49. Satz v. Perlmutter, 362 So.2d 160 (1978), *aff'd* (but limited to the facts of the case), 379 So.2d 359 (Fla. 1980).

Notes to Chapter 3
DISCOVERING DEFECTS BEFORE A BABY IS BORN

1. *Facts about Down Syndrome for Women Over 35* (Washington: DHEW Pub. No. (NIH) 78-536, 1979), p. 10.

2. Michael K. McCormack, "Medical Genetics and Family Practice," *American Family Physician* (Sept. 1979): 143, 144.

3. Consensus Development Conference, *Antenatal Diagnosis* (Washington: NIH Pub. No. 79-1973, 1979), pp. I-27-31, referred to hereafter as *Antenatal Diagnosis*.
4. William Alex McIntosh and Jon P. Alston, "Review of the Polls: Acceptance of Abortion Among White Catholics and Protestants, 1962 and 1975," *Journal for the Scientific Study of Religion* 16 (1977): 295.
5. Glenn Collins, "More Older Women Are Becoming Mothers, Study Shows," *New York Times*, 29 Sept. 1980, p. D-11.
6. NICHD National Registry for Amniocentesis Study Group, "Midtrimester Amniocentesis for Prenatal Diagnosis: Safety and Accuracy," *JAMA* 236 (1976): 1471. Mitchell S. Golbus, et al., "Prenatal Genetic Diagnosis in 3,000 Amniocenteses," *NEJM* 300 (1979): 157.
7. Golbus, ibid., p. 162.
8. J. Howard Turner, T. Terry Hayashi, and Donald D. Pogoloff, "Legal and Social Issues in Medical Genetics," *American Journal of Obstetrics and Gynecology* 134 (1979): 83, 85.
9. Sonography apparently poses little or no danger at levels used by current machines. Still, the machines were put into wide use without a knowledge of side effects. Joseph T. Ferrucci, Jr., "Medical Progress: Body Ultrasonography," Part 2, *NEJM* 300 (1979): 590, 598.
10. Ibid., Part 1, *NEJM* 300 (1979): 538, 539.
11. "AFP: Sometimes an Ominous Clue," *FDA Consumer* (April 1980): 10. See generally James E. Haddow, "Commentary: Prenatal Screening for Neural Tube Defects," *JAMA* 242 (1979): 515.
12. See generally Aubrey Milunsky, "Prenatal Detection of Neural Tube Defects: VI. Experience with 20,000 Pregnancies," *JAMA* 244 (1980): 2731.
13. See Milunsky, "Prenatal Detection of Neural Tube Defects: VI. Experience with 20,000 Pregnancies." The chance of false positives is higher than that of failure to find a defect. George J. Annas, "'Fitness' for Birth and Reproduction: Legal Implications of Genetic Screening," *Family Law Quarterly* 9 (1975): 463, 475.
14. See generally Charles J. Epstein et al., "Prenatal Detection of Genetic Disorders," *American Journal of Human Genetics* 24 (1972): 215-6.
15. A list of recognizable chromosomal disorders is given in McCormack, "Medical Genetics and Family Practice," Table 2.
16. Philip Reilly, *Genetics, Law, and Social Policy* (Cambridge: Harvard, 1977), pp. 238-43. Marc Lappé, *Genetic Politics* (New York: Simon and Schuster, 1979), pp. 86-8.
17. Rosalind Gromet Stark, "My Unborn Child," *Washington Post*, 18 Nov. 1979, p. C-1.
18. Tabitha M. Powledge, "Prenatal Diagnosis: New Techniques, New Questions," *Hastings Center Report* 9 (June 1979): 16.
19. For a judge's criticism of this "new tort," see Becker v. Schwartz, 46 N.Y.2d 401, 417-22, 386 N.E.2d 807, 413 N.Y.S.2d 895 (1978) (Judge Wachtler, dissenting).
20. Jacobs v. Theimer, 519 S.W.2d 846 (1975). See Miriam Kass and Margery W. Shaw, "The Risk of Birth Defects: *Jacobs v. Theimer* and Parents' Right to Know," *American Journal of Law and Medicine* 2 (1976-77): 213, 215, and n. 7.
21. J. W. Pearson, "The Management of High-Risk Pregnancy," *JAMA* 229 (1974): 1439.
22. Becker v. Schwartz. The parents were later reported to have put up their baby for adoption. Presumably, this would reduce their expenses and the amount of damages. "Baby in Malpractice Suit Was Put Up for Adoption," *New York Times*, 17 Feb. 1979, p. 23. See generally Lawrence K. Altman, "Birth Defect Suits Worry Doctors," *New York Times*, 30 Jan. 1979, and George J. Annas, "Medical Paternity and 'Wrongful Life,'" *Hastings Center Report* 9 (June 1979): 16.

23. "Maternal Serum Alpha-Fetoprotein Screening: An Overview." (Background paper prepared for National Conference on Maternal Serum Alpha-Fetoprotein, Washington, D.C., 28–30 July 1980), p. 4.
24. Park v. Chessin, sub nom. Becker v. Schwartz, 46 N.Y.2d 401, 386 N.E.2d 807, 413 N.Y.S.2d 895 (1978).
25. Annas, "Medical Paternity and 'Wrongful Life,'" p. 17.
26. Philip Reilly, "Legal Perspectives on MSAFP Screening," in *Maternal Serum Alpha-Fetoprotein* (Washington, D.C.: DHHS, 1980), pp. 89, 95.
27. Berman v. Allen, 80 N.J. 421, 404 A.2d 8 (1979).
28. See Kass and Shaw, "The Risk of Birth Defects," pp. 231–4.
29. Cf. Stills v. Gratton, 55 Cal. App.3d 698, 127 Cal. Reptr. 652 (1976); Williams v. State, 18 N.Y.2d 481, 223 N.E.2d 343, 276 N.Y.S.2d 885 (1966).
30. Gleitman v. Cosgrove, 49 N.J. 22, 63, 227 A.2d 689, 711 (1967). Accord, Gildiner v. Thomas Jefferson Univ. Hosp., 451 F. Supp., 692, 694 (1978). *Contra*, a ruling in an appellate court recognizing a Tay-Sachs child's right to sue for negligence that led to her birth. Curlender v. Bio-Science Laboratories, 106 Cal. App.3d 811, 165 Cal. Rptr. 477 (1980). See George J. Annas, "Righting the Wrong of Wrongful Life," *Hastings Center Report* 11 (Feb. 1981): 8. See generally Homer H. Clark, Jr., "Wrongful Conception: A New Kind of Medical Malpractice?" *Family Law Quarterly* 12 (1979): 259.
31. V. A. McKusick, *Mendelian Inheritance in Man: Catalogs of Autosomal Dominant, Autosomal Recessive, and X-Linked Phenotypes* (Baltimore: Johns Hopkins).
32. Reilly, "Legal Perspectives on MSAFP Screening," p. 15. Alexander Morgan Capron, "Tort Liability in Genetic Counseling," *Columbia Law Review* 79 (1979): 618, 628–30.
33. Alexander M. Capron, "Autonomy, Confidentiality, and Quality Care in Genetic Counseling," *Birth Defects: Original Article Series* 15, no. 2 (1979): 307, 333–4. Note, "Father and Mother Know Best: Defining the Liability of Physicians for Inadequate Genetic Counseling," *Yale Law Journal* 87 (1978): 1488, 1506–8.
34. William Ristow, "Genetic Counseling: The Third Decade," *New Scientist* 83 (1979): 976, 978.
35. See Gilbert S. Omenn, "Genetic Engineering: Present and Future," in *To Live and Let Die: When, Why, and How* (Springer-Verlag, 1973), pp. 48, 51.
36. Jacobson v. Massachusetts, 187 U.S. 11 (1905).
37. Buck v. Bell, 274 U.S. 200 (1927).
38. J. E. Coogan, "Eugenical Sterilization Holds a Jubilee," *Catholic World*, April 1953, p. 45, cited in Charles W. Murdock, "Sterilization of the Retarded: A Problem or a Solution," *California Law Review* 63 (1974): 917, 921, n. 22.
39. Sandra G. Boodman and Glenn Frankel, "Over 7,500 Sterilized by Virginia," *Washington Post*, 23 Feb. 1980, p. A–1.
40. Seymour Lederberg, "State Channeling of Gene Flow by Regulation of Marriage and Procreation," in Aubrey Milunsky and George J. Annas, eds., *Genetics and the Law* (New York: Plenum, 1976), pp. 247, 262.
41. Jane M. Friedman, "Legal Implications of Amniocentesis," *University of Pennsylvania Law Review* 123 (1974): 92, 131.
42. J. Howard Turner, T. Terry Hayashi, and Donald D. Pogoloff, "Legal and Social Issues in Medical Genetics," *American Journal of Obstetrics and Gynecology* 134 (1979): 83, 95.
43. Lappé, *Genetic Politics*, p. 210.
44. James E. Bowman and Eugene Goldwasser, *Sickle Cell Fundamentals* (Washington: NIH National Sickle Cell Disease Program, 1975), p. 12.
45. Lappé, *Genetic Politics*, n., p. 57.
46. Ibid., p. 23.

47. Seth Lawrence Matarasso, "Sickle Cell Anemia: The Social Context of a Medical Problem," *Forum on Medicine* 3 (1980): 650, 652.
48. See generally Reilly, *Genetics, Law, and Social Policy*, Chapter 3.
49. Reilly, *Genetics, Law, and Social Policy*, p. 82.
50. Yuet Wai Kan, Mitchell S. Golbus, and Richard Trecartin, "Prenatal Diagnosis of Sickle Cell Anemia," *NEJM* 294 (1976): 1039; "Diagnosing Sickle Cell by Amniocentesis," *Medical World News* 19 (11 Dec. 1978): 17.
51. Quoted by George H. Kieffer in *Bioethics: A Textbook of Issues* (Reading, Mass.: Addison-Wesley, 1979), p. 141.
52. "Reproductive Rights and Genetic Disease," in James F. Humber and Robert F. Almeder, eds., *Biomedical Ethics and the Law*, 2d ed. (New York: Plenum, 1979), pp. 373, 381.
53. "Knowledge, Risk and the Right to Reproduce: A Limiting Principle." (Paper delivered at the Second National Symposium on Genetics and the Law, Boston, May 1979), p. 8.
54. See generally Friedman, "Legal Implications of Amniocentesis;" Harold P. Green and Alexander M. Capron, "Issues of Law and Public Policy in Genetic Screening," *Birth Defects: Original Articles Series* 10, no. 6 (1974): 57; and Jon R. Waltz and Carol R. Thigpen, "Genetic Screening and Counseling: The Legal and Ethical Issues," *Northwestern University Law Review* 68 (1973): 696.
55. Loving v. Virginia, 388 U.S. 1 (1967).
56. See generally Gerald Gunther, *Individual Rights in Constitutional Law* (Mineola, N.Y.: Foundation Press, 1976), pp. 255–62.
57. Compulsory screening for genetic traits or disease might be unconstitutional searches. Friedman, pp. 125–30; Waltz and Thigpen, pp. 709–13.
58. Va. Code Sec. 20–5.
59. Lev. 18:7–18.
60. Albert C. Jacobs and Julius Goebel, Jr., *Domestic Relations: Cases and Materials* (Brooklyn: Foundation Press, 1961), pp. 122–3.
61. See Griswold v. Connecticut, 381 U.S. 479, 485 (1965).
62. "Medico-Legal Issues in Prenatal Genetic Disorders," in Milunsky and Annas, eds., *Genetics and the Law*, pp. 53, 59.
63. "'I Am Not What You See,'" in Chester A. Swinyard, ed., *Decision Making and the Defective Newborn*, (Springfield: Thomas, 1978), pp. 465, 467.
64. Bioethicist John Fletcher described the sense of shame as "cosmic guilt." Kieffer, *Bioethics: A Textbook of Issues*, p. 140.
65. Authors state erroneously that each person carries four to eight deleterious genes, according to Lappé, *Genetic Politics*, p. 124.
66. See generally Robert F. Murray, Jr., "Genetic Health: A Dangerous, Probably Erroneous, and Perhaps Meaningless Concept," *Birth Defects: Original Articles Series* 15, no. 2 (1979): 71.
67. Research Group on Genetics, "Ethical and Social Issues in Screening for Genetic Disease," *NEJM* 286 (1972): 1129, reprinted in Tom L. Beauchamp and LeRoy Walters, eds., *Contemporary Issues in Bioethics*, (Encino, Cal.: Dickenson, 1978), pp. 588, 589. See Kurt Hirschhorn, "Practical and Ethical Problems in Human Genetics," in Humber and Almeder, eds., *Biomedical Ethics and the Law*, 2d ed., pp. 361, 371.
68. See Reilly, *Genetics, Law, and Social Policy*, pp. 29–30.
69. Daniel Callahan, "The Meaning and Significance of Genetic Disease: Philosophical Perspectives," in *Ethical Issues in Human Genetics: Genetic Counseling and the Use of Genetic Knowledge* (New York: Plenum, 1973), p. 83; reprinted in Beauchamp and Walters, eds., *Contemporary Issues in Bioethics*, p. 580.

70. Planned Parenthood of Central Missouri v. Danforth 428 U.S. 52, 71, 90 (1976). Doe v. Doe, 365 Mass. 556, 314 N.E.2d 128 (1974).
71. Unless you had contracted a common-law marriage with her, in a state that recognized such marriages.
72. See generally Capron, "Tort Liability in Genetic Counseling," pp. 675–9; Capron, "Autonomy, Confidentiality, and Quality Care in Genetic Counseling," pp. 321–6; and Reilly, *Genetics, Law, and Social Policy*, p. 168. Cf. Simonsen v. Swenson, 104 Neb. 224, 177 N.W. 831 (1920).

Notes to Chapter 4
BABIES IN TROUBLE

1. Anthony Shaw, "Doctor, Do We Have a Choice?" *New York Times Magazine*, 30 Jan. 1972, p. 44.
2. See James M. Gufstason, "Mongolism, Parental Desires, and the Right to Life," in Dennis J. Horan and David Mall, eds., *Death, Dying, and Euthanasia* (Washington: University Publications, 1977), p. 250.
3. Shaw, "Doctor, Do We Have a Choice?" p. 52.
4. "Moral and Ethical Dilemmas in the Special-Care Nursery," *NEJM* 289 (1973): 890.
5. See generally Chester A. Swinyard, Shakuntala Chaube, and Hideo Nishimura, "Spina Bifida as a Prototype Defect for Decision Making: Nature of the Defect," in Chester A. Swinyard, ed., *Decision-Making and the Defective Newborn* (Springfield: Thomas, 1978), p. 17.
6. John Freeman, *Practical Management of Meningomyelocele* (Baltimore: University Park Press, 1974), p. 16, cited by Stanley Hauerwas, "Selecting Children to Live or Die: An Ethical Analysis of the Debate between Dr. Lorber and Dr. Freeman on the Treatment of Meningomyelocele," in Horan and Mall, eds., *Death, Dying, and Euthanasia*, pp. 228, 230.
7. See F. D. Ingraham and H. Hamlin, "Spina Bifida and Cranium Bifidum: II. Surgical Treatment," *NEJM* 228 (1943): 631, discussed by John M. Freeman in "The Shortsighted Treatment of Myelomeningocele: A Long-Term Case Report," *Pediatrics* 53 (1974): 311.
8. J. Lorber, "Results of Treatment of Myelomeningocele," *Developmental Medicine and Child Neurology* 13 (1971): 279, 280–1.
9. J. Lorber, "Early Results of Selective Treatment of Spina Bifida Cystica," *British Medical Journal* 4 (1973): 201, 202.
10. Compare the story of a baby left untreated to die but who lived with extra handicaps, in Freeman, "The Shortsighted Treatment of Myelomeningocele," and a commentary by Professor Lorber, *Pediatrics* 53 (1974): 307 and 311.
11. Ivan Illich discussed medicalization of society in *Medical Nemesis* (New York: Pantheon, Bantam, 1976). Dr. Duff has also said that in some instances the distinction between active and inactive euthanasia is merely a quibble. Beverly Kelsey, "An Interview with Dr. Raymond S. Duff: Which Infants Should Live? Who Should Decide?" *Hastings Center Report* 5 (April 1975): 5, 7. See generally Raymond S. Duff and A. G. M. Campbell "Social Perspectives on Medical Decisions Relating to Life and Death," in John Ladd, ed., *Ethical Issues Relating to Life and Death* (New York: Oxford, 1979), p. 187.
12. "Euthanasia: The Deadly Dilemma," *Family Health* 10 (September 1978): 39.
13. Maureen Hack, Avroy A. Fanaroff, and Irwin R. Merkatz, "Current Concepts: The Low-Birth-Weight-Infant—Evolution of a Changing Outlook," *NEJM* 301 (1979): 1162.
14. "On the Death of a Baby," *Atlantic Monthly* 244 (July 1979): 64.
15. Shaw, "Doctor, Do We Have a Choice?" p. 52.

16. Milton D. Heifetz with Charles Mangel, *The Right to Die* (New York: Putnam, 1974), p. 52.
17. Judge James H. Lincoln, quoted by Joseph Goldstein, "Medical Care for the Child at Risk: On State Supervention of Parental Authority," *Yale Law Journal* 86 (1977): 645, 658, n. 31.
18. Eterna International, P.O. Box 1344, Oak Brook, IL 60521. Eterna also provides services to professionals serving the handicapped.
19. *Facts about Down Syndrome for Women over 35* (Washington: DHEW Pub. No. (NIH) 78-536), p. 6.
20. See Ann Gath, *Down's Syndrome and the Family: The Early Years* (New York: Academic, 1978), p. 121.
21. Eccles. 3:1-2.
22. "Ethical Considerations in Surgery of the Newborn," *Contemporary Surgery* 7 (Dec. 1975): 17.
23. Allen Buchanan, "Medical Paternalism or Legal Imperialism: Not the Only Alternatives for Handling *Saikewicz*-type Cases," *American Journal of Law and Medicine* 5 (Summer 1979): 97, 103-4.
24. *The Morality of Law* (New Haven: Yale, 1964), p. 186. See Richard A. McCormick, "To Save or Let Die: The Dilemma of Modern Medicine," *JAMA* 229 (1974): 172, 175.
25. Goldstein, "Medical Care for the Child at Risk," pp. 144-8. See generally Andrew Jay Kleinfeld, "The Balance of Power Among Infants, Their Parents, and the State," *Family Law Quarterly* 4 (1970): 319, 410, and ibid., vol. 5 (1971): 64.
26. Kleinfeld, "The Balance of Power," vol. 5, p. 107.
27. Roe v. Wade, 410 U.S. 113, 162 (1973).
28. See John Hart Ely, "The Wages of Crying Wolf: A Comment on Roe v. Wade," *Yale Law Journal* 82 (1973): 923, reprinted in part in Tom L. Beauchamp and LeRoy Walters, eds., *Contemporary Issues in Bioethics* (Encino, Calif.: Dickensen, 1978), p. 247.
29. For examples, see House Joint Resolutions 17, 56, 139, and 214 and Senate Joint Resolutions 12 and 22, 96th Congress.
30. Dennis J. Horan, "Euthanasia as a Form of Medical Management," in Horan and Mall, eds., *Death, Dying, and Euthanasia*, pp. 196, 200.
31. See generally John A. Robertson, "Involuntary Euthanasia of Defective Newborns: A Legal Analysis," in Horan and Mall, eds., *Death, Dying, and Euthanasia*, p. 139; *Stanford Law Review* 27 (1975): 213; "Discretionary Nontreatment of Defective Newborns," in Aubrey Milunsky and George J. Annas, eds., *Genetics and the Law* (New York: Plenum, 1975), p. 451; and "Legal Issues in Nontreatment of Defective Newborns," in Swinyard, ed., *Decision Making and the Defective Newborn*, p. 359.
32. Glanville Williams, *Criminal Law: The General Part*, 2d ed. (London: Stevens, 1961), p. 4.
33. *The Common Law* (Cambridge: Harvard, 1963; Boston: Little, Brown), pp. 218-9.
34. United States v. Knowles, 26 Fed. Cas. 800, 801. (N.D. Cal. 1864).
35. See Goldstein, "Medical Care for the Child at Risk," pp. 653-7; and Norman L. Cantor, "Law and the Termination of an Incompetent Patient's Life-Preserving Care," in John A. Behnke and Sissela Bok, eds., *The Dilemmas of Euthanasia* (Garden City, N.Y.: Anchor, 1975), pp. 69, 85-9.
36. Robert A. Burt, "Authorizing Death for Anomalous Newborns," in Milunsky and Annas, eds., *Genetics and the Law*, pp. 435, 437.
37. Michael Wald, "State Intervention in Behalf of 'Neglected' Children: A Search for Realistic Standards," *Stanford Law Review* 27 (1975): 985, 1028, n. 228; and Robert

Bennett, "Allocation of Child Medical Care Decision-Making Authority: A Suggested Interest Analysis," *Virginia Law Review* 62 (1976): 285, 313 at n. 111.

38. This story was related by Anthony Shaw, M.D., from a letter written to him by a Nassau County, N.Y., surgeon, in Swinyard, ed., *Decision-Making and the Defective Newborn*, p. 463.

39. "Passive Euthanasia of Defective Newborn Infants: Legal Considerations," *Journal of Pediatrics* 88 (1976): 883.

40. Maine Medical Center v. H., No. 74–145, Super. Ct., County of Cumberland, Maine, 14 Feb. 1974; accord, Matter of M., No. 1960, P. Ct., Essex County, Mass., 15 Feb. 1978. See also In re Philip B., 92 Cal. App.3d 796, 156 Cal. 48 (1979).

41. Richard A. Mueller and G. Keith Phoenix, "A Dilemma for the Legal and Medical Professions: Euthanasia and the Defective Newborn," *Saint Louis University Law Journal* 22 (1978): 501, 507.

42. Gufstafson, "Mongolism, Parental Desires, and the Right to Life."

43. Swinyard, ed., *Decision-Making and the Defective Newborn*. See also A. R. Jonsen, et al., "Critical Issues in Newborn Intensive Care: A Conference Report and Policy Proposal," *Pediatrics* 55 (1975): 756.

44. I paraphrased Joseph Goldstein in this imaginary quotation. "Medical Care for the Child at Risk," p. 655.

Notes to Chapter 5
THE CHAD GREEN STORY

1. Superintendent of Belchertown State School v. Saikewicz, 373 Mass. 728, 370 N.E.2d 417 (1977). For details on legal steps, see Jonathan Brant and John Graceffa, "Rutherford, Privitera, and Chad Green: Laetrile's Setbacks in the Courts," *American Journal of Law and Medicine* 6 (Summer 1980): 151, 165–170.

2. Stewart Alsop, *Stay of Execution* (Philadelphia: Lippincott, 1973), p. 16.

3. Ezra M. Greenspan and Howard W. Bruckner, "Aspects of Clinical Pharmacology," in Ezra M. Greenspan, ed., *Clinical Cancer Chemotherapy* (New York: Raven Press, 1975), pp. 33–5.

4. Custody of a Minor, Civil No. 78–6816, Super. Ct., Plymouth County, Mass., 18 April 1978, *aff'd*, 78 Mass. Adv. Sheets 2002, 379 N.E.2d 1053 (1978).

5. Ibid., 379 N.E.2d at 1064.

6. Custody of a Minor, Civil No. 78–6816, Super. Ct., Plymouth County, Mass., Interlocutory Order, 22 Jan. 1979.

7. "Parents Could Face Kidnap Charge for Hiding Leukemia-Stricken Son," *Washington Post*, 26 Jan. 1979, p. A–12.

8. Custody of a Minor, Civil No. 78–6816, Super. Ct., Plymouth County, Mass., Findings, Conclusions of Law, and Order for Judgment, 23 April 1979, p. 37, referred to hereafter as "second superior court opinion."

9. Ibid. at 25.

10. Ibid. at 11.

11. Kathleen T. Braico, et al., "Laetrile Intoxication: Report of a Fatal Case," *NEJM* 300 (1979): 238.

12. Second superior court opinion, p. 5.

13. Custody of a Minor, 79 Mass. Adv. Sheets 2124, 393 N.E.2d 836 (1979).

14. "Leukemia Decision is Upheld," AP dispatch in *Atlanta Journal*, 10 Aug. 1979, p. 14–A.

15. "Laetrile Doctors Say Boy Needs Chemotherapy for Leukemia," UPI story in *Washington Post*, 18 Aug. 1979, p. A–8.

16. "Pathologist Tells of Strange Tijuana Autopsy of Chad Green," *Medical World News* 20 (12 Nov. 1979): 20.
17. "Boy's Leukemia Death is Confirmed at Autopsy," AP story in *New York Times*, 22 Oct. 1979, p. B–5.
18. "Judge Declines to Punish Parents in Laetrile Case," AP story in *New York Times*, 9 Dec. 1980, p. B–21.
19. Nils J. Bruzelius, "Greens Apologize; Case Closed," *Boston Globe*, 9 Dec. 1980, pp. 1, 12.
20. "Girl Made Ward of State to Receive Chemotherapy," AP story in *Frederick* (Md.) *Post*, 7 June 1979 (leukemic daughter returned to NIH for treatment despite mother's objection that vitamin therapy was superior); "Parents Win Court Battle over Therapy," *American Medical News*, 9 Mar. 1979 (parents permitted to take leukemic daughter to West Germany for holistic treatment and chemotherapy); In the Matter of Hofbauer, 47 N.Y.2d 648, 393 N.E.2d 1009, 419 N.Y.S.2d 936 (1979) (parents permitted to reject chemotherapy and substitute metabolic treatment for son with Hodgkin's disease; the boy later died).
21. Stephen L. George, et al., "A Reappraisal of the Results of Stopping Therapy in Childhood Leukemia," *NEJM* 300 (1979): 269.
22. See generally Joseph Goldstein, "Medical Care for the Child at Risk: On State Supervention of Parental Authority," *Yale Law Journal* 86 (1977): 645.
23. Prince v. Massachusetts, 321 U.S. 158, 170 (1944).
24. Jehovah's Witnesses in State of Washington v. King County Hosp. Unit No. 1 (Harborview), 278 Fed. Supp. 488 (1967), *aff'd per curiam*, 390 U.S. 598 (1968).
25. Martha M. Hamilton, "Woman Dies for Faith," *Washington Post*, 14 Nov. 1974, p. C–1. I was unable to confirm details in the official court record because the file folder could not be found in the clerk's office for the District of Columbia Superior Court.
26. See generally Eve T. Horwitz, Note, "Of Love and Laetrile: Medical Decision Making in a Child's Best Interests," *American Jnl. of Law and Medicine* 5 (1979): 271.
27. See generally Jane Brody, "The Dangers of Nutritional Misinformation," *New York Times*, 25 Mar. 1981, p. C–19.

Notes to Chapter 6
TEENAGERS: ON DECIDING FOR ONE'S OWN SELF

1. See Anne C. Peterson, "Can Puberty Come Any Earlier?" *Psychology Today* 9 (Feb. 1979): 45. *Contra* (19th century girls reached puberty earlier than has been thought): Vern L. Bullough, "Age of Menarche: A Misunderstanding," *Science* 213 (1981): 365.
2. For a view of the society in which today's teenagers have grown up, see Catherine S. Chilman, *Adolescent Sexuality in a Changing American Society: Social and Psychological Perspectives* (Washington, D.C.: NIH Pub. No. 80–1426, 1980), chapter 4.
3. Oregon v. Mitchell, 400 U.S. 112 (1970).
4. *U.S. Congressional News* 3 (1971): 367. See Harold W. Chase and Craig R. Ducat, *Edward S. Corwin's The Constitution and What It Means Today*, 13th ed. (Princeton: Princeton Univ. Press, 1973), 457–8.
5. Exceptions are Alabama, Alaska, Nebraska, and Wyoming, where the age of majority is nineteen, and Colorado, Mississippi, and Pennsylvania, where it is twenty-one. Mark Holoweiko, "Do You Still Need Parental Consent to Treat a Minor?" *Medical Economics* (17 Sept. 1979): 218, 219–20.
6. Meredith v. Meredith, 216 Va. 636, 638, 222 S.E.2d 511 (1976).
7. Annot., 75 A.L.R.3d 228 (1977).
8. See Walter Wadlington, "Minors and Health Care: The Age of Consent," *Osgoode Hall Law Journal* 11 (1973): 115–6.

9. Note, "Minors' Rights to Medical Care," *Journal of Family Law* 14 (1975–76): 581, 590–1.

10. See generally Mary Grace Kovar, "Adolescent Americans: What of Their Medical and Health Problems?" *The Sciences* (Apr. 1979): 18, reprinted in *Current*, no. 212 (May 1979): 29.

11. See generally Georgia Dullea, "For Adolescents, Pediatrician's Voice is Changing," *New York Times*, 28 Sept. 1976, p. 28.

12. *Health, United States 1980* (Washington, D.C.: DHEW Pub. No. (PHS) 81–1232, 1981), table 4, p. 192.

13. Kovar, "Adolescent Americans: What of Their Medical and Health Problems?" pp. 31–2.

14. Eve W. Paul, "Legal Rights of Minors to Sex-Related Medical Care," *Columbia Human Rights Law Review* 6 (1975–76), 357, 364–5; and "Few Legal Hazards in Treating Teens' Sex-Related Problems," *Medical World News* 20 (2 Apr. 1979): 40.

15. Note, "Minors' Rights to Medical Care," p. 594.

16. *Health, United States 1980*, table 4, p. 192.

17. Holoweiko, "Do You Still Need Parental Consent to Treat a Minor?" pp. 220–3.

18. Carey v. Population Services Int'l, 431 U.S. 678, part IV (1977). See generally Note, "The Minor's Right of Privacy: Limitations on State Action after *Danforth* and *Carey*," *Columbia Law Review* 77 (1977): 1216.

19. Unreported three-judge federal-court decision, aff'd, Danforth v. Rogers, 414 U.S. 1035 (1973).

20. See generally M. David Bryant, Jr., "State Legislation on Abortion after *Roe v. Wade*: Selected Constitutional Issues," *American Journal of Law and Medicine* 2 (Summer 1976): 101.

21. Planned Parenthood of Central Missouri v. Danforth, 428 U.S. 52 (1976).

22. Ibid., p. 74.

23. Bellotti v. Baird, 443 U.S. 622, 649 (1979).

24. H. L. v. Matheson, 49 U.S.L. Week 4255 (U.S.), 23 Mar. 1981.

25. Fred Barbash, "Court Upholds Parental Notice Law in Some Abortions on Minors," *Washington Post*, 24 Mar. 1981, p. A–12.

26. Malcolm M. Manber, "Adolescents: They Seek Care Outside the System," *Medical World News* 20 (2 Apr. 1979).

27. U.S. Congress, Senate, Committee on the Judiciary, *Juvenile Delinquency*, 93d Cong., 2d sess., 1974, S. Rept. 93–1424, p. 6; cited in Robert Bennett, "Allocation of Child Medical Care Decision-Making Authority: A Suggested Interest Analysis," *Virginia Law Review* 62 (1976): 285, 309.

28. Curtis J. Sitomer, "Children in Need: Who Speaks for the Child?" *Christian Science Monitor*, 6, 7, 8 Feb. 1979.

29. See generally Sanford N. Katz, William A. Schroeder, and Lawrence R. Sidman, "Emancipating Our Children—Coming of Legal Age in America," *Family Law Quarterly* 7 (1973): 211; and Wadlington, "Minors and Health Care: The Age of Consent," p. 121.

30. Cited in Rex v. Owen, 4 Carrington and Payne 236, 237n, 172 Eng. Rep. 685, 686n (1830).

31. "Juvenile Gets Life in Slaying," *Washington Post*, 19 Oct. 1978, p. A–7.

32. Garratt v. Dailey, 46 Wash.2d 197, 279 P.2d 1091 (1955); aff'd on second appeal, 49 Wash.2d 499, 304 P.2d 681 (1956).

33. Callicott v. Callicott, 364 S.W.2d 455 (1963) (Civ. App. Tex.).

34. Pat Wald, "Making Sense Out of the Rights of Youth," *Child Welfare* 55 (1976): 379, 382, reprinted from *Quarterly Focus* (Winter 1975). See generally John Holt, *Escape from Childhood: The Needs and Rights of Children* (New York: Dutton, 1974).

35. Wisconsin v. Yoder, 406 U.S. 205, 245 (Justice Douglas, dissenting in part).
36. John E. Schowalter, Julian B. Ferholt, and Nancy M. Mann, "The Adolescent Patient's Decision to Die," *Pediatrics* 51 (1973): 97.
37. Younts v. St. Francis Hosp. and School of Nursing, 205 Kan. 292, 469 P.2d 330, 338 (1970).
38. "Legal Rights of Minors to Sex-Related Medical Care," p. 363. See Wadlington, "Minors and Health Care: The Age of Consent," p. 119.
39. In the Matter of S., 309 N.Y. 80, 127 N.E.2d 820 (1955).
40. Joseph Goldstein, "Medical Care for the Child at Risk: On State Supervention of Parental Autonomy," *Yale Law Journal* 86 (1977): 645, 668.
41. See Brian G. Fraser, "The Pediatric Bill of Rights," *South Texas Law Journal* 16 (1974-75): 245, 272; and Note, "The Minor's Right to Consent to Medical Treatment: A Corollary of the Constitutional Right of Privacy," *Southern California Law Review* 48 (1975): 1417, 1443-56. See Bernard G. Suran and John V. Lavigne, "Rights of Children in Pediatric Settings: A Survey of Attitudes," *Pediatrics* 60 (1977): 715.
42. For a list of applicable state statutes as of 1974, see Fraser, "The Pediatric Bill of Rights," pp. 274-308.
43. Gilbert Sharpe, "Valid Consent: Determining the Minor's Ability to Make Decisions," *Canadian Medical Association Journal* 117 (1977): 934.
44. The age of twelve was suggested by Pat Wald, "Making Sense Out of the Rights of Youth," p. 387; and by Goldstein, "Medical Care for the Child at Risk: State Supervention of Parental Autonomy," p. 663.
45. See Bennett, "Allocation of Child Medical Care Decision-Making Authority: A Suggested Interest Analysis," pp. 320-9.
46. Joel Vernick and Myron Karon, "Who's Afraid of Death on a Leukemia Ward?" *American Journal of Diseases of Children* 109 (1965): 393, 397.
47. David Ferleger, "Kremens v. Bartley: The Right to Be Free," *Hospital and Community Psychiatry* 27 (1976): 708, 711.
48. Bartley v. Kremens, 402 F. Supp. 1039, 1044 (1975), *vacated* 431 U.S. 119 (1977).
49. The new procedures satisfied due process requirements. Secretary of Pub. Welfare of Pennsylvania v. Institutionalized Juveniles, 442 U.S. 640 (1979).
50. In North Carolina, voluntary admission of a minor must be followed by a court review within ten days. Billie F. Corder, Thomas M. Haizlip, and Lawrence D. Spears, "Legal Issues in the Treatment of Adolescent Psychiatric Inpatients," *Hospital and Community Psychiatry* 27 (1976): 712, 713.
51. James W. Ellis, "Volunteering Children: Parental Commitment of Minors to Mental Institutions," *California Law Review* 63 (1974): 840, 842. Ralph Slovenko, "Criminal Justice Procedures in Civil Commitment," *Wayne Law Review* 24 (1977): 1, 3.
52. Addington v. Texas, 441 U.S. 418 (1979).
53. Melville v. Sabbatino, 30 Conn. Supp. 320, 313 A.2d 886 (Super. Ct. 1973).
54. Parham v. J. R., 442 U.S. 584 (1979).
55. Linda V. Tiano, Note, "*Parham v. J. R.*: 'Voluntary' Commitment of Minors to Mental Institutions," *American Journal of Law and Medicine* 6 (Spring 1980): 125, 144. See Ellis, "Volunteering Children: Parental Commitment of Minors to Mental Institutions," p. 868. See generally Mary McCorry, "Patients' Rights: Commitment of Minors to Mental Institutions," *1978 Annual Survey of American Law* (New York: New York University School of Law, 1979), p. 653.
56. In re Gault, 387 U.S. 1, 28 (1967).
57. Melville v. Sabbatino, p. 888.
58. See generally Ellis, "Volunteering Children: Parental Commitment of Minors to Mental Institutions," pp. 886-90.

59. *Parham* decision, 442 U.S. at 633–7 (Justice Brennan, concurring in part and dissenting in part).
60. The American Psychiatric Association said an administrative tribunal could include a psychiatrist, another mental health professional, and a lawyer. "Parents, Children, and Due Process: The Case of Kremens v. Bartley," *Hospital and Community Psychiatry* 27 (1976): 705.
61. Derek Miller and Robert A. Burt, "Children's Rights on Entering Therapeutic Institutions," *American Journal of Psychiatry* 134 (1977): 153.
62. See generally George J. Annas, "Parents, Children, and the Supreme Court," *Hastings Center Report* 9 (Oct. 1979): 21.
63. Slovenko, "Criminal Justice Procedures in Civil Commitment," p. 26. In any event, power relationships in a family may have a stronger influence than natural affection. David J. Rothman and Sheila M. Rothman, "The Conflict over Children's Rights," *Hastings Center Report* 10 (June 1980): 7.

Notes to Chapter 7
DECIDING FOR PATIENTS WHO CAN'T DECIDE FOR THEMSELVES

1. See generally Joseph and Julia Quinlan with Phyllis Battelle, *Karen Ann: The Quinlans Tell Their Story* (Garden City, N.Y.: Doubleday, 1977), referred to hereafter as *Karen Ann*.
2. In the Matter of Quinlan, 137 N.J. 227, 348 A.2d 801, 806 (1975), referred to hereafter as *Quinlan* (Superior Ct.).
3. "The Dangers of Mixing Alcohol and Drugs," *Business Week*, 16 Oct. 1978.
4. *Quinlan* (Superior Ct.), p. 811.
5. See Kathleen Newton Shafer, et al., *Medical-Surgical Nursing*, 5th ed., (St. Louis: Mosby, 1971), pp. 528–9; N.J. Bellergie, "Medical Technology as It Exists Today," *Baylor Law Review* 27 (1975):31, 32.
6. *Karen Ann*, pp. 296–7.
7. *Quinlan* (Superior Ct.), p. 813. For views of doctors' risks in such cases, see generally Donald G. Collester, Jr., "Death, Dying, and the Law: A Prosecutorial View of the Quinlan Case," *Rutgers Law Review* 30 (1977): 304, 306; Alexander Morgan Capron, "Shifting the Burden of Decision Making," *Hastings Center Report* 6 (Feb. 1976): 17, 18; Norman L. Cantor, "Law and the Termination of an Incompetent Patient's Life-Preserving Care," in John A. Behnke and Sissela Bok, eds., *The Dilemmas of Euthanasia* (Garden City: Anchor Press/ Doubleday, 1975), p. 69; and Robert M. Byrn, "Compulsory Lifesaving Treatment for the Competent Adult," *Fordham Law Review* 44 (1975): 1, 27–8.
8. See generally Roy Branson et al., "The Quinlan Decision: Five Commentaries," *Hastings Center Report* 6 (Feb. 1976):8.
9. In the Matter of Quinlan, 70 N.J. 10, 355 A.2d 647 (1976), referred to hereafter as *Quinlan* (N.J. Supreme Ct.).
10. Ex parte Whitbread, 2 Mer. 99, 35 E.R. 878 (1816).
11. Strunk v. Strunk, 445 S.W.2d 145 (1969), annot. 35 A.L.R.3d 683 (1971). See generally John A. Robertson, "Organ Donations by Incompetents and the Substituted Judgment Doctrine," *Columbia Law Review* 74 (1976):48, 67.
12. *Quinlan* (Superior Ct.), p. 814.
13. B. D. Colen, "'We'll Go On,'" *Washington Post*, 18 Dec. 1979, p. A–1.
14. Superintendent of Belchertown State School v. Saikewicz, 373 Mass. 728, 370 N.E.2d 417 (1977). Contra, In the Matter of Storer, Case No. 656, N.Y. Ct. of Appeals, 31 Mar. 1981.
15. See generally Paul Ramsey, "The Saikewicz Precedent: What's Good for an Incompetent Patient?" *Hastings Center Report* 8 (Dec. 1978):36, 40; and George J. Annas,

"Reconciling *Quinlan* and *Saikewicz*: Decision Making for the Terminally Ill Incompetent," *American Journal of Law and Medicine* 4 (Winter 1979): 367, 376.

16. Sharon H. Imbus and Bruce E. Zawacki, "Autonomy for Burned Patients when Survival Is Unprecedented," *NEJM* 297 (1977): 308.

17. *Medical World News* 20 (22 Jan. 1979): 37.

18. Grannum v. Berard, 70 Wash.2d 304; 422 P.2d 812 (1967), annot., 25 A.L.R.3d 1434.

19. Grannum v. Berard, p. 814; In the Matter of Schiller, 148 N.J. Super. 168, 372 A.2d 360 (1977); Lane v. Candura, 376 N.E.2d 1232 (Mass. App. 1978).

20. See Loren H. Roth, Alan Meisel, and Charles W. Lidz, "Tests of Competency to Consent to Treatment," *American Journal of Psychiatry* 134 (1977): 279, 282–3.

21. States having statutes on who may consent include Georgia, Idaho, Louisiana, Maine, Mississippi, Missouri, and North Carolina. James E. Ludlam, *Informed Consent* (Chicago: American Hospital Association, 1978), p. 50.

22. Cantor, "Law and the Termination of an Incompetent Patient's Life-Preserving Care," pp. 80–1.

23. *Quinlan* (N.J. Supreme Ct.), pp. 671–2.

24. Karen Teel, "The Physician's Dilemma; A Doctor's View: What the Law Should Be," *Baylor Law Review* 27 (1975): 7, 8–9.

25. AMA House of Delegates, *Proceedings*, 19–23 June 1977, pp. 107–8.

26. Critical Care Committee, Massachusetts General Hospital, "Optimum Care for Hopelessly Ill Patients," *NEJM* 295 (1976): 362. See Charles Fried, "Terminating Life Support: Out of the Closet!" ibid.; Ned H. Cassem, "When to Disconnect the Respirator," *Psychiatric Annals* 9 (1979): 84.

27. Jane J. Stein, *Making Medical Choices: Who Is Responsible?* (Boston: Houghton Mifflin, 1978), p. 217.

28. See Charles H. Baron, "Medical Paternalism and the Rule of Law: A Reply to Dr. Relman," *American Journal of Law and Medicine* 4 (Winter 1979): 337, 356–7.

29. Kathi Esqueda, "Hospital Ethics Committees: Four Case Studies," *Hospital Medical Staff* 7 (Nov. 1978): 26, 27; Carol Levine, "Hospital Ethics Committees: A Guarded Prognosis," *Hastings Center Report* 7 (June 1977): 25, 27; Corrine Bayley, "Terminating Treatment: Asking the Right Questions," *Hospital Progress* 61 (Sept. 1980): 50.

30. *Saikewicz* decision, p. 435. See Arnold S. Relman, "The Saikewicz Decisions: Judges as Physicians," *NEJM* 298 (1978): 508.

31. Annas, "Reconciling Quinlan and Saikewicz," p. 387.

32. "Dilemmas of Dying," *Medicolegal News* 7 (Fall, 1979): 4, 7.

33. In the Matter of Spring, 80 Mass. Adv. Sheets 1209, 405 N.E.2d 115, 121 (1980).

34. In the Matter of Eichner, Index No. 21242-I-79, Supreme Court, Nassau County, 6 Dec. 1979, *modified and aff'd*, 73 App. Div. 431, 426 N.Y.S. 517 (1980), *modified and aff'd*, Case No. 658, N.Y. Ct. of Appeals, 31 Mar. 1981.

35. Ibid., N.Y. Ct. of Appeals opinion, pp. 13–14.

36. Howard P. Lewis, "Machine Medicine and Its Relation to the Fatally Ill," *JAMA* 206 (1968): 387–8.

37. For an example of a paternalistic attitude, see Arnold S. Relman, "The Saikewicz Decision: A Medical Viewpoint," *American Journal of Law and Medicine* 4 (Fall, 1978): 233, 237.

38. Allen Buchanan, "Medical Paternalism or Legal Imperialism: Not the Only Alternatives for Handling *Saikewicz*-type Cases," *American Journal of Law and Medicine* 5 (Summer, 1979): 97, 101. See generally Dr. Buchanan's "Medical Paternalism," *Philosophy and Public Affairs* 7 (1978): 370.

39. *Special Report on Aging: 1979* (Washington: NIH Pub. No. 79–1907, 1979), p. 24.

40. "Assuring 'Detached but Passionate Investigation and Decision': The Role of Guardians Ad Litem in *Saikewicz*-type Cases," *American Journal of Law and Medicine* 4 (1978): 111, 115.

41. Vincent D. Collins, "Limits of Medical Responsibility in Prolonging Life," *JAMA* 206 (1968): 389, 392.

42. See generally Derek C. Bok, "Can Ethics Be Taught?" *Change* (Oct. 1976): 26; Carleton B. Chapman, "On the Definition and Teaching of the Medical Ethic," *NEJM* 301 (1979): 630; Michael Walzer, "Ethics Makes a Comeback," *New Republic* 178 (10 June 1978): 12; and Howard Brody, "Teaching Medical Ethics: Future Challenges," *JAMA* 229 (1974): 177.

43. See Cristine Russell, "Exploring Medicine's Ethical Dimensions," *Washington Star*, 15 June 1978.

44. Cassem, "When to Disconnect the Respirator," p. 87.

45. J. Engelbert Dunphy, "Annual Discourse—On Caring for the Patient with Cancer," 295 *NEJM* (1976): 313, 314.

46. Bernard Lo and Albert R. Jonsen, "Clinical Decisions to Limit Treatment," *Annals of Internal Medicine* 93 (1980): 764, 765.

47. See "Euthanasia Questions Stir New Debate," *Medical World News* 14 (14 Sept. 1973): 73.

48. See Richard A. McCormick, "The Quality of Life, the Sanctity of Life," *Hastings Center Report* 8 (Feb. 1978): 30, 35.

49. See Allen Buchanan, "Medical Paternalism or Legal Imperialism," pp. 103–5.

50. See generally H. Richard Beresford, "Cognitive Death: Differential Problems and Legal Overtones," *Annals of the New York Academy of Sciences* 315 (1978): 339, 341.

51. See Gerald Kelly, *Medico-Moral Problems* (St. Louis: Catholic Hospital Assn., 1958), pp. 120–30; John Connery, *The Duty to Preserve Life* (Washington: National Conference of Catholic Bishops, 1977).

52. Vatican Congregation for the Doctrine of the Faith, *Declaration on Euthanasia*, 26 June 1980 (Washington: United States Catholic Conference, 1980), pp. 8–10. See Donald G. McCarthy, "Declaration Synthesizes Church Teaching, Stresses Conscience," *Hospital Progress* 61 (Aug. 1980): 25; Kenneth L. Woodward, "To Live and Let Die," *Newsweek* 7 July 1980, p. 58; Henry Tanner, "Vatican Reaffirms View on Euthanasia," *New York Times*, 27 June 1980, p. A–12.

53. J. David Bleich, "The Quinlan Case: A Jewish Perspective," in Fred Rosner and J. David Bleich, eds., *Jewish Bioethics* (New York: Sanhedrin, 1979), pp. 266, 273. See generally Rabbi Bleich's "The Obligation to Heal in the Judaic Tradition: A Comparative Analysis," ibid., p. 1, and his *Judaism and Healing*.

54. For examples, see testimony of Willard Gaylin, U.S. Congress, Senate, Committee on Labor and Public Welfare, *Moral, Ethical, and Legal Questions of Extraordinary Health Care*, 1975, 94th Cong., 1st sess., 6 Nov. 1975, p. 19; and Robert M. Veatch, *Death, Dying, and the Biological Revolution* (New Haven: Yale, 1976), p. 112.

55. A. P. Herbert, *Uncommon Law*, 7th ed., (London: Methuen, 1952), excerpted in William L. Prosser and Young B. Smith, eds., *Torts: Cases and Materials*, 3d ed. (Brooklyn: Foundation Press, 1952), pp. 183, 184.

56. See Richard A. McCormick, "The Quality of Life, the Sanctity of Life," p. 36.

Notes to Chapter 8
LIVING WILLS AND NATURAL DEATH LAWS

1. Milton D. Heifetz with Charles Mangel, *The Right to Die* (New York: G. P. Putnam's Sons, 1975), pp. 40–2.

2. Robert S. Morison, M.D., quoted by Robert M. Veatch, *Death, Dying, and the Biological Revolution* (New Haven: Yale, 1976), pp. 177–8.

3. Luis Kutner, "Due Process of Euthanasia: The Living Will, a Proposal," *Indiana Law Journal* 44 (1969): 539. See Luis Kutner, "The Living Will: Coping with the Historical Event of Death," *Baylor Law Review* 27 (1975): 39.

4. Sissela Bok, "Personal Directions for Care at the End of Life," *NEJM* 295 (1976): 367; Veatch, *Death, Dying, and the Biological Revolution*, pp. 184–7.

5. Arnold S. Relman, "Michigan's Sensible 'Living Will,'" *NEJM* 300 (1979): 1270.

6. For a definition of "persistent vegetative state," see Julius Korein, "Terminology, Definitions, and Usage," *Annals of the New York Academy of Sciences* 315 (1978), 6, 8. See generally D. E. Levy, R. P. Knill-Jones, and F. Plum, "The Vegetative State and Its Prognosis Following Nontraumatic Coma," ibid., pp. 293, 301.

7. I borrowed from Vatican Congregation for the Doctrine of the Faith, *Declaration on Euthanasia* (Washington: United States Catholic Conference, 1980).

8. I borrowed from Sissela Bok, "Personal Directions for Care at the End of Life," p. 369.

9. I borrowed from the Kansas "Declaration," p. 155–56 of this book.

10. See generally Walter Sackett, Jr., "Euthanasia: Why No Legislation," *Baylor Law Review* 27 (1975): 3; and Yale Kamisar, "Some Non-Religious Views against Proposed 'Mercy-Killing' Legislation," *Minnesota Law Review* 52 (1958): 970.

11. Harold J. Logan, "'Death with Dignity' Bill Defeated in Maryland Senate," *Washington Post*, 23 Feb. 1977, p. C–3.

12. Barbara Palmer, "Death and Dignity: Should We Have the Right to Die?" *Washington Star*, 19 Jan. 1977, p. B–1.

13. Dennis J. Horan, "The 'Right to Die': Legislative and Judicial Developments" (Paper delivered before Medicine and Law Committee, American Bar Association annual meeting, 9 Aug. 1977), p. 5.

14. Relman, "Michigan's Sensible 'Living Will'," p. 1271.

15. "The 'Right to Die'," *Southern Medicine* (Oct. 1976): 4.

16. Emily Friedman, "'Natural Death' Laws Cause Hospitals Few Problems," *Hospitals, J.A.H.A.* 52 (16 May 1978): 124.

17. Harold Rubin, "Directive to Physicians: The Right to Die Decently," *The Nation* (4 Feb. 1978): 114, 116.

18. Committee on Evolving Trends in Society Affecting Life, "California Medical Association Survey Results Following One Year's Experience with the Natural Death Act, September 1, 1976–August 31, 1977," (California Medical Association, 1977).

19. Note, "The California Natural Death Act: An Empirical Study of Physicians' Practices," *Stanford Law Review* 31 (1979): 913, 938–9.

20. Arkansas Hospital Association, *Legal News* 4 (Aug. 1977): 7.

21. *1979–1980 Manual* (New York: Society for the Right to Die, 1979), pp. 11–15.

Notes to Chapter 9
YOUR SEARCH FOR MEDICAL INFORMATION

1. H. Waitzkin and J. D. Stoeckle, "The Communication of Information about Illness: Clinical, Sociological, and Methodological Considerations," *Advances in Psychosomatic Medicine*, vol. 8 (Basel: Karger, 1972), p. 180.

2. Martha Weinman Lear, *Heartsounds* (New York: Simon and Schuster, 1980).

3. Philip Harsham, ed., "A Dying Doctor's Last Plea: Treat *Me*, Then Treat My Disease," *Medical Economics* (28 Apr. 1980): 90, 98.

4. Arnold S. Relman, "Here Come the Women," *NEJM* 302 (1980): 1252.

5. Robert L. Dickman, et al., "Medical Students from Natural Science and Nonscience Undergraduate Backgrounds: Similar Academic Performance and Residency Selection," *JAMA* 243 (1980): 2506.

6. "Medicine and Literature: The Human Experience," *UMass Medical Center* 2 (Oct. 1979): 2. See John H. Sorenson, Garrett E. Bergman, and Alton I. Sutnick, "Teaching Humanities in Medical School: The Experience of the Medical College of Pennsylvania," *Forum on Medicine* 3 (Feb. 1980): 114.

7. David R. Kauss, et al., "The Long-Term Effectiveness of Interpersonal Skills Training in Medical Schools," *Journal of Medical Education* 55 (1980): 595. See generally John E. Verby, "The Audiovisual Interview: A New Tool in Medical Education," *JAMA* 236 (1976): 2413.

8. *Medical Opinion*, Dec. 1971, discussed in *Report of the Secretary's Commission on Medical Malpractice* (Washington, D.C.: DHEW, 1973), p. 199.

9. Barbara S. Hulka, et al., "Communication, Compliance, and Concordance between Physicians and Patients with Prescribed Medications," *American Journal of Public Health* 66 (1976): 847.

10. Lawrence D. Egbert, "Reduction of Postoperative Pain by Encouragement and Instruction of Patients: A Study of Doctor-Patient Rapport," *NEJM* 270 (1964): 825.

11. "The Mystification of Meaning: Doctor-Patient Encounters," *Journal of Medical Education* 51 (Sept. 1976): 716, 721.

12. See Humphry Osmond, "God and the Doctor," *NEJM* 302 (1980): 555.

13. Victor R. Fuchs, "The Economics of Health in a Post-Industrial Society," *Public Interest* (Summer 1979): 3.

14. Charles G. Moertel, et al., "Who Responds to Sugar Pills?" *Mayo Clinic Proceedings* 51 (Feb. 1976): 96.

15. Susan Mattern Buttaravoli, "'Doctors' Word Disorder,'" *Washington Post*, 21 Sept. 1978, p. A–24.

16. Derek G. Gill, "Limitations Upon Choice and Constraints over Decision-Making in Doctor-Patient Exchanges," in Eugene B. Gallagher, ed., *The Doctor-Patient Relationship in the Changing Health Scene* (Washington, D.C.: DHEW Pub. No. (NIH) 78-183, 1978), pp. 141, 145–6, referred to hereafter as *The Doctor-Patient Relationship*. For a study of Welsh doctors, see Jean Comaroff, "Communicating Information about Nonfatal Illness: The Strategies of a Group of General Practitioners," *Sociological Review* 24 (May 1976): 269.

17. See discussion and studies cited in Waitzkin and Stoeckle, "The Communication of Information about Illness," pp. 186–7.

18. Rose S. Le Roux, "Communicating with the Dying Person," *Nursing Forum* 16 (1977): 145, 150–1.

19. See generally Sissela Bok, *Lying: Moral Choice in Public and Private Life* (New York: Pantheon, 1978), chapter 15.

20. "The Self-Image of the Physician and the Care of Dying Patients," *Annals of the New York Academy of Sciences* 164 (19 Dec. 1969): 822.

21. "The Death of Ivan Ilyich," in Maynard Mack, et al., eds., *World Masterpieces*, rev. ed. (New York: Norton, 1965), pp. 1035–6.

22. Evan Charney, "Patient-Doctor Communication: Implications for the Clinician," *Pediatric Clinics of North America* 19 (1972): 263, 264–6.

23. See generally John D. Cormican, "Breaking Language Barriers between the Patient and His Doctor," *Geriatrics* 30 (1975): 104; Gustavo M. Quesada, "Language and Communication Barriers for Health Delivery to a Minority Group," *Social Science and Medicine* 10 (1976): 323; and Ann Chappell Mitchell, "Barriers to Therapeutic Communication with Black Clients," *Nursing Outlook* 26 (Feb. 1978): 109.

24. Barnlund, "The Mystification of Meaning: Doctor-Patient Encounters," p. 719.

25. Waitzkin and Stoeckle, "The Communication of Information about Illness," p. 193.

26. John B. McKinlay, "Who Is Really Ignorant—Physician or Patient?" *Journal of Health and Social Behavior* 16 (Mar. 1975): 3, 9.

27. See generally James E. Ludlam, *Informed Consent* (Chicago: American Hospital Association, 1978); Leslie J. Miller, "Informed Consent," *JAMA* 244 (1980): Part I—p. 2100; Part II—p. 2347, Part III—p. 2556, Part IV—p. 2661; and George J. Annas, "Informed Consent," *Annual Review of Medicine 1978*, p. 9.
28. Schloendorff v. Society of New York Hosp., 211 N.Y. 125, 129–30, 105 N.E. 92, 93 (1914).
29. Natanson v. Kline, 186 Kan. 393, 250 P.2d 1093, *rehearing denied* 186 Kan. 186, 354 P.2d 670 (1960). A precursor to this case was Salgo v. Leland Stanford Jr. Univ. Bd. of Trustees, 154 Cal. App.2d 560, 317 P.2d 170 (1957).
30. Natanson v. Kline, p. 1100.
31. Ibid., p. 1104.
32. Canterbury v. Spence, 150 U.S. App. D.C. 263, 464 F.2d 772, 777, *cert. denied* 409 U.S. 1064 (1972).
33. A few courts apply a subjective test—whether the particular plaintiff would have refused the treatment. Miller, "Informed Consent," Part I—p. 2103.
34. Cobbs v. Grant, 8 Cal.3d 229, 245, 104 Cal. Reptr. 505, 502 P.2d 1, 11–12 (1972).
35. For criticism of this standard, see Wilkinson v. Vesey, 110 R.I. 606, 295 A.2d 676, 686–9 (1972).
36. See generally Gregg Orwoll (general counsel for Mayo Clinic), "Informed Consent: A Reincarnation?" *Hospital Medical Staff* (Aug. 1975): 17.
37. See Ludlam, *Informed Consent*, chapter 4, for details.
38. See generally George J. Annas, "Avoiding Malpractice Suits Through the Use of Informed Consent," *Legal Medicine Annual 1977*, p. 219.
39. See California Medical Association, "Special Report: Some Advice on Informed Consent," in Ludlam, *Informed Consent*, p. 71.
40. Canterbury v. Spence, p. 789.
41. See generally Sandra Berkowitz, "Informed Consent, Research, and the Elderly," *Gerontologist* 18 (1978): 237, 240.
42. Canterbury v. Spence, p. 789.
43. Cobbs v. Grant, p. 11.
44. Alan Meisel, Loren H. Roth, and Charles W. Lidz, "Toward a Model of the Legal Doctrine of Informed Consent," *American Journal of Psychiatry* 124 (1977): 285, 287.
45. Dennis H. Novack, et al., "Changes in Physicians' Attitudes Toward Telling the Cancer Patient," *JAMA* 241 (1979): 897.
46. "Doctors Who Tell All," *Washington Post*, 30 July 1978, p. B–8.
47. Joe Von (of the *Chicago Tribune*), "The Hassle of Dying: Too Much Attention," Orlando, Fla., *Sentinel Star*, (10 Oct. 1978), p. 3–B.
48. "The Case against 'Total Candor,'" *Medical World News* 20 (14 May 1979): 94.
49. Elizabeth F. Loftus and James F. Fries, "Informed Consent May Be Hazardous to Health," *Science* 204 (6 Apr. 1979): editorial page.
50. Norman Cousins, "A Layman Looks at Truth Telling in Medicine," *JAMA* 244 (1980): 1929, 1930.
51. "Communicating with the Dying," *Journal of Medical Ethics* 1 (Apr. 1975): 18, 20.
52. Patricia McCormack, "Keeping a Lid on Medical Records," UPI story in *Washington Post*, 11 Feb. 1979, p. H–2.
53. *Health Records Confidentiality Law in the States* (Washington, D.C., National Commission on Confidentiality of Health Records, 1979), p. 4.
54. Alan F. Westin, "Medical Records: Should Patients Have Access?" *Hastings Center Report* 7 (Dec. 1977): 23, citing *Boston Evening Globe*, 1 Mar. 1974, p. 1.
55. Privacy Protection Study Commission, *Personal Privacy in an Information Society* (Washington, D.C.: GPO, 1977), p. 298. See generally Budd N. Shenkin and David C.

Warner, "Sounding Board: Giving the Patient His Medical Record: A Proposal to Improve the System," *NEJM* 289 (1973): 688.

56. U.S. Congress, House Committee on Government Operations, *Federal Privacy of Medical Information Act: Report to Accompany H.R. 5935*, 96th Cong., 2d sess., 1980, H. Rept. 96–832, pt 1. *Privacy of Medical Records: Hearing on H.R. 2979 and H.R. 3444*, 96th Cong., 1st sess., 1979.

57. David Karp, "How to Keep Legal Bombshells Out of Your Records," *Medical Economics* (14 Apr. 1980): 228.

58. David P. Stevens, Rhonda Stagg, and Ian R. Mackay, "What Happens when Hospitalized Patients See Their Own Records," *Annals of Internal Medicine* 86 (1977): 474.

59. Robert M. Moore, Jr., "Consent Forms—How, or Whether, They Should Be Used," *Mayo Clinic Proceedings* 53 (1978): 393, 394.

60. The patient's actions can imply consent. O'Brien v. Cunard S. S. Co., 154 Mass. 272, 28 N.E. 266 (1891).

61. Ludlam, *Informed Consent*, pp. 83–4.

62. Moore, "Consent Forms—How, or Whether, They Should be Used," p. 394.

63. Rogers v. Lumbermen's Mutual Casualty Co., 119 So.2d 649, 652 (App. La. 1960). See George J. Annas, *The Rights of Hospital Patients* (New York: Dutton, 1975), pp. 69–70.

64. Mark Flannery et al., "Just Sign Here . . . " *South Dakota Journal of Medicine* 31 (May 1978): 33.

65. Barbara Rubin, "Medical Malpractice Suits Can Be Avoided," *Hospitals, J.A.H.A.* 52 (1 Nov. 1978): 86, 87.

66. T. M. Grundner, "On the Readability of Surgical Consent Forms," *NEJM* 302 (1980): 900. See Gary R. Morrow, "How Readable are Subject Consent Forms?" *JAMA* 244 (1980): 56.

67. Barrie R. Cassileth, et al., "Informed Consent—Why Are Its Goals Imperfectly Realized?" *NEJM* 302 (1980): 896. See generally Desmond Rennie, "Informed Consent by 'Well-Nigh Abject' Adults," ibid., pp. 917, 918.

68. "Why You Can't Rely on a Hospital Consent Form," *Medical Economics* (26 May 1980): 127.

69. Gary Morrow, Jon Gootnick, and Arthur Schmale, "A Simple Technique for Increasing Cancer Patients' Knowledge of Informed Consent to Treatment," *Cancer* 42 (1978): 793.

70. Isadore Rosenfeld, *The Complete Medical Exam* (New York: Simon and Schuster, 1978). Excerpt in *San Francisco Chronicle*, 11 July 1978, p. 13.

71. Harry E. Munn, Jr., "Communication between Patients, Nurses, Physicians, and Surgeons," *Hospital Topics* 55 (Mar.–Apr. 1977): 6, 7.

72. Wilson, "Communicating with the Dying," p. 19.

73. Mary Jo Jupst, et al., "Improving Physician-Parent Communication: Some Lessons Learned from Parents Concerned about Their Child's Congenital Heart Defect," *Clinical Pediatrics* 15 (Jan. 1976): 27.

74. Galen L. Barbour and Micahel J. Blumenkrantz, "Videotape Aids Informed Consent Decision," *JAMA* 240 (1978): 2741, 2742.

75. *Contra* (use of tape recorder makes doctor appear anxious), Jack E. Horsley with John H. Lavin, "An Up-to-Date Guide to Informed Consent," *Medical Economics* (21 March 1977): 150.

76. Hugh R. Butt, "A Method for Better Physician-Patient Communication," *Annals of Internal Medicine* 86 (1977): 478. The tape recorder does not inhibit conversation. Malcolm Coulthard and Margaret Ashby, "Talking with the Doctor: 1," *Journal of Communication* 25 (Summer 1975): 140.

77. Ruth R. Faden and Tom L. Beauchamp, "Informed Consent and Decision Making:

The Impact of Disclosed Information," *Social Indicators Research*, discussed in *Principles of Biomedical Ethics*, by Tom L. Beauchamp and James F. Childress (New York: Oxford, 1979), p. 73.

78. Claire O. Leonard, Gary A. Chase, and Barton Childs, "Genetic Counseling: A Consumer's View," *NEJM* 287 (1972): 433.

79. John Stuart Mill, *On Liberty*, in Max Lerner, ed., *Essential Works of John Stuart Mill*, (New York: National General, 1961), p. 315.

80. On the principle of autonomy, see generally Beauchamp and Childress, *Principles of Biomedical Ethics*, chapter 3.

81. Robert Veatch, "Three Theories of Informed Consent: Philosophical Foundations and Policy Implications," in *The Belmont Report: Ethical Principles and Guidelines for the Protection of Human Subjects of Research* (Washington, D.C.: DHEW Pub. No. (OS) 78-0014, 1978), Appendix, Vol. II, p. 26-18.

82. Beauchamp and Childress, *Principles of Biomedical Ethics*, p. 64.

83. Fuchs, "The Economics of Health in a Post-Industrial Society," p. 6. Quaere: Does good health lead to good schooling, rather than vice versa?

84. Lois V. Pratt, *Family Structure and Effective Health Behavior: The Energized Family* (Boston: Houghton Mifflin, 1976).

85. Lois V. Pratt, "Reshaping the Consumer's Posture in Health Care," in *The Doctor-Patient Relationship*, pp. 197, 198.

86. Rose Kushner, *Why Me?*, rev. ed. (New York: New American Library, 1977). The hardcover book, *Breast Cancer: A Personal History and Investigative Report*, was published by Harcourt Brace Jovanovich in 1975. Revised editions of *Why Me?* are scheduled by Holt, Rinehart & Winston, New York (hardcover) and W. B. Saunders, Philadelphia (softcover).

87. *The Treatment of Primary Breast Cancer: Management of Local Disease* (NIH Consensus Development Conference Summary, Vol. 2, No. 5, 5 June 1979). "New Era in Treatment of Localized Breast Cancer," *JAMA* 242 (1979): 14. See generally Maya Pines, "Reducing the Trauma of Breast Cancer," *New York Times Magazine*, 6 Apr. 1980, p. 35; and Craig Henderson and George P. Canellos, "Cancer of the Breast: The Past Decade," *NEJM* 302 (1980): 78.

88. Leonard R. Derogatis, Martin D. Abeloff, and Nick Milisaratos, "Psychological Coping Mechanisms and Survival Time in Metastatic Breast Cancer," *JAMA* 242 (1979): 1504.

89. Norman Cousins, *Anatomy of an Illness* (New York: Norton, 1979), p. 48.

SELECTED READING

A Selected Bibliography

Annas, George J. "Reconciling *Quinlan* and *Saikewicz*: Decision Making for the Terminally Ill Incompetent." *American Journal of Law and Medicine* 4 (Winter 1979): 367.

Barnlund, Dean C. "The Mystification of Meaning: Doctor-Patient Encounters." *Journal of Medical Education* 51 (1976): 716.
  Why factors that inhibit communication do so to the extreme in medical settings.

Baron, Charles H. "Medical Paternalism and the Rule of Law: A Reply to Dr. Relman." *American Journal of Law and Medicine* 4 (Winter 1979): 337.

Beauchamp, Tom L., and Childress, James F. *Principles of Biomedical Ethics*. New York: Oxford University Press, 1979.
  Enlightening and outstanding.

Beauchamp, Tom L., and Walters, LeRoy, eds. *Contemporary Issues in Bioethics*. Encino, Cal.: Dickenson Publishing Co., Inc., 1978.
  Basic writings, many of them condensed.

Bok, Sissela. "Personal Directions for Care at the End of Life." *New England Journal of Medicine* 295 (1976): 367.
  A recommendation that you name a proxy to make decisions for you.

Brown, Norman K., and Thompson, Donovan J. "Nontreatment of Fever in Extended-Care Facilities." *New England Journal of Medicine* 300 (1979): 1246.
  The authors reveal that physicians intentionally fail to treat some patients.

Buchanan, Allen. "Medical Paternalism." *Philosophy and Public Affairs* 7 (1978): 370.

———. "Medical Paternalism or Legal Imperialism: Not the Only Alternatives for

Handling *Saikewicz*-type Cases." *American Journal of Law and Medicine* 5 (Summer 1979): 97.

Byrn, Robert M. "Compulsory Lifesaving Treatment for the Competent Adult." *Fordham Law Review* 44 (1975): 1.

Capron, Alexander Morgan. "Tort Liability in Genetic Counseling." *Columbia Law Review* 79 (1979): 618.

Cassem, Ned H. "When to Disconnect the Respirator." *Psychiatric Annals* 9 (1979): 84.

Charney, Evan. "Patient-Doctor Communication: Implications for the Clinician." *Pediatric Clinics of North America* 19 (1972): 263.

Collester, Donald G., Jr. "Death, Dying, and the Law: A Prosecutorial View of the Quinlan Case." *Rutgers Law Review* 30 (1977): 304.

Cousins, Norman. *Anatomy of an Illness as Perceived by the Patient.* New York: W. W. Norton & Co., 1979.

The well-known editor tells how he marshaled his life forces, working with his doctor to defeat a supposedly irreversible illness.

Dionisopoulos, P. Allan, and Ducat, Craig R. *The Right to Privacy: Essays and Cases.* St. Paul: West Publishing Co., 1976.

Duff, Raymond S., and Campbell, A. G. M. "Moral and Ethical Dilemmas in the Special-Care Nursery." *New England Journal of Medicine* 289 (1973): 890.

The article that set off a widespread discussion about treatment for severely defective babies.

Ellis, James W. "Volunteering Children: Parental Commitment of Minors to Mental Institutions." *California Law Review* 63 (1974): 840.

Fletcher, Joseph. *Morals and Medicine.* Princeton, N.J.: Princeton University Press, 1954.

———. *Humanhood: Essays in Biomedical Ethics.* Buffalo: Prometheus Books, 1979.

Gallagher, Eugene B., ed. *The Doctor-Patient Relationship in the Changing Health Scene.* Washington, D.C.: DHEW Pub. No. (NIH) 78–183, 1978.

Goldstein, Joseph. "Medical Care for the Child at Risk: On State Supervention of Parental Authority." *Yale Law Journal* 86 (1977): 645.

Brilliantly reasoned.

Grundner, T. M. "On the Readability of Surgical Consent Forms." *New England Journal of Medicine* 302 (1980): 900.

Gufstafson, James M. "Mongolism, Parental Desires, and the Right to Life." *Perspectives in Biology and Medicine* 16 (1973): 529.

A theologian concludes that the famous Baltimore baby should have been treated instead of being allowed to die.

Heifetz, Milton D., with Mangel, Charles. *The Right to Die: A Neurosurgeon Speaks with Candor.* New York: G. P. Putnam's Sons, 1975.

Horan, Dennis J., and Mall, David, eds. *Death, Dying, and Euthanasia*. Washington, D.C.: University Publications of America, Inc., 1977.

Horwitz, Eve T. Note, "Of Love and Laetrile: Medical Decision Making in a Child's Best Interests." *American Journal of Law and Medicine* 5 (Fall 1979): 271.
About the Chad Green and Joseph Hofbauer cases.

Illich, Ivan. *Medical Nemesis*. New York: Pantheon Books, Inc.; New York: Bantam Books, 1976.
The priest and social critic says that the medical system itself is a health hazard. Pioneering but overstated.

Imbus, Sharon H., and Zawacki, Bruce E. "Autonomy for Burned Patients when Survival Is Unprecedented." *New England Journal of Medicine* 297 (1977): 308.
Lucid, competent patients who apparently have no chance of recovery are asked whether they wish to choose maximal treatment or, instead, ordinary care.

Kushner, Rose. *Why Me?* (Originally titled *Breast Cancer: A Personal History and Investigative Report*). New York: Harcourt Brace Jovanovich, 1975; revised, New York: New American Library, 1977.
Reveals the value of seeking information and making decisions about one's own medical treatment.

Jonsen, A. R.; Phibbs, R. H.; Tooley, W. H.; and Garland, M. J. "Critical Issues in Newborn Intensive Care: A Conference Report and Policy Proposal." *Pediatrics* 55 (1975): 756.

Kutner, Luis. "Due Process of Euthanasia: The Living Will, a Proposal." *Indiana Law Journal* 44 (1969): 539.

Lo, Bernard, and Jonsen, Albert R. "Clinical Decisions to Limit Treatment." *Annals of Internal Medicine* 93 (1980): 764.

Lorber, John. "Early Results of Selective Treatment of Spina Bifida Cystica." *British Medical Journal* 4 (1973): 201.

Ludlam, James E. *Informed Consent*. Chicago: American Hospital Assn., 1978.

McCormick, Richard A. "To Save or Let Die: The Dilemma of Modern Medicine." *Journal of the American Medical Association* 229 (1974): 172.
The question of whether babies have the potential to relate to other humans can be crucial in deciding on their treatment.

Milunsky, Aubrey, and Annas, George J., eds. *Genetics and the Law*. New York: Plenum Press, 1975.

———. *Genetics and the Law II*. New York: Plenum Press, 1980.

Novack, Dennis H.; Plumer, Robin; Smith, Raymond L.; Ochitill, Herbert; Morrow, Gary R.; and Bennett, John M. "Changes in Physicians' Attitudes Toward Telling the Cancer Patient." *Journal of the American Medical Association* 241 (1979): 897.

Paul, Eve W. "Legal Rights of Minors to Sex-Related Medical Care." *Columbia Human Rights Law Review* 6 (1975–76): 357.
Powledge, Tabitha M., and Fletcher, John. "Guidelines for the Ethical, Social, and Legal Issues in Prenatal Diagnosis: A Report from the Genetics Research Group of the Hastings Center." *New England Journal of Medicine* 300 (1979): 168.
Quinlan, Joseph and Julia, with Battelle, Phyllis. *Karen Ann: The Quinlans Tell Their Story.* Garden City, N.Y.: Doubleday and Co., Inc., 1977.
   A devout family confronts a tragedy and makes legal history. Told in saccharine style.
Ramsey, Paul. *The Patient as Person.* New Haven: Yale University Press, 1970.
   A pioneering study on problems such as a right to die, organ donations, etc., by the noted theologian.
———. *Ethics at the Edges of Life.* New Haven: Yale University Press, 1978.
Redleaf, Diane Lynn; Schmitt, Suzanne Baillie; and Thompson, William Charles. Note, "The California Natural Death Act: An Empirical Study of Physicians' Practices." *Stanford Law Review* 31 (1979): 913.
Reilly, Philip. *Genetics, Law, and Social Policy.* Cambridge: Harvard, 1977.
   The relationship between eugenic programs and personal freedom; other discussions of issues caused by the explosive knowledge of genetics. Indispensable.
Relman, Arnold S. "The Saikewicz Decision: A Medical Viewpoint." *American Journal of Law and Medicine* 4 (Fall 1978): 233.
   Dr. Relman's view, that judges should have only a limited role in deciding the medical care of incompetent patients, led to a debate on physicians' paternalism. See entries under "Baron" and "Buchanan."
Robertson, John A. "Involuntary Euthanasia of Defective Newborns: A Legal Analysis." *Stanford Law Review* 27 (1975): 213.
Rosner, Fred, and Bleich, J. David, eds. *Jewish Bioethics.* New York: Sanhedrin Press, 1979.
Schowalter, John E.; Ferholt, Julian B.; and Mann, Nancy M. "The Adolescent Patient's Decision to Die." *Pediatrics* 51 (1973): 97.
Shannon, Thomas A., ed. *Bioethics: Basic Writings on the Key Ethical Questions that Surround the Major, Modern Biological Possibilities and Problems.* New York: Paulist Press, 1976.
   A well-chosen anthology.
Shaw, Anthony. "Doctor, Do We Have a Choice?" *New York Times Magazine,* 30 Jan. 1972, p. 44.
   On whether to treat Down syndrome children who have a life-threatening defect.
Shenkin, Budd N., and Warner, David C. "Giving the Patient His Medical Record: A Proposal to Improve the System." *New England Journal of Medicine* 289 (1973): 688.

Stevens, David P.; Stagg, Rhonda; and Mackay, Ian R. "What Happens When Hospitalized Patients See Their Own Records." *Annals of Internal Medicine* 86 (1977): 474.

Stinson, Robert and Peggy. "On the Death of a Baby." *Atlantic Monthly* 244 (July 1979): 64.
On doctors' "heroic" but cruel efforts to keep a premature baby alive.

Stoddard, Sandol. *The Hospice Movement: A Better Way of Caring for the Dying.* New York: Stein and Day; New York: Vintage Books, 1978.

Swinyard, Chester A., ed. *Decision Making and the Defective Newborn.* Springfield, Ill.: Charles C Thomas, 1978.

Turner, J. Howard; Hayashi, T. Terry; and Pogoloff, Donald D. "Legal and Social Issues in Medical Genetics." *American Journal of Obstetrics and Gynecology* 134 (1979): 83.
Readily understood by laymen. Excellent.

Vatican Congregation for the Doctrine of the Faith. *Declaration on Euthanasia.* Washington, D.C.: United States Catholic Conference, 1980.

Veatch, Robert M. *Death, Dying, and the Biological Revolution: Our Last Quest for Responsibility.* New Haven: Yale University Press, 1976.
A scholarly, informative study of social and ethical problems.

Wadlington, Walter. "Minors and Health Care: The Age of Consent." *Osgoode Hall Law Journal* 11 (1973): 115.

Wald, Pat. "Making Sense Out of the Rights of Youth." *Child Welfare* 55 (1976): 379, reprinted from *Quarterly Focus* (Winter 1975).

White, Laurens P. "The Self-Image of the Physician and the Care of Dying Patients." *Annals of the New York Academy of Sciences* 164 (19 Dec. 1979): 822.
"Doctors can be just as fearful and unrealistic as can be anybody else, according to Dr. White."

Cases

In the following list, *United States Reports*—the official compilation of U.S. Supreme Court decisions—is abbreviated "*U.S.*" Volume numbers precede, and page numbers follow titles of volumes. When more than one set is listed for a case, it means the decision appears in each.

Becker v. Schwartz; Park v. Chessin, 46 *New York Court of Appeals Reports*, 2d Series 401, 386 *North Eastern Reporter*, 2d Series 807, 413 *New York Supplement*, 2d Series 895 (1978).
In companion cases, court rules that physicians must warn mothers who face risks of bearing abnormal babies.

In re Brooks, 32 *Illinois Reports*, 2d Series 361, 205 *North Eastern Reporter*, 2d Series 435 (1965).
A Jehovah's Witness successfully refuses blood transfusions.

Canterbury v. Spence, 150 *U.S. Court of Appeals for the District of Columbia*

208 MAKING YOUR MEDICAL DECISIONS

Reports 263, 464 *Federal Reporter*, 2d Series 772, *certiorari denied*, 409 U.S. 1064 (1972).
A leading informed-consent case, along with Cobbs v. Grant, in which judges hold that a physician must explain significant risks.

Cobbs v. Grant, 8 *California Reports*, 3d Series 229, 104 *California Reporter* 505, 502 *Pacific Reporter*, 2d Series 1 (1972).

Custody of a Minor. First court hearing: 78 *Massachusetts Advance Sheets* 2002, 379 *North Eastern Reporter*, 2d Series 1053 (1978). Second hearing: 79 *Massachusetts Advance Sheets* 2124, 393 *North Eastern Reporter*, 2d Series 836 (1979).
The Chad Green case.

In the Matter of Eichner, Case No. 658. New York Court of Appeals, 31 Mar. 1981.
Court rules that respirator can be disconnected from Brother Fox, who, while competent, opposed extraordinary medical treatment.

Green, Chad, case. See "Custody of a Minor."

Maine Medical Center v. H., No. 74–145, Superior Court, Cumberland County, Maine, 14 Feb. 1974.
A judge rules that a defective baby must be operated on, because life in itself is the highest value.

Parham v. J. R., 442 *U.S.* 584 (1979).
Supreme Court refuses to overturn Georgia procedures by which parents "volunteer" children into mental institutions.

Planned Parenthood of Central Missouri v. Danforth, 428 *U.S.* 52 (1976).
Supreme Court rules parents cannot have veto power over their underage daughter's abortion decision.

In the Matter of Karen Ann Quinlan. 70 *New Jersey Reports* 10, 355 *Atlantic Reporter*, 2d Series 647 (1976).

Roe v. Wade, 410 *U.S.* 113 (1973).
The abortion decision.

Satz v. Perlmutter, 362 *Southern Reporter*, 2d Series 160 (1978), *affirmed*, 379 *Southern Reporter*, 2d Series 359 (Florida 1980).
Abe Perlmutter rejects a respirator that might extend a burdensome life.

Superintendent of Belchertown State School v. Saikewicz, 373 *Massachusetts Reports* 728, 370 *North Eastern Reporter*, 2d Series 417 (1977).
Justices refuse to order chemotherapy to treat leukemia of mentally retarded adult.

Union Pacific Ry. v. Botsford, 141 *U.S.* 250 (1891).
Supreme Court rules woman has right to refuse physician's examination and thus control her own person.

Younts v. St. Francis Hospital and School of Nursing, Inc., 205 *Kansas Reports* 292, 469 *Pacific Reporter*, 2d Series 330 (1970).
Court rules that seventeen-year-old girl, being a mature minor, can on her own consent to surgery.

INDEX

ABC News-Harris Poll, 2
abortion:
   constitutionality of, 19, 28–29, 74–75
   and prenatal testing, 37–38, 51–52, 58
   public acceptance of, 39
   saline method for, 38
   in teenagers, 106–7
adolescents. *See* teenagers
AFP. *See* alpha-fetoprotein
aging population, 9
alpha-fetoprotein:
   in amniotic fluid, 39, 41–43
   in maternal blood, 48–49, 57–58
American Hospital Association, 18
American Medical Association, 11, 12, 127
American Medical Record Association, 169
amniocentesis:
   doctor acceptance of, 48
   indication for, 39
   procedure, 39, 41–44
   risks of, 39–40
amyotrophic lateral sclerosis, 33–36
antibiotics, role of, 9, 11
Arkansas Hospital Association, 157
Arkansas natural death law, 154–55
Ashkenazi Jews, 60
Asimov, Isaac, 2
audiovisual aids in doctor-patient communication, 175–76
authority, distrust of, 2–3

autonomy in medical treatment:
   AMA views of, 11, 12
   for burn patients, 124–25
   in cancer therapy, 6, 21–22, 167, 176–77, 179–80
   among Europeans, 6
   false reasons for, 31
   leaving hospital "AMA", 22, 35
   limitations on, 31–33
   movement toward, 5–8
   principle of, 176–77
   women's influence on, 7–8

babies, defective:
   abuse statutes, 75
   as constitutional "persons," 75
   Down syndrome, 63–65
   family suffering, 70–71
   hydrocephalus, 67–68
   institutional care, 70–71, 74
   lawsuits:
      informed consent, 46–50
      wrongful birth, 50–51
   meningomyelocele, 67–68
   prematures, 69–70
   quality of life, 71–72
   respiratory distress syndrome, 66
   treatment:
      "active," 65
      doctors' views on, 65–70
      legal framework for, 74–80
      parental control of, 98
   see also (Chad) Green

Bander, Martin, 87
Barnlund, Dean C., 159
Baron, Charles H., 133
battery by doctors, 22, 103
Berdon, Robert I., 115
"best interest" test, 124
Bingham, Carol Ann, 15–16
birth rates, teenagers', 104
Blackmun, Harry A., 28, 106
Bleich, J. David, 138–39
blood transfusions and Jehovah's Witnesses, 30–31, 32–33, 99, 148
bodily integrity, right of, 23–24
Bok, Sissela, 147
Borer, William, 21–22
Boston University Law School, 169
Botsford, Clara L., 23–24
Brady, Mary Frances and Ray, 17
Brandeis, Louis D., 24–26, 29
breast cancer:
    biopsy, 174, 178–79
    consent for mastectomy, 173
    Halsted operation, 178–79
    refusing treatment for, 21–22
Brennan, William J., 27–28, 106
Bristow, Lonnie R., 171, 176–77
Brooks, Bernice, 30–31
Brown, Carol, Gene, and Chad, 73–74
Buck, Carrie, 52–53
Buchholz, Carol and Karen, 73
Burger, Warren, 115–16
Byrnes, John Carroll, 152

California Medical Association, 154
California natural death law, 151, 153–54
Callahan, Daniel, 61
Callan, John P., 7
Campbell, A.G.M., 65–66
cancer:
    autonomy in treating, 6, 21–22, 167, 176–77, 179–80
    unpredictability of, 134
    war on, 3
    see also breast cancer, chemotherapy, (Chad) Green, leukemia
Capron, Alexander Morgan, 55–56, 58
Cardozo, Benjamin N., 163
Caroline, Nancy L., 10–11
Catholic view of therapy for incompetents, 121, 138–39

case law, evolving, 20, 79–80
Cassem, Ned H., 127–28, 135
Cayce, Edgar, 7
Central State Regional Hospital, 115
cesarean deliveries, 4
Chaminade community, 131
chemotherapy:
    combining chemicals, 85, 97
    incompetent patients, 123–24
    as "poisons," 84–85
    rejection of, 6, 82–83, 86–87, 94, 96
    side effects of, 84, 86, 88, 96, 123
children:
    as inhibiting autonomy, 32, 33
    as martyrs, 98–99
    see also babies (Chad) Green, teenagers
Children's Hospital National Medical Center, 71
Christian Affirmation of Life, 146–47
chromosomal abnormalities, 44–45
City of Hope National Medical Center, 65
Clift, Elaine, 7
code words for therapy, 137–39
colostomy, 176–77
communication, doctor-patient:
    alert consumers, 177–80
    audiovisual aids, 159, 175–76
    autonomy, principle of, 176–77
    compliance, effect on, 159
    consent forms, 170–74
    with dying patients, 158, 160–61
    informed consent, 162–67
    lack of time for, 159
    malpractice suits, effect of on, 159
    medical records, 168–70
    placebo effect, 159–60, 167–68
    sociocultural influences, 132–33, 161–62
competency:
    burn patients, 124–25
    definition of, 125–26, 148, 150
    risk-benefit measurement, 126
    see also incompetent patients
Concern for Dying, 143–46, 152
Connecticut mental hospitals, 115
consent for therapy. See autonomy, babies, consent forms, (Chad) Green, incompetent patients, informed consent, substituted judgment, teenagers

consent forms, 49, 120, 170–74
constitutions, interpretation of, 19
consumerism movement, 158, 167
contraceptives, 26–28, 106
Contreras, Ernesto, 92, 93–94, 95
Coogan, J.E., 53
Coolidge, Calvin, Jr., 8–9
counselors, bioethical, 129
Cousins, Norman, 180
Crick, Francis, 55

death and dying, 8–17, 160–61
Diamond, Sondra, 59
"disproportionate" therapy, 138–39
Douglas, William O., 19, 27, 109
Down syndrome
  and abortion, 37, 46
  heart defects in, 63, 73
  intelligence in, 39, 64, 71
  intestinal blockage in, 64, 73, 76
  in older women's babies, 37
  triple chromosomes in, 44
drug abuse, teenagers, 104, 105
drugs, prescription:
  deaths from, 4
  failure to take, 22
Duff, Raymond S., 65–66, 68–69
Dumont, Belinda, 4
Dunne, Robert Jerome, 30–31

education and health, 177–78
Ehlers-Danlos syndrome, 168–69
Eichner, Philip K., 131
Eldon, Lord, 122
emancipation in youths, 107–8
emergency therapy, 104, 166
energized patients, 178
ethics committees, 126–29
ethics training, 133–34
"extraordinary" therapy, 121, 137–39
eugenics, 52–61
Euthanasia Educational Council, 152

Ferholt, Julian B., 110
Ferris, John G., 34–36
fetoscopy, 40
Field, Stephen J., 76
Finkelman, Fred, 134–35
First Amendment, 31
Fletcher, John, 79–80, 129
Fletcher, Joseph, 55, 78
Foley, Genevieve V., 81, 82, 86, 87

Forsman, Dale H., 127
Fortas, Abe, 117
Fost, Norman, 77
Fourth Amendment, 25
Fox, Brother, case, 131–32
free exercise of religion, 30–31, 56, 99
Freund, Paul, 29
Friedman, Emily, 153
Fromme, Alex M., 111
Fuller, Lon L., 72
fundamental rights, 27, 31–33, 56

Gastel, Barbara, 49
Gault, Jerry, case, 116–17
Gehrig, Lou, disease, 33–36
Geier, Mark R., 37–46, 51
Genetic consultants, 38
genetic defects, 39, 51, 59–60
  see also amniocentesis, chromosomal
    abnormalities, eugenics, prenatal
    testing, sonography, and *names of
    diseases*
genetics laws, 52–61
Georgia mental hospitals, 115–16
German measles (rubella), 47, 50
Gray, Harold, 23–24
Green, Chad, Diana, and Jerry:
  cancer, experience with, 84
  chemotherapy:
    rejection of, 82–83, 86–87, 94, 96
    side effects, 84, 86, 88, 96
  court hearings, 87–92, 95–96, 99
  death, autopsy, 94–95
  diet, 86, 90–91
  laetrile, 90, 92, 93, 95
  leukemia:
    first signs of, 83
    recurrence, 82, 95
    remissions, 81, 87
  metabolic therapy, 89–93
  Mexico, flight to, 90, 92–95
Green, Vera and Hollis, 81, 84–85
Griswold, Estelle T., 26–27

Handler, Philip, 2
Hardy, George W., Jr., 172
Harris, Sidney J., 4
Heifetz, Milton D., 70, 141
Herbert, A. P., 139
Hinde case, 122
Hoines, David A., 33–36
holistic health movement, 7

212 INDEX

Holmes, Oliver Wendell, Jr., 52–53, 75
Hosford, Frances, 162, 175
hospices, 12–17, 146
Hughes, Charles Evans, 19
Hughes, Richard J., 29, 121
hydrocephalus, 67–68, 73
hysterectomies, needless, 3–4

Illich, Ivan, 4
Ilyich, Ivan, 161
"imminent death," 155
incompetent patients:
  and autonomy, 32–33
  bioethical counselors, 129
  Brother Fox case, 131–32
  Catholic views on, 121, 138–39
  code words, use of, 137–39
  competency, definition of, 125–26, 148, 150
  court decision-making, 130–32
  ethics committees, 126–29
  family decisions, 126, 135–36
  Jewish view, 138–39
  physicians' decisions, 132–35
  Quinlan case, 119–23
  Saikewicz case, 123–24
  substituted judgment, 122–24, 140, 147
infections, decline of, 8–9, 11
informed consent:
  consent forms, 49, 120, 170–74
  emotional damages, 50
  legal doctrine, 163–67
  prenatal tests, 46–52
Ingelfinger, Franz J., 79
insane asylums, and minors, 113–18
insurance, as eugenics weapon, 58

Jacobson, Henning, case, 31–32
Jehovah's Witnesses, 30–33, 98–99, 148
Jewish view, therapy for *goses*, 138
Johnson, Lyndon, 145–46

Kaback, Michael M., 60–61
Kampmeier, R. H., 153
Kansas natural death law, 155–56
karyotypes, 44–45
kidney disease, 62, 109–10
Klaman, Carol, 36
Klinefelter's syndrome, 44
Korein, Julius, 120, 137
Kushner, Rose, 178–80
Kutner, Luis, 142–43

Lack, Sylvia A., 146
laetrile, 6, 90, 92, 93, 95
law and social changes, 17–20, 79
Lear, Harold, 158
leaving hospital against medical advice, 22, 35
Letts, Gavin K., 35–36
leukemia:
  childhood:
    form of cancer, 81
    research on, 97
    survival rates for, 84, 97–98
    treatment of, 81–87, 97
  discussing, with others, 167
  Saikewicz case, 123–24, 130
Lewis, Howard P., 132
Liacos, Paul J., 130
living wills:
  Brother Fox case, 132
  Christian Affirmation of Life, 146–47
  Concern for Dying, 143–46
  Kansas Declaration, 155–56
  Medical Care Directive, 147–51
  natural death laws, 8, 151–57
  proxy decisions, 146, 147, 151
Lorber, John, 68
Los Angeles County-UCLA Medical Center, 124
low-birth-weight babies, 69–70

Magno, Josefina B., 15, 146
majority, age of, 102–3
malpractice suits, 1–2, 47, 159
  see also informed consent
Mann, Nancy M., 110
Marieskind, Helen I., 4
Martinez, Carmen, 22–23
Massachusetts:
  medical-records law, 169
  patients' bill of rights, 18
Massachusetts General Hospital, 81, 83, 84, 96, 127–29, 135
"material risk" test, 165–66
mature minors, 108–13
Mayo Clinic, 171, 175
medical ethics training, 133–34
medical records, 168–70
Mehling, Alice V., 152–53
Mendelsohn, Robert S., 4–5
meningomyelocele. *See* neural tube defects
metabolic therapy, cancer, 6, 89–93

INDEX 213

Michigan mental hospitals, 117
Mill, John Stuart, 176
Milunsky, Aubrey, 58
mongolism. See Down syndrome
Montefiore Hospital, 129
Moore, Robert M., Jr., 171
Morris View Nursing Home, 122–23, 126–27
Munn, Harry E., 174

National Association of Children's Hospitals, 112
National Cancer Advisory Board, 180
National Hospice Organization, 14–15
National Institutes of Health, 40, 97, 129, 178, 179–80
natural death laws, 8, 18, 151–57
neural tube defects, 39, 42, 43, 48–49, 67–68, 71, 73, 77
New Mexico Hospital Association, 157
Newton Memorial Hospital, 119
New York Academy of Medicine, 11
nitrogen mustard, 84–85
Nixon, Richard M., 3

Olmstead, Roy, 25–26
omission, crimes of, 75–76
Optimum Care Committee, 127–29
"ordinary" therapy, 137–39
O'Rourke, Kevin D., 146–47
Osler, William, 9

Packard, Dorothy, 114
pain control, 13, 146, 151
parent-child. See babies, children, (Chad) Green, teenagers
patients' bills of rights, 18, 112
Paul, Eve W., 111
Pediatric Bill of Rights, 112
Pennsylvania mental hospitals, 113–14
Perlmutter, Abe, case, 33–36
Perlmutter, Jerry and Lee, 33, 36
Perry, Seymour, 5–6
persistent vegetative state, 11, 120, 131–32, 136, 148
"persons," babies as, 75
physicians, esteem for, 3–5
placebos, 159–60, 167–68
Platt, Eleanor, 29
pneumonia, antibiotics for, 9, 11
Podoll, Elliott, 158

polycystic kidney disease, 49
Popper, David, 23
Powell, Lewis F., Jr., 107
Pratt, Lois V., 178
pregnancy, teenage, 102, 104–6
prenatal testing. See alpha-fetoprotein, amniocentesis, fetoscopy, sonography
privacy. See right of privacy
Privacy Act of 1974, 169
Privacy Protection Study Commission, 169–70
Privitera, James S., 6
"professional standards" test, 165–66
prognosis, certainty of, 134–35
"proportionate" therapy, 138–39
proxy consent, 121–24, 126, 140, 146, 147, 151
puberty, age of, 102

quality of life, 71–72, 137
Quinlan, Karen Ann, case, 11–12, 29, 119–27, 148

Randolph, Judson C., 71–72
"reasonable" person, 139
Reavley, Thomas M., 48
Reilly, Philip, 46–47
religion:
   free exercise of, 30–31, 56, 99
   medicine as, 159
Relman, Arnold S., 152
respiratory, 9–10, 34–36, 119–27 131–32, 137
respiratory distress syndrome, 66
Rh incompatibility, 170
right of bodily integrity, 23–24
right of privacy:
   development of, 19, 24–30
   in eugenics laws, 56
   of families, 98, 101
   in Perlmutter case, 35–36
   in Quinlan case, 121
   of teenagers, 106
right-to-die movement, 8–12
Robertson, John A., 77
Robinson, Spottswood W., III, 164
Rochester, University of, Cancer Center, 173
Rosenfeld, Isadore, 174
Royal Melbourne Hospital, 170
rubella, and fetal defects, 47, 50

Saikewicz, Joseph, case, 123–24, 130
St. Christopher's Hospice, 13–14
St. Clare's Hospital, 120
St. Joseph Hospital, 129
St. Luke's Hospital, 13
St. Mary's Hospital, 17
Sandy, Paula, Richard, Tommy, and Matthew Paul, 37–46
Saunders, Cicely M., 13–14, 146, 148
Schloerndorff, Mary E., 163
Schniedermeyer, Paul, 16
Schowalter, John E., 110
Schroeder, Alfred G., 164
Shaw, Anthony, 65
sickle cell, 54–55
side effects, 4, 84, 86, 88, 96, 123
Society for the Right to Die, 152–56
sonography, 40–42
Speck, Richard, 44
spina bifida. See neural tube defects
Spingarn, Natalie Davis, 167
Staniforth, Robert O., 6
statutes, interpretation of, 19
Stead, Eugene A., Jr., 141–42
sterilization of insane, 52–54
Stinson, Peggy, Robert, and Andrew, 69–70
substituted judgment, 121–24, 126, 140, 146, 147, 151
surgery:
    consent forms, 170–74
    unnecessary, 3–4
Stoddard, Sandol, 15
syphilis, premarital test for, 57

Taft, William Howard, 25–26
Tay-Sachs, 39, 60–61
Teel, Karen, 126, 127
teenagers, medical treatment:
    abortions, 106–7
    age of consent, 102–4, 112–13
    contraception, 106
    drug abuse, 104, 105
    emancipation, 107–8
    health problems, 104–5
    "mature minors," 108–13
    mental problems, 113–18
    Pediatric Bill of Rights, 112
    pregnancy, 102, 104–6
    venereal disease, 105
Theisen, Rita, 58–59
therapeutic privilege, 166
Thompson, Acors W., 127, 152, 174
Tolstoy, Leo, 161
Trapasso, Thomas A., 121
Truman, John T., 81–87, 91–92, 93, 96
Turner's syndrome, 44

Ulrich, Lawrence P., 55
Underwood, Robert C., 31
"unreasonable" person, 139

Veatch, Robert M., 147
vegetative state, 11, 120, 131–32, 136, 148
venereal disease, 57, 105
Veterans Administration Hospital, 175
Volterra, Guy, 86, 88, 90–92, 99

Warren, Samuel, 24
Washington Home Hospice, 15–16
Washington natural death law, 155
Weddington, Sarah, 28
White, Laurens P., 161
White, William Allen, 8
Whitman, Walt, 8
Williamson, William P., 10
Wilson, J. Michael, 168
women, influence of, 7–8, 158
Wright, J. Skelly, 32–33
wrongful birth lawsuits, 50–51

Yale Legislative Services, 155
Yale-New Haven Hospital, 66, 109–10
Young, John L., 37–39, 41–42
Younts, Nancy, 110–11

Zawacki, Bruce E., 125